DUQUESNE STUDIES
Philosophical Series
8

CONTEMPORARY
EUROPEAN THOUGHT
AND
CHRISTIAN FAITH

DUQUESNE STUDIES
Philosophical Series
8

CONTEMPORARY EUROPEAN THOUGHT AND CHRISTIAN FAITH

by

ALBERT DONDEYNE, Ph.D., S.T.L.

TRANSLATED
by
ERNAN McMULLIN, Ph.D.
and
JOHN BURNHEIM, Ph.D.

Second Impression

DUQUESNE UNIVERSITY PRESS
Pittsburgh, Pa.
EDITIONS E. NAUWELAERTS, LOUVAIN
1963

DUQUESNE STUDIES

Philosophical Series

Andrew G. van Melsen, D.Sc., D.Ed., and Henry J. Koren, C.S.Sp., S.T.D., editors.

Volume One—*Andrew G. van Melsen*, From Atomos to Atom. Pp. XII and 240. Price: paper $3.50, cloth $4.25. Published also in Dutch, German, Spanish and Italian.

Volume Two—*Andrew G. van Melsen*, The Philosophy of Nature. Pp. XII and 265. Third edition, fourth impression. Price: paper $3.75, cloth $4.50. Published also in Italian and Dutch. Polish edition in preparation.

Volume Three—*P. Henry van Laer*, Philosophico-Scientific Problems. Out of print.

Volume Four—*Cajetan's*, The Analogy of Names and the Concept of Being. Pp. X and 93. Second edition. Price: $2.25, cloth.

Volume Five—*Louis de Raeymaeker and others*, Truth and Freedom. Pp. VII and 132. Second impression. Price: $3.00, cloth. Published also in French.

Volume Six—*P. Henry van Laer*, The Philosophy of Science. Part One: Science in General. Pp. XVII and 164. Price: cloth $3.75.

Volume Seven—*Stephan Strasser*, The Soul in Metaphysical and Empirical Psychology. Pp. X and 275. Second impression. Price: cloth $6.00. Published also in German, Dutch and French.

Volume Eight—*Albert Dondeyne*, Contemporary European Thought and Christian Faith. Pp. XI and 211. Second impression. Price: paper $5.00, cloth $5.75. Published also in French.

Volume Nine—*Maxwell J. Charlesworth*, Philosophy and Linguistic Analysis. Pp. XIII and 234. Second impression. Price: paper $4.75, cloth $5.50.

Volume Ten—*Remy C. Kwant*, Philosophy of Labor. Pp. XI and 163. Price: paper $4.50, cloth $5.25.

Library of Congress Catalog Card Number 58-4327

© 1962, by Duquesne University

Printed in the United States of America by

The Ad Press, Ltd., New York, N. Y.

Volume Eleven—*Remy C. Kwant*, ENCOUNTER. Pp. VIII and 85. Price: cloth $3.25. Published also in Dutch.

Volume Twelve—*William A. Luijpen*, EXISTENTIAL PHENOMENOLOGY. Pp. XIII and 355. Second impression. Price: paper $6.00, cloth $6.75. Published also in Dutch.

Volume Thirteen—*Andrew G. van Melsen*, SCIENCE AND TECHNOLOGY. Pp. X and 373. Price: paper $6.20, cloth $6.95. Published also in Dutch.

Volume Fourteen—*P. Henry van Laer*, PHILOSOPHY OF SCIENCE. Part Two: A STUDY OF THE DIVISION AND NATURE OF VARIOUS GROUPS OF SCIENCES. Pp. XIII and 342. Price: paper $5.75, cloth $6.50.

Volume Fifteen—*Remy C. Kwant*, THE PHENOMENOLOGICAL PHILOSOPHY OF MERLEAU-PONTY. Pp. VIII and 257. Price: paper $4.50, cloth $5.25.

IN PREPARATION:

John Peters—METAPHYSICS
M. G. Plattel—SOCIAL PHILOSOPHY
Joseph Kockelmans, PHENOMENOLOGY AND THE PHYSICAL SCIENCES

OTHER SERIES OF DUQUESNE STUDIES:

Philological Series (three volumes to date)

Psychological Series (one volume to date)

Spiritan Series (six volumes to date)

Theological Series (one volume to date)

PERIODICALS PUBLISHED BY DUQUESNE UNIVERSITY PRESS:

Annuale Mediaevale. $4.00 per year.

Duquesne Hispanic Review. $3.00 per year.

Duquesne Review. A Journal of the Social Sciences. $2.25 per year.

Duquesne Science Counselor. $3.00 per year (foreign $3.25).

Review of Existential Psychology and Psychiatry. $5.00 per year.

TABLE OF CONTENTS

PART TWO

Christian Faith

CHAPTER FIVE—The Relevance of Thomism

TRANSLATORS' FOREWORD

To the English-speaking reader, the philosophical movement loosely called "existentialism" usually appears as an exotic post-war growth, born of the despair of a disillusioned generation. He has heard of the emphasis it places on such themes as boredom and anguish; he may even have applied the label "existentialist" to a play or novel he thought depressing or morbid. He cannot quite see what such a movement has in common with the academic and aseptic philosophizing of what the French persist in calling "*le monde anglo-saxone.*" If he were asked whether such a mood (for he is more likely to regard it as a mood than as a philosophical movement in the proper sense) could contribute any new insights to the thesaurus of philosophy, he would be likely to answer with a decided negative, following the example of the majority of British (and perhaps even of American) philosophers of the last few decades. If he happens to be devoted to the tradition of Christian philosophy (if we may use a controverted phrase), the denial is likely to be even more emphatic, when he recalls Sarte's strident denial of God's existence and the vaguely raffish air of the nightclub that appears to hover about the whole enterprise.

To such a reader, the aim of this book will come as a shock. The author, who is equally versed in old and new, is determined to show that existential phenomenology, far from being fundamentally antipathetic to the *philosophia perennis*, actually has much to contribute to it. He argues that the relativism, irrationalism and atheism so often taken to be characteristic of it are really second-order features or optional choices that obscure the real success existential phenomenology has had in recovering the median position between rationalism and empiricism, denied to philosophy since the time of Descartes. Its analyses of intentionality, of pre-reflective consciousness, of temporality, are held to recapture the wholeness of the mediaeval view and to enrich the Greek and mediaeval insights in metaphysics as well as in the theory of knowledge.

This is a controversial thesis, as its author well realizes. It is up to the reader to decide whether he has succeeded in his task or not. The enthusiasm with which his presentation of this difficult and delicate theme was greeted when it first appeared in article form in the *Revue Philosophique de Louvain* in 1951 encouraged him to present his case in a book (*Foi chrétienne et pensée contemporaine*) that ran through several printings within a year. For the present edition, the author has completely revised the original text. The first two chapters are new, and smaller changes have been made in the remaining chapters. In addition, the translators have added subheadings and have altered the divisions and order of the later sections (in chapter five particularly). Because of its original format as a series of articles, the text contained many repetitions; these have been eliminated as far as possible. References to works in English have been added, and some of the original footnotes have been amplified or incorporated in the text.

The translation itself presented many difficulties. There are no agreed English equivalents for many of the phenomenological terms used. The author wishes us to come to *see* reality as he sees it; to this end, he frequently tries to convey an *attitude*, to persuade rather than to prove. His reliance on metaphor and analogy, his linking together of more or less synonymous phrases to increase the suggestive effect of his analyses, derive from his highly personal view of the nature of philosophical dialogue (outlined in his final chapter). The English-speaking reader, brought up on more "tough-minded" fare, will be apt to find the rhetorical outweighing the logical at times. But if he perseveres, he will find a penetration of insight and a sudden illumination that may often be missing from the sober-toned arguments to which he is more accustomed. To help the reader, we have been liberal in our translation policy, taking the paragraph rather than the sentence as our basic unit, to convey the thought and the overtones of the original as far as possible.

There are those who hold that the most pressing task facing the Western philosopher to-day is the sort of "re-thinking" of our philosophical and cultural heritage of which Professor Dondeyne speaks so forcefully. Even those who disagree with his findings will admit that he has faced this task squarely and added an effective voice to the vital and continuing dialogue between Christian and non-Christian, between old and new.

ERNAN McMULLIN

JOHN BURNHEIM

INTRODUCTION

This work attempts in a modest way to reach an understanding of the age in which we live and to grasp the significance of Christianity for this age. It is a work of philosophical reflection chiefly; it is a dialogue with contemporary philosophical thought, especially with existential phenomenology. The reader may, perhaps, ask why one should go to philosophy in search of a better understanding of our epoch, for an appreciation of the hopes which animate peoples and the dangers that threaten them. Is not philosophy by definition a search for eternal and immutable truths? Can there be any relation between philosophy and the contingencies of history?

Humanist Import of Philosophy. It is true that the philosopher's task is to aim at a total explanation of the total real; from this point of view, every philosophy tries to reach an understanding which will be universal and valid for all time. But this does not mean that it breaks all connection with the concrete existence of individuals and peoples. How else could it present itself as a search for the ultimate meaning of existence? "Is life worth being lived out or not?"—this is the poignant question which disturbs and quickens the meditations of the philosopher, gives to philosophy its seriousness and prevents it from becoming a mere scaffolding of concepts lacking any real relation to everyday life. Every philosophy worthy of the name is rooted in concrete human existence and is elaborated with a view to illuminating and guiding this existence. This the history of philosophy abundantly confirms. The great philosophical systems had, every one of them, a humanist import; each reflected the epoch in which it first arose as well as contributing to the formation of this epoch. This is evident, for example, in mediaeval philosophy which was created by the people who were most representative of Christian humanism, namely, intellectuals who were also saints. The same can be said too of Cartesian philosophy which expresses the humanism of the Renaissance and is characterized by a boundless confidence in human reason. Contemporary existential philosophy is no exception to this rule; its success is due to the fact that it mirrors the situation of the man of today with his fears and hopes. The best way, then, to meditate upon our time and to understand its problems is to examine the philosophies of our time.

Why Existential Phenomenology is chosen. But, someone will say, why concern ourselves so much with existential phenomenology? How can this choice be justified? Phenomenology is assuredly not the only factor

1

in the present philosophical situation; the importance for our time of Marxism, neo-positivism, and psychoanalytic thought, for example, ought in no way to be minimized. Nevertheless, one cannot deny that in the philosophical life of today existential phenomenology holds a privileged place, not only because of the growing number of thinkers who draw their inspiration from it, but even more because it attempts to integrate the partial truths of other approaches into a higher synthesis. It is in this that the secret of its success is to be found. Merleau-Ponty notes that "before reaching complete philosophical selfconsciousness, phenomenology already existed as a movement. It has been on the way for a long time; its disciples are to be found everywhere along this way; one will find in their number not only Hegel and Kierkegaard, but also Marx and Nietzsche and Freud".[1] One might almost say that it is so close to the temper of modern thought that "many of our contemporaries have had the feeling of finding in it much less a new philosophy than something for which they have always been looking."[2]

Division of this Book

The book is divided into two parts, the first being a detailed discussion of existential phenomenology, and the second, a brief survey of Christian philosophical thinking, leading to an appraisal of the part existential phenomenology could play in this developing tradition.

Existential Phenomenology as the Bridge Between Naturalism and Intellectualism. In the first chapter, existential phenomenology is seen to be an explicit attempt to bridge the chasm between the empiricist and intellectualist traditions which has so disturbed the philosophy of the past three centuries. The main defects of empiricism and rationalism are brought out; to put it very summarily, they do not face the human situation. By their concentration on one or other extreme of the "I-world" relation which is directly given to us in consciousness, they distort this relation and fail to explain our existence as an "I-with-others-in-a-world." Existential phenomenology, by taking this existence, this relation, as the primitive given fact from which all philosophizing ought to begin, is able to achieve a satisfying philosophical synthesis which finds some resonances in the Christian tradition. There are, however, certain characteristics

---

[1] M. Merleau-Ponty, *Phénoménologie de la perception*, Paris, 1945, p. II. This book (which will be taken as a sort of standard reference on existential phenomenology) will be referred to as *Phénoménologie*.

[2] *Ibid.*, p. XVI.

which dominate this synthesis and which would—at first sight, at least —appear to make it ultimately quite inimical to the Christian world-view. The first of these is its emphasis on the historicity of human existence; the other is its distrust of the rational. A chapter is devoted to each of these themes.

Historicity. The most characteristic trait of European thought, particularly since World War II, is its realization of the historical dimension of man's existence. Thus, *historicity* has become a central theme in contemporary philosophy, whether it be of Hegelian, Marxist, or phenomenological inspiration. Such an emphasis can easily lead—and has, in fact, quite often led—to a form of relativism which would be impossible to reconcile with the notion of a Divine Revelation, of an immutable Truth, or of an absolute moral law. It is argued that the idea of historicity ultimately excludes the possibility of any sort of permanent and unchanging strand in the rope of history; thus, the existence of a universal, immutable human nature as well as that of a moral law that has its source in such a nature, are alike challenged. "Man invents man. . . . life has no *a priori* sense."[3] The argument is carried even further; the question is raised whether there can even be a Being outside history, if man's properly historical character be admitted. Hegel and Marx saw in the affirmation of a transcendent God an abdication of human freedom.

According to Sartre, "if man is free, God does not exist"; while Merleau-Ponty declares, in a much-quoted phrase, that "metaphysical and moral consciousness perishes at the touch of the Absolute." We shall have to examine the cogency of these claims; it is a task no Christian philosopher can shirk.

The Irrational. Another characteristic of contemporary humanism is its interest in the *irrational*; this will be the concern of Chapter Three. One of the most obvious preoccupations of modern thought, as it manifests itself in art, philosophy, depth-psychology, literature, is the exploration of the multiple forms of the irrational that seem to lie deep within us, influence our behavior, and underlie even our highest activities. From this point of view, contemporary European thought has left the rationalism, whether scientific or idealist, of the last century far behind. This is a welcome progress. It is, however, true that within this anti-rationalist reaction, one can discern a tendency to discredit the human intelligence and its instrument, the concept; to exalt the emotions and the liberty of

---

[3] J. P. Sartre, *L'Existentialisme est un humanisme*, Paris, 1946, pp. 38, 89.

the will beyond measure, to declare impossible the attainment of an objective and universally valid truth in domains other than that of mathematics and, perhaps, positive science. Once again, all this seems hard to reconcile with the spirit of Christianity. Faith opens our minds to the mystery of a transcendent God and allows us enter into personal relations with Him; it is a light meant to illuminate *every* man that comes into the world. But this can be so only if the human intelligence is somehow capable of recognizing universal and objective truths which transcend the narrow limits of scientific verification. The universality of the Christian faith cannot be reconciled with either voluntarism of fideism.

Critique of Existentialism. Chapter Four summarizes the contributions that existentialism has made to our philosophical understanding, and then goes on to examine some of its technical defects. It is argued that it has not quite rid itself of traces of both empiricism and idealism; it is further suggested that this is due to an inadequate analysis of its point of departure. The way is left open for a more thorough analysis which will, at last, get beyond Cartesian dualism.

The Relevance of Thomism. This brings us to Part Two, where it is pointed out that such an analysis, though it will not be found ready-made in the Thomist tradition, could profitably follow the general lines laid down by Aquinas. The argument of Chapter Five is directed towards three conclusions: first, the Thomist notion of existence, especially when enriched by contemporary insights, allows us to avoid the difficulties under which existential phenomenology is presently laboring; second, the new analysis thus provided eliminates the dangers of relativism and irrationalism inherent in much of the current existentialist writing; third, such an analysis will be possible only if Thomists are willing to enter into a living dialogue with contemporary thought. Christian faith is not, of course, a philosophical system, nor does it, of itself, impose any particular philosophy, but this does not mean that any and every philosophy is compatible with it. As everyone knows, the Catholic Church has for a long time past given its preference to the philosophy of St. Thomas. It is important to grasp the philosophical implications of such a preference. The "neo-Thomist" movement is just now passing through a crisis, a crisis of growth, in our opinion. This crisis has been brought about by many factors, not least the distrust, mentioned by Pope Pius XII (in his Encyclical, *Humani generis*) among those who think that Thomism is "outmoded in its form and rationalist in its method." It is urged that a mutual reappraisal may be of considerable value to existential phenomenology as well as to Thomism.

The Life of Faith and the Quest of the Spirit. In the final chapter, the discussion is broadened. The problem every Christian faces is not simply that of the choice of a philosophical tradition. There is the more general issue of the relation between faith and unfettered research, between the spiritual and the temporal, between believer and unbeliever. These are not new questions, but they pose themselves in a more compelling way than ever before for an age which has so profound a realization of the historical vocation of man. If man lives within history, we are told, it is not so much to suffer it as to create it. Whereas Christianity—so the modern unbeliever will often argue—kills the sense of the terrestrial and the historical by its insistence that man has not here a lasting city. "Seek ye first the things that are from above, not those that are from the earth," St. Paul cries to all generations of Christians. To walk with feet directed firmly to earth and eyes no less firmly to heaven requires careful balancing. It must be shown that the immutability of Christian faith is reconcilable with the practical requirements of historical existence. A proper understanding of the Christian doctrines of the supernatural (which, far from overthrowing nature, presupposes and respects it) and of the Incarnation, fruit of Infinite Love, is seen finally to provide the basis for a true humanism.

Such are the principal problems we propose to examine. Our purpose is not to try to treat them exhaustively, but rather to use them in bringing Christian faith and contemporary thought into some sort of relationship so that a genuine dialogue may develop. To set over against one another two more or less divergent positions is not to enter into a dialogue. Dialogue is a common effort of many, directed towards a mutual understanding and a mutual enrichment. But to understand one another means first to learn from one another, and to learn from one another means to show oneself responsive and open. Nothing is more dangerous to the human spirit than to believe that one has understood everything and that one has no more to learn from anyone. By taking up this attitude, one renders oneself impervious not only to the thought of others but even, in a sense, to one's own thought, since it is only by confronting ideas with one another that the mind begins to awaken and that the unreflecting anonymous consciousness gives way to the reflective personal one. From this stems the necessity of dialogue for every man who thinks, and for the Christian, in particular. To be open to the problems posed by modern thought is, for the Christian, not only the best means of attaining to an understanding of his age but also a way to deepen his own faith and to make it bear a more efficacious witness.

PART ONE

EXISTENTIAL PHENOMENOLOGY

CHAPTER ONE

A GENERAL DISCUSSION OF EXISTENTIAL PHENOMENOLOGY

It would be rash to try to limit phenomenology by a neat definition. Even in Husserl's work, one finds that the idea of phenomenology revealed itself very gradually, passing first through a long series of metamorphoses,[1] so that historians of philosophy are wont to distinguish many Husserls within his writings. And as to the subsequent work inspired by him, one can say without much exaggeration that there are as many phenomenologies as there are phenomenologists. Besides the work of Scheler and Hartmann, which is dominated by the Husserlian theme of an *eidetic intuition*, there is the extensive literature of existentialism which is related rather more directly to the Husserlian concept of the "world." Then the existentialist label itself covers many widely divergent, and indeed in some ways diametrically opposed, views.[2]

Nevertheless, despite these divergences and oppositions, the term "phenomenology" is not an empty nor an equivocal one. It designates a certain "style" of thinking, a certain manner of taking up and treating the age-old problems of the *philosophia perennis*. Like every other authentic philosophy, phenomenology draws its sustenance from a central enlightening intuition which bestows upon it a direction and organic unity and therefore a kind of "style", and gives it a definite power of penetration and truth-value. This central philosophical intuition is, as it were, the privileged place where the philosopher takes up his sojourn, the light

---

[1]See M. Farber, *Phenomenology as a Method and as a Philosophical Discipline,* Buffalo, 1928; *The Foundation of Phenomenology,* Harvard, 1943; E. Welch, *The Philosophy of Edmund Husserl,* New York, 1941; Q. Lauer, *Phénoménologie de Husserl,* Paris, 1955. In the chapters devoted to existential phenomenology which follow, no attempt will be made to give extensive documentation since many excellent bibliographies are available for this field already. See K. Douglas: *A Critical Bibliography of Existentialism,* New Haven, 1950; V. Yanitelli: "A Bibliographical Introduction to Existentialism," *The Modern Schoolman, 26,* 1949, 345-63; J. Collins, *The Existentialists,* Chicago, 1952, (Appendix).

[2]The names that come immediately to mind are those of Heidegger and Jaspers in Germany, and those of Sartre, Marcel, Merleau-Ponty, Ricoeur, and Camus in France. Many general accounts of existentialism are available in English, such as J. Wahl, *A Short History of Existentialism,* tr. by F. Williams and S. Maron, N. Y., 1949; P. Foulquié, *Existentialism,* tr. by K. Raine, London, 1948; H. Kuhn, *Encounter with Nothingness: an Essay on Existentialism,* Chicago, 1949. The work of J. Collins (*supra*) can be particularly recommended.

that guides his steps, and the inspiration which makes his work an addition to the philosophical heritage.

Because of it, his work is not a pointless chattering but something which gives an insight into the matters it studies. If phenomenology, as a general mode of thought, represents a major philosophical event— and there can be no doubt of this—it is because there lies hidden somewhere within it, despite its imperfections and shortcomings, some sort of intuition of this kind which gives it a permanent interior truth, not in any static sense but in the dynamic sense of a power of penetration which enables the phenomenologist to tell us something of permanent value.

It is just this permanent truth-value which we shall try to grasp in this chapter. The first merit of existential phenomenology is that it constitutes one of the most successful attempts to bypass the classical dilemma of naturalism and intellectualism.

1. The Dilemma of Naturalism and Intellectualism

Man and the Universe. There is a paradox about man and the universe that the philosopher will never cease to find worthy of contemplation since it is, in a sense, the mainspring of all philosophical reflection. One might express it as follows: man is at once lord over and slave to the universe. He is lord because the universe for him is an object which he interrogates in order to judge; it is a possession which he cultivates and dominates ever more successfully, thanks to the progress of science and technology. But if man can thus judge and master the world, he is still not its creator. He is himself part of the world, he depends on it for his very existence, he is carried along and nourished by it. One might, therefore, say that the relation between man and world is a reciprocal one like that between "container" and "contained." This is why it is impossible to understand man without considering his universe, just as it is impossible to describe the universe correctly without referring to man. Even those branches of science which appear most objective— those which speak of "laws" of nature like the "laws" of thermodynamics, for example—always imply some reference to man, to the intervention of man in natural events. In order to discover the laws of thermodynamics, man needs a thermometer which is, in its turn, his own invention. Man and the universe are like two parts of the same book which can be understood only by means of one another.

Two Opposed Views. There exists, then, a strong bond between man and the universe, and it becomes of paramount importance to elucidate the nature of this bond. On this subject, there are two classical views. One (naturalism) treats man as the resultant of physical, physiological, and sociological influences which determine him from the outside and make of him a thing among other things. The other (idealist intellectualism) sees in man an acosmic liberty insofar as he is spirit and constructs the representation of those very causes which are thought to act upon him.[3]

That there should be in this way two quite opposed views of the relation between man and the universe is not surprising when one remembers that to "comprehend" always involves in some way a "taking together," a reduction of the diverse to a unity. But this unity can be sought in two quite different directions. One manner of comprehending endeavors to reduce the superior to the inferior, the diverse to the simple, the heterogeneous to the homogeneous, the qualitative to the quantitative. Such explanation by what may be termed "reductive analysis" ends by making man a perfectly ordinary part of nature. The other manner of interpretation sees in the inferior a reflection or anticipatory realisation of the superior. Thus the superior provides, as it were, the light which enables one to understand the inferior. The key to this kind of explanation is found in the idea that it is through thought, considered as the highest element in man, that one grasps the sense of the lower elements. Man is in this way enabled to unravel the significance of the universe; he is no longer an ordinary part of Nature, since it is he who gives a sense to Nature.

Such is what is often called the dilemma of naturalism and intellectualism. It is worth-while to examine each of these terms more closely.

A. Naturalism

Why Naturalism is so Attractive. The naturalist type of explanation represents a spontaneous and permanent tendency of the human mind, and this is why one finds some form or other of materialist naturalism at almost all moments in the history of philosophy. Democritus and Epicurus had, and always will have, their disciples. The success of this type of explanation is easy to understand if one remembers the following two facts. First, of all, it is a kind of explanation which automatically commends itself to the human mind because of its reduction of the complex

---

[3]M. Merleau-Ponty, *Sens et Non-Sens*, Paris, 1948, p. 142. This book will henceforward be referred to as "*Sens*." In general, we shall give our own translations of passages quoted from the French or German in order to keep the terminology of the book reasonably constant. References will thus be given to the originals rather than to translations.

to the simple or, as Meyerson put it, when speaking of physical explanation, of diversity to identity. The aborigine sees no relation between heat, electricity, and mechanical work; he cannot understand how heat can cause an iron bar to expand or a locomotive to move. But these things become already much clearer if one can classify all these phenomena by a single mathematical equation, and establish a mechanical equivalent of heat or of electrical energy. For the physicist, there is nothing extraordinary about the fact that heat makes metals expand since, according to the kinetic theory, a rise in temperature is the same as an increase in the average velocity of the colliding molecules in the metal. In this way, heat and mechanical movement are identified with one another.

Such reductive explanations are not, however, simply a fascinating game for a mind in search of clarity and identity. It must be emphasized —and this is the second fact alluded to above—that the game *succeeds*, to a great extent, at least. The great scientific discoveries of today owe their origin to the progressive application of the naturalist hypothesis to ever wider domains. Medicine made no real progress until it drew upon biology. Biology itself became an explanatory science only when it left behind the stage of morphological description and began to consider life as a biochemical process. And biochemistry, in turn, is itself a sector of chemistry which is now inseparable from physics. That the universe of man should thus lend itself to a naturalist type of explanation is a consequence of the fact that it manifests within itself hierarchical order of genera and species. The genus-species structure implies that the lower is like a substratum of the higher, the stuff of which the higher is made, thus leading to the consideration (from certain points of view, at least) of the higher as a differentiation within the lower. Man is a species of animal; an animal is a higher form of organic life; a living organism is a biochemical entity; a biochemical entity has a particular kind of physical nature. Here one can see the reason why explanation by means of a reduction of the higher to the lower appears as a permanent tendency of the human mind.

Contemporary Naturalism. Modern naturalism is characterized above all by its close relation with positive science, hence the labels "positivism" or "scientism."[4] It must be carefully noted that "scientism" and "science" are by no means synonymous. Phenomenologists know this perfectly well; they will have nothing to do with naturalist scientism but they do

---

[4]The naturalism of the 17th and 18th centuries was less scientific. It often took its origin in psychological empiricism (associationism).

not decry positive science itself, even though this latter inevitably possesses some naturalist characteristics. There is, they would say, a "good" naturalism, that of positive science, and a "bad" one, that of positivist science. What is the difference between them?

The most important feature of modern scientific knowledge is its doubly empirical character. Not only does it begin from empirical facts, but it pursues a type of explanation which terminates in, and is verifiable by, other empirical facts and finds its intelligibility in them. As Claude Bernard, the founder of experimental medicine, puts it:

> When using the experimental method, one performs experiments solely to see and to prove, that is, to control and verify. The experimental method, insofar as it is scientific, is based entirely upon the experimental verification of the scientific hypothesis.[5]

In this, science differs profoundly from philosophy. When the philosopher starts out to prove the existence of God or the immortality of the soul, he *begins*, it is true, from the data of experience, broadly speaking, but the conclusion he reaches is not directly verifiable in experience. Whereas when the physicist sets up a theory of the atom, this latter is of value only insofar as it is open to direct verification by the facts. For the man of science, to "explain" means to establish relations between phenomena and their phenomenal antecedents, to unite phenomena by increasingly inclusive mathematical equations which admit a phenomenal type of verification. Positive science is restricted, therefore, to "nature", taken as an *a priori* totality lending itself to scientific experimentation.

In this sense, science is, by definition, "naturalist," but the naturalism in question here is a purely *methodic* one. It is a manner of marking off the field of scientific experimentation, of tracing the limits within which science must operate. This methodic naturalism is in every way legitimate and salutary; should an avowedly scientific explanation make surreptitious appeal to transphenomenal or metaphysical factors which escape experimental control, it would cease to have any properly scientific value.

Philosophical Naturalism. It must immediately be added, however, that the man of science may easily err by attributing a uniqueness to his method which it does not possess, by maintaining that the only truth is scientific truth and that the only real being is that revealed by positive science. By doing this, such a scientist shows himself unfaithful to the

---

[5]C. Bernard, *Introduction à l'étude de la médecine expérimentale*, Geneva, 1945, p. 409.

scientific spirit, since he is asserting something which, by definition, is not subject to scientific verification. It is this unjustified glorification of positive science as the unique source of truth and certitude that is called scientism or positivistic naturalism. There is no longer question here of merely methodic naturalism; we have here a *philosophical* naturalism which reduces the total field of intelligibility and truth to a particular mode of understanding, namely, the mode which is proper to scientific explanation. This is the sort of naturalism that phenomenology never ceases to combat.

Yet this philosophical naturalism is not, perhaps, the most important factor when it comes to explaining the anti-naturalist attitude of phenomenology. The principal merit of this new philosophy would seem to be that it has shown with an extraordinary perspicacity that there are varieties of naturalism which are much more insidious and dangerous than the straightforward one we have called positivist. Naturalism—and we shall see that the same is true of intellectualism—is not just a philosophical system, it is also a spontaneous tendency of our minds, which unceasingly threatens our thinking and spoils even our best efforts to describe man and his place in the universe. Naturalism in this wider sense is the temptation to visualize the whole real (including the realms of consciousness and freedom, intersubjectivity, and even the mysterious depths of the Godhead) in terms of cosmological categories, that is, in terms of categories borrowed from the world of nature, from the world of "things," as Bergson would put it. Among these categories, two deserve special attention, those of "thing" and "impersonal causality."

A "Thing." To be a "thing" is to be a quantified reality, subject to manipulation and measurement; it is to occupy a determinate place in the spatiotemporal world. The "being-there" of such a thing possesses perfectly definite contours, which permits one to situate it as a thing among other things. This is no longer the case when one is treating of persons, of beings endowed with consciousness and freedom. The "being-there" of man, his "Da-sein," his mode of presence, does not allow itself to be shut off behind clearly defined barriers. It lacks the contours which would allow us to circumscribe it. When a father announces to his children that Mother is about to return home after a long absence in hospital, it is evident that such expressions as "absence," "return," "being-at-home," express much more than a simple localization. The absence of Mother was everywhere a sort of "void," her return gives a "presence" which cannot be sharply localized as that of an object in space could, since it tends to fill space. Indeed, in a certain sense, it can almost be said to create a "space," to make it exist. It is precisely this "presence of Mother" which makes the "home" much more than a concrete-and-brick structure whose dimensions were exactly determined by its architect. Instead, it is an open and welcoming space, a little world in which it is good to live. The presence of a person in the world has not got the definite contours that the presence of a thing would have; it has a certain ubiquity. The "being-there" of a person is identically his "being-in-the-world"; it is as vast and varied and mobile as the world which it fills and to whose existence it contributes. The phenomenological discussion of "being-to-the-world" is an effort to rediscover our primitive experience of presence, so alien to the current emphasis on "things."

Impersonal Causality. A second important category of the world of nature is that of natural causality, or *impersonal causality*, (*"causalité en troisième personne,"*) as recent writers tend to call it. By this, they mean a causal process in which there is no place for the person, for the intervention of liberty. Such, for example, would be the necessary causal process in which rain is formed by a sudden cooling of clouds. Here again, there is a great temptation to treat of the mystery of incarnate liberty or of the interaction between different liberties according to one's notions of natural causality. To excuse our faults, we sometimes throw the responsibility for them on our education, on the books we have read, on the people with whom we have been forced to live. It is true that in our thoughts and actions we owe much to our education and environment. But it would be wrong to look upon this dependence as if it were the expression of an impersonal causal process. My environment for the most part forms me only insofar as I accept it and allow myself to be formed by it.

Even religious or theological thinking does not always succeed in resisting the temptation of naturalism. We are easily led to regard faith and the life of grace as a kind of supernatural "having" which automatically confers upon us the love of God and neighbor and a morality higher than that of the unbeliever by an impersonal causal process. We forget that the love of God is a *personal* attitude, the response to an appeal, and that faith (*fides*) is at once a gift from above and a demand for *fidelity*. This point will be more fully developed later. For the moment, it is enough to remember that the category of natural causality can aid us but little in correctly describing the universe of man and its intersubjectivity; it is even more to be distrusted when we try to grapple with the mysteries of Creation and Providence where the freedom of man encounters the freedom of God. Here again, phenomenology by its elaboration of a philosophy of encounter has done us a valuable service.

B. Intellectualism

While naturalism tends to understand the higher (that is, the life of spirit) in terms of the lower (the subhuman universe), intellectualism follows just the opposite path. It interprets the lower in the light of, and in function of, the higher, because it is the higher which gives the lower its sense. This sense is a sort of reflection of the higher, a preparation for its coming, a mirroring in which the higher can find its own reflection and can thus arrive at a full knowledge and possession of self. Why should the man of science or the philosopher pore so much over the subhuman world, which at first sight seems so distant and mysterious and hostile, if not to bring it closer by revealing its *rational* structures, in other words, its fundamental kinship with human reason, with the Logos which inhabits us and enables us to understand ourselves in understanding the world? Far from being reducible to the lower as if it were merely a product of the lower, the higher is, in fact, its principle and terminus.

It goes without saying that the "higher" in question here is the life of the intelligence envisaged in its highest manifestations: the pure concept, reflection, and reasoning. Intellectualism might, then, be defined for our purposes as a manner of philosophizing which considers the intelligence, independently of its reference to sense-experience, as the unique and self-sufficient source of all authentic knowledge. The intelligence is taken to be the locus of truth and authentic being; in the return of the intelligence upon itself, man discovers deep within himself the presence of the Absolute.

Various Forms of Intellectualism. There are, however, many ways of interpreting the life of the intelligence according to which of its three "moments" one emphasizes most. These "moments" are: the formation of the concept, the judgment as an absolute positing of existence, and the discursive or dialectical process. Because of this diversity, what one is wont to call intellectualism in philosophy is really a general mode of thought which can manifest itself in a thousand ways. If the reason is taken primarily to be the faculty of clear and distinct ideas (as it is in Cartesian intellectualism), then the locus of authentic truth will be sought in the self-sufficiency of notional evidence, and it is here that the Absolute will finally be encountered. If, on the other hand, the life of the mind is understood rather in terms of act and action, one enters into the climate of idealist intellectualism characteristic of post-Kantian philosophy; the pure essence of thought will be defined as an active identity of self with self which must be manifested in and realized by reflection. Philosophy becomes a discourse on subjectivity which is taken to be a knowledge of self consequent to a return upon self.

Whatever about the varied forms which intellectualism has taken in the history of thought, it is important to note that it contains a measure of eternal truth, just that measure, in fact, which naturalism neglects. This is why it forms the other term of the contrast which we are discussing. This permanent truth of intellectualism is an insight into what scholastic philosophers called the immanent character of cognitive life, or in more modern terms, its interiority and spontaneity. By this is meant that the cognitive life cannot in any way be interpreted as the product of an impersonal causality. As we shall see later in more detail, the appearance of a *cogito*, that is, of that mysterious presence-to-self which constitutes the knowing person, is a primitive and irreducible fact. Conscious life was regarded by the scholastics as a type of immanent operation. Such an operation proceeds from the agent while remaining within the agent as its own perfection.[6] It is a "self-movement"; it is a manner of acting and existing which makes one appear to oneself as a self with one's own proper existence. We find the same idea in modern guise in those who define cognitive life as "being-of-itself-and-for-itself" (*"aus sich und für sich sein"*).

Monist Tendency. Doubtless, this manner of being, this "being-of-itself-and-for-itself," does not necessarily imply that the cognitive consciousness also exists *"durch sich,"* that is, as the absolute source of its own being. There is, however, a great temptation to carry out the process of passing to the limit and to attribute to cognitive life the perfect and absolute aseity by which the being of God is properly defined. This temptation is all the greater in that there is question here of what the scholastics called a "simple" perfection, that is, one whose formal definition excludes all imperfection and which is therefore somehow "unlimited" in itself. It is central to the kind of intellectualism we have been considering to make this passage to the limit right away; subjectivity and aseity are taken as synonymous. "To posit oneself and to be are one and the same thing with regard to the being of the Self."[7] But if the self is defined by perfect aseity, it must be identified with the Absolute; the non-self exists only by and for the self. This leads directly to monism.

The same monist tendency is found in Spinoza's concept of substance; he reaches this concept through an aseity based on a conceptual type of

---

[6]The word "immanent" is used in a rather different sense nowadays, chiefly in connection with the Cartesian theory of consciousness. For the scholastics, however, it indicated a definite opening of oneself to the other *qua* other.

[7]J. Fichte, *Grundlagen der gesammten Wissenschaftslehre*, Leipzig, 1908, vol. i, p. 292.

evidence. To be a substance, it is not enough that a thing should exist of itself; it must also be capable of being *conceived* without reference to anything else: *substantia est quod per se est et per se concipitur.* Now this is true only of God; God is the unique Substance, because He is the only Essence that carries within itself its own justification. By identifying the immanence which characterizes the cognitive life with the divine Aseity, intellectualism always leads to one or other form of metaphysical monism.

"Monism" of Truth. This metaphysical monism (or monism of being) entails a sort of "monism" of truth as well. Intellectualism, whether rationalist or idealist, recognizes only one authentic form of intelligibility and certitude, that of the apodictic evidence which philosophical reflection aims to reach. Once the cognitive life has been identified with aseity, pure and simple, one must conclude that there is no authentic knowledge nor truth except at the moment when the mind becomes conscious of this aseity, that is, when it discovers itself as the self-sufficient source of the entire system of truth and being. It is just this self-revelation of thought, this "phenomenology of Spirit," as Hegel put it, that philosophical reflection sets out to accomplish. Philosophy thus becomes the reflexive act by which Spirit becomes conscious of itself, makes explicit what was already implicit; it is the ultimate act which justifies itself to itself and in so doing, justifies all the rest. Once philosophy is achieved, thought and being coincide in the translucent identity of self with self. In this way, human consciousness in its search for light and certitude arrives eventually at an intimacy with being and truth, thanks to philosophy. Thus philosophy becomes the unique foundation of all certain knowledge. Sense-experience, of itself, does not have any validity nor definitive value. Philosophical discourse alone, by deploying its apodictic evidences, can transform experiential judgment into valid and necessary truth.

In a well-known metaphor, Descartes likens philosophy "to a tree whose roots are metaphysics, whose trunk is physics, and whose branches are all the other sciences."[8] One finds the same idea in Spinoza's theory of the four degrees of knowledge. Only knowledge of the fourth degree, that which comes through the very essence of God, can be called true and certain in the strict sense. Within the framework of post-Kantian idealism, this would be expressed by saying that there is no true *Wissen* or knowledge except that which comes to a man who, having traversed the *Wissenschaftslehre* (philosophy), at length succeeds in reconstituting the world, beginning from the constituting consciousness.

---

[8]Letter to Picot, *Oeuvres,* Adam et Tannery ed., vol. 9, p. 14.

Primacy of Knowledge. In summary form then, intellectualism is a manner of philosophizing which gives the primacy to knowledge, more specifically, to reflective and philosophical knowledge. This is why it leads to a monism of truth and being, and consequently to a vision of the world where there is scarcely any room left for contingency, liberty, or historicity. Every authentic truth, and ultimately every authentic being, is said to be *in materia necessaria.* As we shall see later, existential phenomenology introduces the ideas of "intentional consciousness" and "existence" precisely in order to challenge this alleged primacy of knowledge and reflection. Human consciousness is not originally and primarily a "knowing" one, in the narrow intellectualist sense of this word; it is first and foremost "being-with," a lived experience of presence. This is why reflection never approaches the self-sufficiency of apodictic evidence, but instead reaches toward something that was already there before the reflection began, namely, the perceptive or pre-reflective life of consciousness.

Reification. Before finishing, it might be well to add—as we have already done with regard to naturalism—that intellectualism, too, is more than a style of philosophizing. It is also a natural tendency of the human mind which inclines one to exaggerate or distort the part played by the concept in cognitive life. Bergson labelled it "reifying abstraction." Man cannot, of course, think without the aid of concepts, yet it must always be remembered that the concept is not the ultimate terminus of thought. It is rather a sign which thought requires in order to grasp reality directly. To confuse this reality with the concept we form of it is to reify the concept and to miss the reality entirely. One can all too easily do just this, however. Plato's realism of the Ideas, Descartes' dualism of body (*res extensa*) and soul (*res cogitans*), and Leibniz' realism of the world of Possibles, are well-known examples of it. There is a subtler form of reifying abstraction, too, one which amounts to a reification of the human ideal. This occurs when one confuses the idea of the transcendent infinity of God with the "limit-ideas" normally used for conveying the unlimited and inexhaustible character of our aspirations towards the true, the good, and the beautiful. In this way, one may be inclined to situate the mystery of creation in the prolongation (by a simple limit-process) of what one does in fashioning a utensil or work of art. The only distinction made in such a case between our miserable effort and the creative omnipotence of God is to say that God, in creating, meets with no resistance on the part of the object. But it is clear that this can give only a poor image of the creative Word. In this way too, one may be tempted to compare Divine Providence with the administration of a mighty enterprise, or perhaps with the loving guidance given by a parent to his children. One fashions God thus to the image of a world-emperor or father of a family.[9] But this is to stray far from the Christian mystery of Providence which was made manifest in the Passion and Resurrection of Jesus Christ, the First-born Son of God.

The significance of these remarks will appear more fully later. As we shall see, naturalist or intellectualist conceptions of God will be found somewhere in the background when modern atheism rejects the mystery of God and His Providence on the grounds that belief in God involves a surrender of man's humanity.

2. Phonomenological Critique of Naturalism and Intellectualism

A. First Objection: Dogmatic Presuppositions

Philosophy is the search for "ultimate foundations" of two kinds: the ultimate foundations of being, *rationes essendi*, and the ultimate foundations of our knowledge of being, *rationes cognoscendi*. Philosophy has a metaphysical aim in view when it tries to reveal the ultimate foundations of being; insofar as it seeks a solid basis for human knowledge, it banishes all dogmatic presuppositions and takes the form of a critical or epistemological reflection aimed at discovering the "primary" truths which bear the whole edifice of our knowledge. "Primary" has a double sense in this context. It is synonymous first with *"irreducible"*: a truth is said to be "primary" if it is immediate, that is, if it stands on its own without any need of support from outside. "Primary" also indicates something which is the principle of something else. Thus, a truth is said to be "primary" in this sense when it appears as the basis or part of the basis of other derived truths. Every philosophy, insofar as it is regarded as a work of criticism, is an incessant effort to discover primary truths beyond the derived truths with which it is presented.

Naturalism. Naturalism, when examined epistemologically, is seen to be a sort of critical empiricism. It can take two forms, one psychological (associationism), the other deriving from empirical science (scientism or positivism). According to the former, all human truth derives ultimately from sense-impressions which convey elementary sense-qualities. According to the latter, there is no authentic truth other than that which "positive" science establishes. It is not difficult to show that the so-called "sense-quality," when understood as an elementary and primary

---

[9] J. Maritain, *La signification de l'athéisme contemporain*, Paris, 1949, pp. 25, 28.

datum, is in reality an abstraction, a construction of the mind. That which first presents itself to me is not a color nor a rough surface, taken separately, but a colored or rough object.

> It is impossible to describe the color of a tapestry completely without saying that there *is* a tapestry, a tapestry made, say, of wool, and without implying in that color a certain tactile quality, a certain weight, a certain opaqueness to sound.[10]

That which we call a "rough surface" is not an abstract geometrical space, nor an immanent content of consciousness but a real aspect of a real object. In a certain sense, this object manifests itself only by concealing itself. This is why it presents multiple "aspects": it can be seen from the "front" or from the "back" but not ordinarily from both sides at the same time. In a sense, it is present, whole and entire, in each of these aspects, since "front" has meaning only when relative to a "back"; it invites me, so to speak, to look at the other side.[11]

What we have just said of the alleged elementary sense-qualities of psychological empiricism applies with even greater weight to the "scientific fact" delivered by the experiments of positive science. This "fact" is not an absolutely first datum because scientific experiment is a work of man which presupposes prescientific contact with the world. The best-established laws of mechanics or of geology, and the concepts used in them (like the concepts of particle, of motion, of stratification, of folding, and so on) would not have any sense for me if my everyday perceptive experience had not presented to me objects which approach me and move away from me, or landscapes where terraces rise, one upon the other. The world of scientific research lies just over the horizon of the lived world of natural perceptive experience; this why the latter contributes so much towards giving a sense to our scientific image of the world.

> The universe of science is constructed upon the lived world. If science is to be carried on rigorously, with an exact appreciation of its meaning and implication, it is necessary to awaken within us first that experience of the world of which science is a second expression.[12]

This is why scientism, which claims to reduce the field of intelligibility and truth to the rationality of positive science, appears as an excellent example of what Le Senne so aptly calls "detotalization of the

---

[10]M. Merleau-Ponty, *Phénoménologie de la perception*, p. 373.

[11]Husserl expresses this by the notion of *Abschattung;* real things, according to him, are seen only *Abschattungsweise*, in different profiles.

[12]Merleau-Ponty, *Phénoménologie*, p. III.

totality."[13] Scientific experiment, insofar as it endeavors to disclose functional relations between objects, universally verifiable "facts," is evidently a process of abstraction. It leaves to one side the quality of individuality which the experience possesses as *my* body. It also abstracts from the aspect of "meaning-and-value-for-consciousness" which affects the data of experience; it does this when even the data are themselves psychological events.[14] The scientific "object," therefore, represents only a sector of our total experience; scientific rationality is only one manifestation among many of human reason, understood in its widest and existential sense. In this sense, reason is that *lumen naturale*, that natural light which is in us, which enables us to give a human meaning to our behavior, to discover all round us a world full of significances and values, and to find in the "other" a center of initiative and a companion who shares our situation in the world.

Thus we may justifiably claim that science is not *all* that man has to say, nor even that which is most important to say. Besides the work of science, there is the aesthetic, the social, the moral life; there is the encounter with other selves through the medium of language in its multiple forms. More generally, there is the grasp of existence itself as a synthetic unity, opening on the world in all its intersubjectivity.

Intellectualism. If the mistake of empiricist naturalism is to take either the sense-impression or the scientific "fact" as the primary datum, the mistake of intellectualism is to make either the clear and distinct idea or philosophical reflection the primitive and all-sufficient source of truth. But here again, there is no human idea which does not refer to some perceptive experience from which it has been abstracted; reflection is always a turning-back on a pre-reflective stage which preceded it and which continues to act as its referent. Even the most radical kind of reflection, such as the philosopher's search for ultimate foundations, has meaning only when it retains "a consciousness of its peculiar dependence on a non-reflective life which is its initial, constant, and final situation."[15]

---

[13] *Obstacle et valeur*, Paris, 1934, p. 27. By this he means "the operation by which one passes from the consideration of the whole, in the broad sense, to that of the whole less one of its parts, and attributes to this latter imperfect whole the name and properties of the original whole."

[14] In empirical or "objective" psychology, events of the psychical order (such as, for example, the consciousness of passing from one sensation to another of a greater intensity, the perception of a *Gestalt*, the perception of a relation between things or events) are regarded as objective facts to be put in relation with other objective facts, such as the physical structure of the stimulus. The aim is to set up functional relations between variables and not to elucidate the "internal meaning" of the variables.

[15] Merleau-Ponty, *Phénoménologie*, p. IX.

Existential Phenomenology Exposes These Dogmatic Presuppositions. If these remarks are accurate, it is easy to understand why the primary preoccupation of phenomenological and existential thought has always been to expose the unexamined presuppositions which underlie naturalist and intellectualist systems, and to show that they are second-level constructions of the human mind. One must return to things themselves as they present themselves in the primitive revealing intuition which first gives us knowledge of things and of which perception is the prototype. This is the meaning of the famous Husserlian motif: *Zu den Sachen selbst* ("return to things themselves"). It also indicates the meaning of "phenomenon" in the terminology of Husserl and Heidegger: the real as it appears, as it shows or gives itself, as it reveals a meaning to consciousness by its significant presence. The aim of phenomenological reduction is to make this return to things themselves; as Merleau-Ponty expresses it, it must enable us to bring to light and formulate "an experience of the world, of a contact with the world."[16] It is this experience which first gives us access to truth.

To describe this primary and primitive relation between man and the real, phenomenology makes use of several expressions all of which mean more or less the same thing, though they are not altogether synonymous. It speaks of the "prereflexive" or "antepredicative" or "perceptive" life of consciousness. It describes man as "being-to-the-world" ("*être-au-monde*," "*in-der-Welt-sein*") in order to emphasize that conscious life is not just a succession of impressions or of immanent contents; it is originally an experience of "presence" or of "compresence," a "being-with" or a "being-near." The terms "existence" and "intentional consciousness" are intended to emphasize the same idea. Before examining the meaning of these expressions more closely, let us review the second objection which existential phenomenology levels against naturalism and intellectualism.

B. Second Objection: a Faulty Philosophical Anthropology

Every philosophy is at once a theory of truth and of certitude (an epistemology and a noetic), a doctrine of being (metaphysic) and a conception of man (philosophical anthropology). We shall return again and again to this. Concentrating on the last-mentioned aspect, it is clear that naturalism and intellectualism by their reduction of truth to a single mode cannot but truncate the being of man and make his relation to the world unintelligible.

---

[16]*Sens*, p. 55.

Naturalism. This truncation is clear where naturalism is concerned. First of all, if man were nothing more than a point of encounter of a series of impersonal forces, it is hard to see how he could appear to himself as an "I" who knows his existence to be his own, who knows his body to belong to him. When, for example, I am gazing at a landscape, I know myself to exist as an incarnate being because my view of things is peculiarly *mine*. This experience which I have of my own "incarnation" is not the same as that which I have of a neutral object over against me, but rather that of a personal tending—corporeally implemented—towards things.

This entails a consequence which naturalism cannot explain. Because of this intention, I am at every instant "beyond" that which I am actually sensing, while at the same time previous perceptions are still influencing me. My exploratory intention anticipates in some fashion a future which does not yet exist, a whole world yet to be explored; it leaves behind a horizon of past perceptions which no longer exist yet which are somehow retained. My "project of exploration," insofar as it has a *meaning* for me (that is, insofar as it appears to me as directed towards something and at the same time beginning from something), cannot be the simple resultant of physical forces which are acting at this moment upon me since it is guided largely by what no longer exists and by what does not yet exist. Looking at this in another way, the world appears to me as a world to be explored; it reveals itself by hiding itself, as it were; it appears as an inexhaustible potentiality of interconnected aspects. It is a "hodological" world (Lewin) in which everything appears as a "way towards" something else, as pointing out something other than itself. For this reason, it already has a "meaning" of sorts. As *Gestalt* psychology has shown so definitively, a signification (even the very minimal "form-background" one) cannot be adequately explained by the objective structure of physical stimuli acting upon the perceiving organism.

Intellectualism. Intellectualism is untrue to man because it reduces him to a sort of disembodied spirit. If human consciousness is not first and foremost a relation-to-the-world, if it is a pure interiority shut up in its internal representations, there is no way of distinguishing perception from image since their only differentiation is an extrinsic relation to an extramental reality which is, in principle, inaccessible.[17] Furthermore, if it is true that we are the pure and translucid interiority of which Descartes and the post-Kantian idealists speak, how is it that the human

---

[17]See J. P. Sartre, *L'imagination*, Paris, 1948, pp. 91-113.

psyche appears to us as a mystery, an enigma? How can we explain the empirical, always partial, historical character of our existence? If human consciousness is at bottom an impersonal Logos, it is hard to understand how such an interiority could ever manifest itself through an exteriority (through a gesture, a glance or a smile, for example); the phenomena of incarnation and of intersubjectivity become unintelligible; above all, man is reduced to a being without soul and without destiny, for whom nothing whatever can be done.[18]

To summarize, then, naturalism and intellectualism do not succeed in enabling us to understand our position in a world; they refuse to face the human condition.

> The merit of the new philosophy is to seek in the notion of existence a means of understanding the human condition. Existence in the modern sense is the movement which impels man towards a world and engages him in a physical and social situation which determines his point of view on the world.[19]

This we must now examine in more detail.

3. Existence: Central Reference-Point of Existential Phenomenology

In presenting existential phenomenology as a reaction against naturalism and intellectualism, we have defined it in rather a negative manner. It is time to provide a more positive analysis. Existential phenomenology appears in the history of philosophy as a manner of philosophizing centered round the notion of existence. What is meant by "centered round" in this context?

A. The Notion of a "Central Reference-Point" or a "Primitive Fact"

Every philosophy proceeds from a central intuition, in the light of which it describes and evaluates everything it meets. This intuition is not necessarily a conceptual evidence, capable of being developed into a *mathesis universalis* by means of an *a priori* deductive process. It may just as well be—in fact, it will much more often be—an "existential" experience, a certain manner of grasping our "presence-to-the-world" on the basis of a particular sensitivity towards some general aspect of things or towards some fundamental value, in consequence of which the world is

---

[18]This point is treated at some length in Chapter 3.
[19]Merleau-Ponty, *Sens*, p. 143.

viewed in a certain way. What we shall mean here by a "central intuition" is not an idea nor an isolated fact, but a first intelligible or meaningful moment which is primitive, central, all-embracing, the source of universal intelligibility. It confers a certain intelligible clarity on all things and permits us to situate them, each in its place, in the totality of the real. Some examples may help to make this clearer.

Examples. Mediaeval philosophy was elaborated in the light of the "primary intelligibles": *ens, unum, verum, bonum,* which were regarded as the heart of the intellectual life. As soon as the intellect is awakened, as soon as it "passes into act," it knows the meaning of *ens, unum, verum, bonum*; it possesses a certain understanding of them, prephilosophical doubtless, but enlightening nevertheless; because of this, the intellect is by nature capable of understanding all things and of philosophizing. These *prima intelligibilia,* or naturally known concepts, though incomplete as principles of knowing, characterize the human intelligence as a *lumen naturale,* a power of understanding.[20]

When Descartes suppressed the natural relationship of man to the world which his predecessors called "sensation," he took the primary intelligibles to be the *Cogito,* with the immediate evidences which are contained in it. These governed the Cartesian reflection in the same way as geometry is governed by its fundamental postulates. Under the influence of Kant's well-known "Copernican revolution," post-Kantian idealism was dominated by what was later called the "discovery of the Self," by the recognition of a critical and ontological priority of the subject over the object. This "discovery of the Self" is not a datum of common experience but rather the end-product of a critical and metaphysical reflection upon that subject-object relationship which constitutes cognitive life.

In a philosophy which emphasizes experience in the wide sense and regards conceptual and discursive thought as a derivative kind of knowledge, things are naturally quite different. The primitive point of reference will no longer be an idea nor a datum which is capable of being expressed as a universal concept or as a predicative proposition. It is now a primary significant *fact.* Some speak of a "primitive fact" (Maine de Biran), others of an *"intuition originaire"* (Bergson) or even of an

---

[20]"There are in us by nature some conceptions which are known to all, such as those of being, of unity, of good, and so on. The intellect proceeds from these to the knowledge of the quiddity of a thing in the same way as it proceeds from *per se* known principles to the knowledge of conclusions." St. Thomas, *Quodlibetum* VIII, q. 2, a. 4. He related them to the activity of the agent intellect. See *Summa Theol.,* I, q. 79, a. 5, ad 3.

experience which is "pure" or "*a priori*" (Madinier) or transcendental (Husserl). Lavelle developed his "dialectic of the eternal present" in the light of an "initial experience which is implied in all the others," namely "the experience of the presence of being . . . the immediate bond between being and the self which is the foundation of each of our actions and gives each of them its value."[21] Marcel took "incarnate existence" to be the "central reference-point" ("*repère central*") of philosophical reflection.

Philosophical Importance. These few examples should suffice to show the philosophical importance of what we have called variously the "primary intellectual point of reference," the "first intelligible or meaningful moment," the "central reference-point," the "primitive intuition," or as we shall usually call it, the "primitive fact." It dominates and orients the philosophical dialectic, allowing it to be at once radical and transcendental. It is characteristic of philosophy to seek the widest syntheses, to search for the ultimate and definitive unity which gathers together all beings in one, yet allows each to be what it is and to act its proper part, to have its proper significance. We can define philosophy as "radical and transcendental thinking," as "interrogation of the being of beings," or as a "search for the ultimate meaning of things"; all of these say the same thing but they help to bring out the fact already mentioned that every philosophy is at once a metaphysic, an episte- mology and a philosophical anthropology.

B. METAPHYSICS - EPISTEMOLOGY - PHILOSOPHICAL ANTHROPOLOGY

Being. The intermingling of these three aspects is worth examining more closely because of its importance for what follows. What is meta- physics if not a reflection by man upon the meaning of being in general, a reflection which is guided by some accepted view of what constitues "true" being or at least of what constitutes an approach to, a rough model of, "true'" being? Thus naturalist scientism will recognize as "being" only that which positive science reveals, all the rest being illusion and counterfeit. The scientific object is thus considered to be the prototype of anything which deserves to be called a "being." Intellec- tualism, on the other hand, sees authentic being rather in the line of the clear and distinct idea, the essence which bears in itself its own evidence and whose being consists precisely in its being manifested. It is because of the aseity of the conceptually evident that Spinoza, for example,

---

[21]*La présence totale*, Paris, 1934, pp. 25, 27.

regards God as *natura naturans*, as an infinite Essence whose proper activity is to manifest Itself in Its attributes and modes in somewhat the same way as the concept of "triangle," if it is truly a concept, shows forth to us all the possible properties and modalities of a triangle. For post-Kantian idealism, the selfsufficiency of the Self shows the presence in us of the Absolute Being, of the Being who justifies Self and everything else.

Truth. If these diverse conceptions of being are examined more closely, however, they are seen also to be diverse ways of interpreting *truth.* It is sufficient to look back at the examples just cited to see that being is defined in each case by its mode of appearance, of showing itself to someone. This is perfectly natural since metaphysics is man's search for an ultimate meaning of being. If being is meaningful for us, it is because in one way or another it manifests itself to us, or to put this in another way, it is because there is a primitive connection between being and truth, *ens* and *verum.*

Man. Carrying this a little further, it is clear that *man* is implicitly mentioned in all these different approaches to being and truth. Once again, this is not to be wondered at since—for us at least—man is the first meeting-point of being and truth. This is indeed in a certain sense the very essence of man. To put this in scholastic fashion, if man is distinguished from other animals by his intelligence, the "faculty of being," then he can be called a "metaphysics-making animal." In all metaphysics, then, there must be some reference to man. Further, in defining *verum* and *bonum* as attributes of being precisely as being, the scholastics introduced a reference to human intellect and will, respectively. Heidegger reaches the same conclusion, for him an all-important one, though he expresses it somewhat differently. According to him, the essence of man is to "exist," to be "open to being," to abide in the midst of being as an opening or "openness." This implies that man possesses a preontological understanding of being which philosophical reflection must bring to light and transform into explicit knowledge. But if this be so, then "the problematic of philosophy centers around the essence of man," and metaphysics is at once an enquiry into being and into man. [22]

One of the fundamental characteristics of contemporary existentialist thought is to have recognized with singular clarity this interrelation of metaphysics, noetics and philosophical anthropology. This is intimately connected with phenomenology's emphasis on the notion of existence.

---

[22] Heidegger, *Kant et le problème de la métaphysique.* Tr. by A. de Waelhens and W. Biemel, Paris, 1953, p. 261.

C. EXISTENCE AND INTENTIONALITY

It would be impossible to do justice in a few lines to the wealth of significance attached by recent writers to the word "existence." Existential phenomenology is not a well-defined system; it is, rather, a philosophical style of thinking. Thus "existence" has a different shade of meaning from one author to another: in Merleau-Ponty and Sartre it is one thing, in Marcel and Jaspers another, in Heidegger something else again. Despite these differences, however, it possesses a common core of meaning in all of these writers.

Existence. Insofar as it serves to express the fundamental category, or more precisely, the "central reference-point," of existential philosophy, the term "exist" no longer signifies—as it did for Kant—the simple fact of being real; it means rather the manner of being which is proper to *man*. In this sense, only man "exists." Not that there is nothing outside man; man has, however, a mode of being called "existence" by which he is distinguished from all other beings that inhabit the universe. Man is not simply a *thing* among other things, nor a pure interiority turned inward upon itself, shut up in its own immanent representations, like the soul in Descartes' philosophy or the monad in that of Leibniz or the Self in post-Kantian idealism. Man realizes himself as an interiority with consciousness and freedom, a "for-itself," only by going *outside* himself, so to speak. He must get *near* to things by way of a living contact with the world and with other people. Human consciousness is essentially and from the beginning an openness towards what is other than itself. Man is a "subject bound to the world" (Merleau-Ponty), a "summoning of being" (Sartre). It is this openness towards what is other than itself that contemporary philosophy, following Kierkegaard, wishes to emphasize by stressing the prefix "ex-" of "exist" or the *"Da"* of Heidegger's *"Dasein."* The term "exist" thus becomes synonymous with "being-to-the-world"; it is ultimately only another way of expressing what Husserl meant by the "intentionality of consciousness" (*Welterfahrendes Leben*).[23]

Intentionality. This notion of intentionality, that dominates all philosophizing which derives its inspiration from Husserl, is more complex than it appears to be at first sight; the time is not yet ripe for us to develop it in its multiplicity of aspects. It will be sufficient for the moment

---

[23]See G. Brand, *Welt, Ich und Zeit nach unveröffentlichten Manuscripten Edmund Husserls*, The Hague, 1955.

to remark that the concept of intentionality, like that of existence or of "being-to-the-world," is used in order to bring out the essence of consciousness, namely, openness to that which is other than consciousness; to employ an expression dear to Merleau-Ponty, it is a "paradox of immanence and transcendence." For phenomenology, the primitive relation between man and the universe is not the relation of *knowledge*, strictly speaking. From this point of view, phenomenology might be characterized as the refusal to give primacy to knowledge.

This statement could easily prove misleading, however, unless it is carefully taken. To "know," in the strict sense, is to be able to say to oneself (and to others) what the real is and how it is; it is to be able to formulate a judgment about the real with full confidence that it is conformed to the real as it is. Knowledge, therefore, if understood strictly, pertains to the representative and predicative consciousness, or, as St. Thomas puts it, it belongs to the order of reflection.[24] For this reason it cannot be primitive because it presupposes an "antepredicative" exchange with the real directly (*die Sachen selbst*). Every judgment, according to Husserl, refers to an experience of presence (*Erfahrung*) in which consciousness is in contact with the real and gives an intentional union with the real.

Presence. This experience of *presence* constitutes our first relation with the real, and makes the real present to me as a "real-for-me," that is, as something which has a meaning and value for me. It enables me to realize myself as a being-to-the-world. It goes without saying that this primordial relation is not one of simple spatial juxtaposition: consciousness is not a thing among other things. Nor is it a pre-established harmony between the two worlds of thought and being (Descartes, Leibniz). It is not a relationship of causality, whether of a causality which proceeds from the object towards the subject to produce knowledge in the subject (materialism) or of a causality which goes from subject to object and makes of human subjectivity a consciousness which constitutes its object (idealism). If we are to "think" (that is, to "fix in concepts") this primitive or antepredicative life of consciousness, terms like "cause" and "effect" are no longer appropriate. We must rather look to the notion of "dialogue" and to the categories entering into the structure of the "encounter."[25] Such are, for example, the notion of "exchange,"

---

[24]*De Veritate*, I, q. 9; *Summa Theol.*, I, q. 16, a. 2.

[25]Indeed, the notions of dialogue and encounter themselves also prove inadequate in dealing with the structure of the intentional consciousness, since this latter is a primitive fact of which dialogue and encounter, in the ordinary senses of these terms, are already particular forms.

the relation of intention and datum, the dialectical bond between engagement and situation.

> The (primary) bond between subject and object is no longer the relation of knowledge of which classical idealism spoke and according to which the object always appeared to be constructed by the subject. It is rather a bond of being in virtue of which, paradoxical as it may seem, the subject *is* his body, his world, his situation.[26]

In the same way, Marcel considers the primitive relation between the self and the world to be one of exchange, involvement, participation, in the double sense of taking part in and of being a part of that in which one takes part. This, he claims, is why the world appears to me as "my" world, a world in which I feel "at home." The human *Dasein*, says Heidegger, insofar as it realizes itself in the world, associates the world with its projects and sees the world in the light of these projects. Man is thus a "world-builder"; he arranges a world around himself. Thus we speak of the "world" of the farmer, of the doctor, of the physicist. These different "worlds" are so many different ways of arranging the world-in-general which is so to speak, the farthest encircling horizon of every human project, the guarantee of our meeting one another in one and the same arena.

Noema - Noesis. One important consequence of this is that all intentional behavior manifests a so-called "noetic-noematic" structure. By "*noema,*" contemporary writers mean the object of the intentional consciousness, the grasped, the "seen," with the meaning it possesses for consciousness. The "*noesis*" is the manner in which the subject orients himself intentionally towards things, the way in which he views or "pro-poses" objects to himself, the grasping. Since intentional behavior brings about the meeting of intention and datum, *noesis* and *noema* always go together; the meaning of one points to the meaning of the other. It is impossible to describe one without bringing in the other.

Let us take an example. If a picture is to appear to me as a portrait, that is, as the representation of someone, it must, of course, possess a definite objective structure. A white wall could not appear as the image of my mother. It is, however, equally necessary that I should take up a definite attitude towards it. I must direct a certain "intention" towards it, and this intention must be incarnated in a certain kind of conduct. If I intend simply to note the kind of material used or the manner in which the painter has manipulated his colors, I shall adopt the line of conduct usually called "observation" and the picture will appear to me

---

[26]Merleau-Ponty, *Sens*, p. 144.

as an ensemble of lines and colors. It will not possess the sense of a portrait since it has no reference to a person represented. Because of this, my consciousness in this case will appear to itself not as evoking images but as perceiving or observing. Another example: if a landscape seems sombre and sad to me, this may well be due to the fact that I am feeling sad or discouraged; it is also true, of course, in reverse that sunless weather tends to make me feel sad.

The activity of the scientist reveals the same kind of correlation between *noesis* and *noema*. If the scientific object is to reveal itself in its proper structure to the human consciousness, it is necessary to adopt a scientific attitude towards the real, to "interrogate" it in a proper scientific manner, to go to meet it with hypotheses which we try to verify. Science, however empirical it may be, is never the result of a merely passive attitude towards the world. It is a human "work" in the strictest sense. The same is true in the domain of aesthetics or in the world of instruments or of human relations. To the eyes of a child or of a savage with no knowledge of writing, a pen will appear as a toy or perhaps as a weapon. If it is to take on the significance of an instrument for writing, it must at some time be associated with the action of writing, that is, with a type of behavior, a particular kind of intentional relation towards the world. Again, in order to find someone worthy of my love, I must be disposed to love him; anyone who treats men as things will always remain closed to the mystery of "thou."

Traditional Character of "Intentionality." Such is, in brief, the meaning of "intentionality" and the concepts connected with it, which have dominated much of philosophy since the time of Husserl. Our knowledge of the real depends on an experience of *presence* which, in turn, is interpreted as the coming together of a guiding intention (*noesis*) and a given (*noema*). By means of this analysis, existential phenomenology takes up from a new angle the old problem of the nature and structure of finite human knowledge. Human knowledge, because it is finite, does not create its object; the object is already there but this does not mean that human consciousness is pure passivity, receiving impressions from outside by way of transitive causality. For existential phenomenology, as for Aristotle, Aquinas, Kant, human knowledge is a mixture of passivity and of revealing spontaneity. In this sense, one might say that this new philosophy is an inheritor of the tradition of moderate realism coming from Aristotle, a tradition in which the dilemma of empiricism and intellectualism does not arise. That which Aristotle regards as a light provided by agent intellect, and Kant as an *a priori* of the subjectivity (the *a priori* forms of sensibility and the *a priori* concepts of the understanding), here becomes an intentional grasping, constitutive of its horizons and ultimately of the world. This "world" is not the sum of things known, but the "horizon of horizons" within which every object appears and takes on a sense for us. A thing is intelligible and comprehensible only in a context. The world is, then, the "context of all contexts."

D. Existence as the Central Reference-Point of Philosophical Reflection

We have seen that existential phenomenology is a way of philosophizing which is dominated by the notion of existence or of intentional consciousness. Existence is its central reference-point, its "primitive fact," in the sense of being *irreducible* and *primary*.

It is, first of all, *irreducible*; it cannot be reduced to or reconstructed from, simpler elements such as the sense-impressions of empiricism or the clear and distinct ideas of intellectualism. Existence, as being-to-the-world giving rise to a paradox of immanence and transcendence, is a first datum. It is something which cannot be denied nor called in question because it is presupposed in the very attempt to deny it.

Secondly, it is *primary*. It is at the origin of all the most complex manifestations of the life of consciousness; it is the point of reference for all significance and comprehension, for our everyday comprehension of things, for scientific explanation as well as for philosophical reflection. It is the foundation for all that is to come after. Every philosophy is a return to foundations. For the existentialist, these foundations are no longer the pure diversity of sense-impressions of classical empiricism nor the scientific facts unveiled by positive science. Nor are they first truths revealed by an analysis of clear and distinct ideas. Nor is the foundation a reflexive act by which consciousness attains perfect self-identity, revealing itself to itself as a creative subjectivity which is eternal, impersonal, the *a priori* source of all ideas. For existential phenomenology, the ultimate foundation of human truth is nothing other than our "being-to-the-world," to the elucidation and clarification of which philosophical reflection must be dedicated.

E. The Tasks of Phenomenology

Phenomenology is a work of reflection. Like any other philosophical reflection which aims to be radical and transcendental, it finds itself confronted with a multiplicity of tasks. The first is that of *phenomenological reduction*, whose purpose, as we have already seen, is first to uncover hidden assumptions in positions which are being criticized, and second, to discover the significant "primitive fact" with its character of irreducibility, inevitability and primacy. The second task is an *analysis and elucidation of the phenomenal field*. By the latter is meant the complex group of noetic-noematic structures which constitute the "world" of man. The name "phenomenology" indicates that it is a science of the "phenomenon" so that it must tackle the phenomenal field from both the noetic and the noematic points of view, bringing to light the intentions and fundamental meanings it contains.

This latter work is clearly an immense one, having many facets. There is the so-called "regional phenomenology" which studies the different domains that make up the world of man, such as the world of inanimate nature, the world of living things, the world of culture. There is also the phenomenological study of man himself as a being-to-the-world. It may be made from an analytic point of view, taking each of the diverse modalities of being-to-the-world for specific treatment. Along these lines, we find a phenomenological analysis of emotion, of the image-forming consciousness, of perception, of memory, of symbolism, of predicative knowledge, of the affective life, of will. Or the study might be carried on from a synthetic point of view in order to arrive at the general structures of what Ricoeur calls "the movement of existence which underlies every authentically human act,"[27] in particular, the structure of temporality which is so basic to human action.

Phenomenology in Metaphysics. Even more radically, phenomenological reflection may be employed at the level of *ontology* and *metaphysics*. In this domain, it tries, for instance, to reach the ultimate ontological implications of the human *Cogito*, understood as a *Cogito* which opens on the real. It seeks to know the nature of that human presence-to-the-world which enables us to encounter the real as it is. It asks about the first and fundamental phenomenon which permits man to know himself to be among things and near to them, not as an animal—prisoner in its surroundings—would be, but rather as a free being who can tell what the real is in itself (*quod quid est*) and take this real as the norm of his conduct. This is "the question of the essence of truth, that is, of uncovering as such, an uncovering in virtue of which we find ourselves from the very first in a reality opened to us."[28]

It would seem that that which makes the different "existents" (*Seiendes*)

---

[27]In an essay contributed to *Problèmes actuels de Phénoménologie*, Paris, 1952, p. 115.
[28]Heidegger, *Qu'est-ce que la métaphysique?*, tr. by H. Corbin, Paris, 1937, p. 7. See also "The way back into the ground of metaphysics," Introduction to the 5th edition of the foregoing, separately translated in W. Kaufman's excellent little anthology, *Existentialism from Dostoevsky to Sartre*, N.Y., 1957, p. 210.

appear to me as being, cannot be itself a "being." Thus existential philosophy eventually meets the age-old problems of being and truth at this profound level of reflection.

Let us conclude. Existential philosophy is more than a philosophical propaedeutic aimed at an accurate analysis of problematics. It is a rethinking of the problems of the *philosophia perennis*, the problem of the unity of the things despite the diversity of its aspects, the problem of the unity of the "world" as a last horizon within whose bounds we meet together as an incarnate subjectivity, the problem of the origin and the essence of Truth, the problem of Being. All these problems are now treated over again, but in a new perspective. The world of nature is not regarded as a world of realities which can be studied apart from all reference to man. Human subjectivity is not assumed to be an interiority closed on itself, having a meaning for itself independently of the world. The primitive revealing experience which underlies our concepts and judgments is not of a sense-world separated from man nor of a spiritual *Cogito* separated from the world. It is a living bond between man and the universe.

Human "existence" is the central reference-point of the new philosophy, and this "existence" is essentially temporal. Thus the notion of *historicity* is of vital importance in contemporary thought; to it the next chapter will be devoted.

CHAPTER TWO

THE HISTORICAL CHARACTER OF HUMAN
EXISTENCE AND CONTEMPORARY RELATIVISM

1. Historicity and Humanism

The sense of becoming, or more precisely the historical dimension of things, (the two terms are not synonymous) is perhaps the most characteristic trait of our times. So profoundly is it embedded in the humanism of to-day that it is scarcely an exaggeration to say that it defines it. This sense of history is the resultant of two factors which ought to be carefully distinguished.

A. The Effect of Scientific Discoveries

In the first place, modern science, by expanding our knowledge of the past, has accustomed us to a picture of the world of which our ancestors had no conception, a world whose dimensions exceed the wildest imaginings, and which is yet continually expanding and evolving. Compared to the Universe as we see it, the world as the medievals conceived it looks like a toy. Its history was a mere five or six thousand years in length. It comprised only things with neatly defined boundaries, things that could be classified by genus and species with clarity and precision. There was no room for things "in transition," for links between the species, literally neither fish or fowl. With the progress of modern science, we have seen the world-view of the ancients left behind with incredible rapidity. Instead of something static, we have an "expanding universe." The galaxies and clouds of stars are counted by the millions, and we photograph nebulae a thousand million light years away. More important still, we find that this expanding universe has come about by a development, a sort of history with periods and sub-periods. Lemaître tells us that the duration of the expansion is probably of the order of four to ten thousand million years.[1] The age even of our earth

---

[1] *The Primeval Atom*, New York, 1950, p. 101. There has more recently been considerable discussion of the expansion hypothesis on which this figure is based and of the whole methodological basis of arguments of this type. See, for instance, the November, 1954 issue of *The British Journal for the Philosophy of Science* which is entirely devoted to this question. See also *The Advancement of Science*, vol. XII, issue 45, 1955; M. Munitz, *Space, Time and Creation*, Glencoe, 1957.

is generally supposed to be about two to four thousand million years. The first beings who seem to have been capable of activities resembling those of human beings appeared some six hundred thousand years ago; more and more intermediaries between them and *homo sapiens*, represented by the Cro-Magnon man, are constantly being found.[2] Though the distance which separates modern man from Cro-Magnon man is practically insignificant from the point of view of skeletal change, it is of tremendous importance from the point of view of civilization and culture. New sciences, unknown to our ancestors, have come to confirm this, sciences like prehistory, archaeology, ethnography, the history of science and technique, the history of ideas, the philosophy of culture, and the comparative study of religions. Together with astrophysics, geology and paleontology, these sciences have contributed to broaden the horizons of the past; they have allowed us to look at the world and at humanity on a vaster scale, to see them, as it were, in their totality.

Seen thus, the most striking thing about our universe is the fact of development, evolution, continuity, historical structure. It is not surprising, then, that modern man sees and feels things in a rather different way than his ancestors did. Yet this is only one of the components of what we have called the new sense of the historical dimension of things.

B. THE MAKING OF THE FUTURE

Besides seeing further and further into the past, the man of today has become more actively aware of the future. The future is not just the other half of the film which remains to be shown before the end of the world comes. In the modern view, man has other roles to play besides that of the spectator who sits and waits. He knows that he is not the omnipotent master of his future, but he also realizes quite clearly that by his personal activity he contributes to the making of the future. The future is not so much something which happens to him as it is a horizon of possibilities to be realized, into which he must "project" himself. The awareness of history which characterizes our time is bound up with the fact that we have a vivid consciousness of our being an "embodied liberty," a "being-towards-the-world," or, in Marxist terms, a "worker-being." "The labor on which history rests," says Merleau-Ponty, "is not . . . the mere production of wealth, but more generally the activity by which man projects around him a human environment, and

---

[2] See G. Vandebroek, "The origin of man and the recent discoveries of the natural sciences," in *God, Man, and the Universe*, N.Y., 1953, pp. 93-143.

rises above the natural data of his life.''[3] This is why we emphasize that man is a ''historical'' being. Because we are embodied spirits, the material world is not so much an obstacle as a support and an instrument which we need in order to liberate ourselves. Even our most immaterial activities can be accomplished only with the help of matter. There is no science without laboratories, no true aesthetic emotion without a work of art, neither poetry nor thought without language. To cultivate ourselves we must cultivate the world. This is the sense in which man is a worker-being.

Man's historical character is inseparable from the history of civilization. Civilization is a give-and-take between man and the world. Man, in order to free himself, puts his stamp on the world, transforms it into a world of civilization and culture. The world in turn molds man and gives him the opportunity for further freedom, or freedom in new dimensions. It is for this reason, too, that one can speak of a *meaning* in history. History is not a bundle of events without order and continuity, without lines or vectors; it is not ''a tale told by an idiot . . . signifying nothing.''

This consciousness of being-in-history is bound to become more acute as it becomes daily clearer that our world is at a turning point, that humanity finds itself faced today with the task of building a new world. Such a turning point occurs when, at that moment where past and future touch, the concrete situation inherited from the past meets an ensemble of radically new possibilities. This is just what is happening today. The incredible expansion of the positive sciences and of industrial techniques has opened to us new horizons of technical, cultural and social possibilities. The idea of a greater participation by the masses in the benefits of culture and civilization is no longer a Utopian dream, but rather a program to be realized in the immediate future. A new ideal of justice has been born. This is the explanation of the awakening of the working class and of the upsurge of the great mass of dispossessed peoples in the Orient and in Africa.

C. THE HISTORICAL DIMENSION

This sense of the historical dimension of things, which is characteristically modern, is not to be confused with the doctrine of Heraclitus, according to which terrestrial things are fundamentally transient and unstable. It has nothing in common either with the belief in a universe governed by a law of iron, a so-called ''evolution,'' to which man can only submit. Even the historical determinism dear to Marxist thought

---

[3]Merleau-Ponty, *Sens*, p. 215.

is not a physical determinism, but a "dialectical" one which recognizes in history an interchange between man and the world and takes the aspirations of men to be the most important factor in history. Insistence on instability or on pure becoming in the universe leads to scepticism and epicureanism. Belief in an iron law, even in the law of evolution, engenders fatalism and stagnation. But the sense of the historical dimension of our living contributes in a most powerful way towards an understanding of ourselves and our tasks.

This sense of history is inseparable from the consciousness of our being-towards-the-world, and powerfully strengthens this consciousness. Though it can lead, as we shall see, to a certain relativism in regard to truth and to value, yet this relativism is no scepticism. It does not maintain that all values are equal or, what amounts to the same thing, that nothing has any value. There is a *sense* in history, and for a humanism animated by the sense of being-in-history this sense provides a principle of discrimination. There is a *better* world waiting to be built, *greater* justice waiting to be achieved, a future to be made which will be more worthy of man and permit a more effective recognition of man by man. Thus the sense of being-in-history becomes the motive force of humanity in moments of crisis. It brings to the humanism of today not only a special orientation but also a singularly powerful vitality.

D. HISTORICITY AND THE ABSOLUTE

This point is all the more important in view of the fact that contemporary atheism often launches its attacks on Christianity from the standpoint of a history-centered humanism, objecting to the revealed and supernatural character of the Christian religion. Christianity, it is argued, kills our feeling for the things of earth, for the pulse of history, because of its habit of regarding everything *sub specie aeternitatis*. The Christian has his dwelling in heaven. "Our conversation is in heaven."[4] Does not St. Paul recommend us to put aside the things of this world? "Mind the things that are above, not the things that are upon earth."[5] Christianity is supposed to impede our following the vocation of being truly human and of striving to eliminate the man-made restrictions which weigh down humanity. "Religion," says the Marxist slogan, "is the opium of the people." The idea of a revealed truth, immutable, defined once for all, is regarded as a danger to all that is great and vital in contemporary humanism, to the almost tragic sense of the complexity

---

[4]*Philippians*, III, 20.
[5]*Colossians*, III, 2.

of the truth, of the incompleteness of human knowledge, of the necessity of renewing over and over again our scale of values in order to adapt them to the new possibilities which arise as man's situation in the world is transformed. Thus the Christian is supposed to be reactionary and conservative by vocation. Furthermore, since Christians regard themselves as sole possessors of the truth, and since error has no rights, they are supposed to be intolerant and inclined to dictatorship.

> Recourse to an absolute foundation is either useless or destructive of the very thing which it is meant to establish. For, if I consider myself able to seize the absolute principle of all thought and all evaluation . . . I have the right to withdraw my judgments from the scrutiny of others. My judgments take on a sacred character . . . and I can piously condemn my adversaries.[6]

Where the Christian is supposed to be wrong is in placing "the foundation of truth and morality outside of experience." Belief in God, by clouding the sense of being-in-history, leads to rigidity of thought and finally kills all reflection. "The metaphysical and moral consciousness dies once it comes in contact with the absolute."[7] Is it true that belief in God and in an after-life stifles in us any feeling for man or for history? This is the all-important question which the modern world puts to the Christian conscience, and particularly to the Christian moralist, whether he be philosopher or theologian. This question must be taken seriously. It is not to be dismissed as an idle objection cooked up to disconcert believers. It is by no means a simple task to reconcile belief in a Divine, immutable revelation with a healthy and vigorous humanism that respects the historical character of human life. The bringing together of time and eternity, and even more the entry of the eternal into history, (which is, after all, the essence of the Christian religion, centered as it is around the mystery of the Incarnation of God) pose multiple problems both in theory and in practice.

Among the theoretical problems (we shall return to the practical ones in our final chapter), there are two in particular that merit special attention. First, is historicity consistent with the presence of an immutable factor within history? Without such a factor, historicity becomes historicism and there is no way of avoiding a relativism of truth and value. Second, is historicity consistent with the existence of an Absolute outside history, an Absolute which is yet in constant relation with history? This is the problem of the co-existence of the eternity of God and the

---

[6]Merleau-Ponty, *Sens*, p. 190.
[7]*Ibid.*, pp. 190-1.

contingence of history, of the sovereignty of the Creator and the liberty of the creature. It is characteristic of contemporary atheism to declare such a co-existence unthinkable. According to Merleau-Ponty, theology adverts to the contingence of the being of man only when pointing out its origin in a necessary Being, and so for all practical purposes ignores it.[8] Our first task, then, must be to examine the theme of historicity in present-day philosophy.

2. The Theme of Historicity

Although it is easy to see that the notion of historicity occupies a central place in modern thought, it is quite difficult to define this notion or explain how it has attained its present importance. What do contemporary thinkers mean to stress when they make "historicity" (rather than, say, "becoming" or "duration," two not dissimilar concepts which have had their vogue) the key to their systems?

A. What "Historicity" is Not

Fleetingness. "Historicity" must not be confused with "fleetingness." The contemporary stress on the historical dimension of things has nothing to do with the "*fugit irreparabile tempus*" of the poet, or the "*vanitas vanitatum, omnia vanitas*" of Ecclesiastes, or the eschatological warnings of preachers. The feeling that earthly things are unstable and transitory generally indicates a mind which is turned towards the past or else is haunted by the Absolute. Whereas those who emphasize historicity suggest that one should "project" oneself towards the future, as it were, in order to come to grips more adequately with the present. This does not mean that modern thought underestimates the past. There are two rather different ways of regarding the past; it may be thought of as falling back into non-being, as something which has been but no longer is in any way, or it may be considered as that which has been present and which still contributes to anchor us in this present moment by a process of "retention" or "reactivation." Although Plato no longer exists, it is true that in a certain sense, he still lives among us; without him, our philosophy would not be what it is; our awareness of the mystery of being would not be as keen, our experience of our presence in being would not reach the same spiritual depths. Heidegger distinguishes between these two different notions of the past as *Vergangenheit* and as *was gewesen ist* (with the emphasis on "*ist*").

---

[8] *Eloge de la philosophie,* Paris, 1953, p. 61.

Motus. Nor is historicity synonymous with the vague and general notion of *motus* (change, movement), in the manner in which this is developed in some neoscholastic manuals which make it cover the appearance of any new determination, no matter of what kind. Understood in this way, "*motus*" is more of a linguistic schema than a concept. To include under the same phrase, "new determination," events as diverse as spatial movement, qualitative change, philosophical reflection, artistic creation, response to the call of duty, is to stop at the externals of these events and leave out of account that which matters most, namely, the *content* of that which comes to be. This vague idea of *motus* has an almost limitless extension, but its comprehension, its revelatory power, is almost nil. It tells us little about the structure of the real; it is not a very significant concept. It can, of course, take on a metaphysical meaning, that is, one which tells us something about the nature of being.

In any case the concept of historicity is something quite different, since it designates not every kind of *motus* but the manner of being which is proper to man.

Becoming and Evolution. "Becoming" is a more satisfactory notion than *motus*. It introduces us to the living world and designates, not just the coming to be of determination, but the manner of being and changing which is proper to the living thing, to the world of "nature" in a narrow sense. That which characterizes living beings is the progressive actualization of that which was already present in germ. The acorn becomes an oak; the child becomes an adult. "Become that which you are," said Goethe. In all these expressions, "become" gives the idea of development, of evolution, of springing forth. In each case, the final terminus of the activity is pre-contained, as it were, in the initial situation. Thus, becoming implies a natural finality and a tendency towards that finality. This unformed presence of the end within the beginning assures the continuity of becoming and the natural movement from one term to the other.

With the notion of historicity, however, we pass over to the world of liberty and intersubjectivity. Continuity is not excluded, but is no longer assured by the gradual unfolding of what was already present. Liberty, in fact, involves a rupture of sorts, since it is the power we possess to separate ourselves from the past in order to see it as it was and to take up a position regarding it. Phrases like "the evolution of art" or "the evolution of philosophy" do not, therefore, express their meanings very aptly; it would be better to speak of the *history* of art or of philosophy. Modern art is not the resultant of a slow progressive evolution; it is a new creation, the work of liberty. Neo-Thomism is not the product of a long maturing process within Thomism; it is an act of fidelity to the thought of St. Thomas. Here we are in a world, not merely of organic life, but of intersubjectivity.

Duration. It is true that Bergson's idea of "duration" is not unlike the present concept of historicity, since it is closely linked with the notions of qualitative time and of liberty. On this view, time would involve discontinuity, novelty, discovery as well as a certain continuity. Nevertheless, this conception of time is somewhat ambiguous because it is still too dependent upon introspective psychology and biology. The well-known "snowball" metaphor, the categories of *élan vital* and creative evolution, illustrate this dependence since they are adapted from the world of inanimate nature. When applied to man, they may easily obscure that which precisely makes man be man. As we have seen in the first chapter, however, one of the main characteristics of contemporary European thought is its reaction against naturalism, against all attempts to make man just another part of nature, another moment in the evolution of the cosmos. It is just this irreducibility of man to physical nature that the notion of historicity aims to emphasize.

B. THE NOTION OF HISTORICITY

Contemporary existentialist thought, though strongly opposed to naturalism, also avoids the opposite intellectualist or idealist extreme which would make of man a disembodied consciousness. Because of his physical and biological bonds with the world, man occupies a definite place in the scheme of evolution, a place which natural science must try to define. In this sense, man can be called an animal; the subhuman everywhere underlies the human. This does not mean, however, that man's behavior, insofar as it presents itself as significant, can be reduced to a play of conditioned reflexes. Man may be classed among animals, it is true, but only if we remember, as Hegel put it, that he is a "sick animal."

The irrational animal is at rest (in a certain sense) within the natural world which surrounds and supports it. His needs and natural instincts are blind forces which waken him to the world and yet shut him off from it and from himself. In comparison with this, man is an anxious questing animal. Snatched by his gifts of wonder, interrogation, and anguish, from the anonymity of being the plaything of natural forces, he feels himself alone in the midst of things; there is an abyss between him and the universe because he knows his existence to be his own, something to which he must himself give meaning.

Liberty. This abyss is constituted by what contemporary writers call "liberty," using this traditional term in a special sense. Liberty is here understood to be a manner of being which permits us to liberate ourselves from nature, both the nature that we are and the nature that surrounds us. It is thus the power of saying "no" to nature, of standing back and asking questions, of giving rise to multiple forms of "negativity" within the complex net of cosmic determinism. "I am other than the universe." "This is not that." "The past no longer exists." "You shall not do that." "Is life really worth living?" Among all these forms of "negativity," there is one which is fundamental, that which permits us to grasp the other-as-other and ourselves as present to it. Merleau-Ponty expresses this as follows:

> Man is not a force but a weakness at the core of being, not a cosmological factor but a focus where all cosmological factors, by an ever-incomplete transmutation, gain significance and become history.[9]

In what sense do they "become history?" By defining liberty as the possibility of standing back from the real in order to make it appear as something already given, we have emphasized its negative aspect. But liberty is also that which permits me to project myself into the future, to plan ahead, to give things a *sense*.[10] Sense implies direction, a viewpoint on the future. "Time is the 'sense' of life ... one speaks of the 'sense' of a river, the 'sense' of a phrase, the 'sense' of smell."[11] Considered it itself, a road has not got a 'sense'; it must be taken as the road *to* somewhere before its 'sense' can be determined. In other words, it must be associated with a project of some sort. If the door of my room appears to me as something which permits me to pass from one place to another, it is only because it has become for me more than a geometrical figure on a neutral background. It is associated in my mind with the intention I have of leaving the room once my work is finished; it is thus implied in my manner of being-towards-the-world, which is always a presence-absence, a paradox of ubiquity and engagement in a definite situation. If I recognize something as an ashtray or a pen, it is because I am familiar with the cultural intentions of a society in which tobacco is smoked and writing is done. Thus we are brought back to the concept of intentionality.

---

[9]*Loc. cit.*

[10]The English word, "sense," lacks many of the overtones of the French *"sens"* on which this passage relies (Transl.).

[11]P. Claudel, *Art Poétique*, Paris, 1907, p. 28.

Intentionality. A 'sense' is born of the encounter between an intention and a datum; this is why all intentional behavior presents the noetico-noematic structure we have already seen when discussing the phenomenological theory of consciousness in the first chapter. At first sight, it might appear that this conception is applicable only to the recognition of a cultural object, like a door or an ashtray. But this is not so. In the passage just quoted, Claudel brings together under one word the meaning of life, the direction of a river, the sense of smell. This is no mere play on words. The life of perception, by which natural things present a sense to me, is already a preliminary manner of ordering the world and humanizing it. Perception can never be reduced to the simple conscious presence of a pure diversity of unrelated sense-qualities. We may recall the passage in which Merleau-Ponty points out that it is impossible to describe the color of a tapestry adequately without saying that it is the color of a *tapestry*. This is how the color comes to have a sense for me; the consciousness does not stop at it but is carried on towards an indefinite horizon of possible perceptions. This is also why the color appears to me as real, as the color of a real thing; the real is "where every moment is not only inseparable from all others but is somehow synonymous with all others, where all aspects signify one another."[12] What is true of the reality of a thing is true *a fortiori* of the reality of the world; a thing appears as real only because of its "insertion into" the world.

Consciousness is, therefore, an encounter, a never-ending dialogue with a world which appears to us as a horizon opening up an indefinite number of perspectives.[13] This implies that human existence has a temporal structure. Human time is neither a pure succession of events which last only an instant before vanishing, nor an eternal present which encompasses the world with a single non-temporal all-seeing gaze. Our presence to the world is admixed with absence; the unveiling of the world which makes it a world-for-me is the continuing work which constitutes history. The continuity of history is assured by the unity of the world which is the correlate of my intentional grasp, but the presence-absence character of this grasp makes it a history which is always incomplete, always beginning again. My past ought not be regarded as a sort of "snowball"; its presence to me rather implies that I can stand back and look at it, situate myself with regard to it and take it as the starting-point for new projects.

---

[12]Merleau-Ponty, *Phénoménologie*, p. 373.
[13]See *Philosophical Essays in Memory of Edmund Husserl*. Ed. by M. Farber, Cambridge (Mass.), 1940, pp. 106-24.

Intersubjectivity. The description of intentionality above assumes that I am alone in the world, that my consciousness is a solitary dialogue with the universe and my past. But I am not alone; the world which opens its illimitable perspectives to me is also that which makes the intersubjectivity of different consciousnesses possible. It is intentionality, then, that allows us to share the *same* world. "If I take my perceptions to be simple sensations, they belong to me alone. If I regard them as acts of intelligence . . . communication with other selves becomes possible."[14] It is characteristic of the intentional situation that "the thing imposes itself not as true for every intelligence but as real for every subject who shares my situation."[15]

The "unveiling" of the world which occurs when it takes on form and value as a world-for-me, is always a shared community work. Thus the world I find around me is one which has already been humanized by others. It bears the imprint of past generations as well as of those who now share my situation. I become fully present to the world only with the help of others, in communion with others, for the benefit of others. The "sense" of a utensil, of a work of art, of a social institution, of language, is not only to make the world more habitable for me but also to allow me to encounter others by means of the world. It is this trait especially which characterizes historicity. History, in the sense in which we use that term here, is made possible by the intersubjectivity within which my presence to the world makes itself felt. Man cannot, in fact, exist without forming a part of history.

The consciousness of being (in some sense) *everywhere* which defines the wide horizon of our presence to the world extends not only to the world but also to the history of mankind. Every trace left by man has a sense for us; it is as if it were a dialogue with the past. This is why the past which we are always reliving is not merely our own but also the past of all those with whom we communicate on the basis of what Hegel called "the world of spirit made objective," especially the ambiguous world of linguistic signs. This is what gives a history to science, art, philosophy. As we have already noted above, the philosophic past helps to anchor us in the present. Without Plato, St. Thomas, Kant, and all the rest, our sensitivity for the mystery of being would not be as keen as it is. Once again, this view of the past does not make it a sort of snowball which gathers up all that has gone before; this would be to describe the world of intersubjectivity by a purely physical concept. The reason

---

[14]Merleau-Ponty, "Le primat de la perception," *Bull. Soc. Franc. Philos.*, vol. *41*, 1947, pp. 124f. This article will be cited as: "Le primat".
[15]Merleau-Ponty, *loc.cit.*

why the philosophic past can make the present fruitful is that we are
able to stand back and examine it as it was. In this way, the thoughts
and acts of those who no longer exist can be reactivated and scrutinized.
History is thus a combination of continuity and discontinuity, anonymity and originality, generality and singularity.[16]

Rethinking. Within the history of philosophy, "rethinking" (what
Heidegger calls *Wiederholung*) is the central and transforming activity.
Every great philosophy is a return to the same problems, but this return
is not simply a repetition or a new answer to clearly-posed questions.
It is rather a rethinking of the problems themselves right from the
beginning.

> By the rethinking of a fundamental problem, we understand the
> bringing to light of the potentialities it conceals. The unfolding
> of these transforms the problem itself and in this way conserves
> its authentic content. To conserve a problem means to liberate,
> as well as to safeguard, the interior force which is the source of
> its appeal and which makes it appear to us as a problem.[17]

This kind of "rethinking" gives philosophy its continuity so that one
can speak meaningfully of a *philosophia perennis*; it also indicates that
philosophy is not an empty series of repetitions, that it will have turning-
points and crises, and that every great philosophy is assured of a fruitful
posterity.

To conclude, "historicity," "temporality," "embodied liberty,"
"being-towards-the-world," "intentional consciousness" are obviously
closely related terms. Historicity represents an essential aspect of human
existence, and has three strands: the noetico-noematic structure of
consciousness, the temporal character of man, and the intersubjectivity
in which man lives. This is the concept which has come to have a central
place in contemporary French and German philosophy. What we have
said in the first chapter about the key role of the concept of "existence"
in contemporary thought holds good, *mutatis mutandis*, for historicity too.
In the next section, we shall see how it has affected metaphysics and
epistemology.

3. Historicity in Contemporary Philosophy

The notion of historicity made its first appearance in philosophy
with Hegel. Nevertheless, it would be wrong to take Hegel's metaphysics

---

[16]P. Ricoeur, *Histoire et Verité*, Paris, 1955, pp. 6off.
[17]Heidegger, *Kant et le problème* . . ., p. 261.

as a true philosophy of historicity, since according to it, historicity was destined to disappear with the advent of the absolute truth of the Hegelian philosophy.

A. HISTORICITY AND CONTEMPORARY METAPHYSICS

According to existential phenomenology, the concept of man's historicity has a consistency and status which no subsequent reflection can attenuate. (The concept of existence has somewhat the same sort of consistency for Thomists; they too hold that the attribution of a proper mode of being to the creature is not a provisory affirmation destined for later correction in the light of the affirmation of God). In the philosophies of existence, man's being is envisaged as a presence-to-the-world revealing itself in a temporal and intersubjective way. This being becomes, then, the "primitive fact" for these philosophies; it is at once something irreducible, final, and a first intelligible which affords us access to being and indicates the lines our thought should follow. According to this view, absolute being cannot be handled by concepts applicable primarily to the physical world nor by a self-sufficing conceptual evidence. It is neither one nor the other of the Absolutes it is often taken to be. There is, first, the Absolute of *naturalism*, the infinitely full and perfect density of Nature, ruled by deterministic law. In such a world of causal necessity, everything happens just in the way it *must* happen, without surprise or accident. There is no place there for contingency or evil or any sort of negativity. Whether the earth blooms or grows arid, whether the rivers flow tranquilly in their courses or ravage crops and towns, all this is indifferent because it must happen thus. Such a world is a perfectly tuned machine which cannot conceivably go wrong; it is perfect, without any fissure or fault. It is, in brief, a world without history.

The other Absolute is that of *intellectualism*. Here we have an immanent and necessary dialectic based on conceptual evidence, like the absolute Knowledge of Fichte, the absolute Spirit of Hegel, the God of Spinoza. As before, all that happens happens necessarily. Everything has a sufficient and determining reason. There is no room for chance, evil, liberty, historicity. Everything is for the best in this best possible of worlds . . . Some have held that this is the view defended by classic theology. If holding that God is a "necessary" Being implied that the mystery of creation, of the co-existence of God and man, is thinkable only in terms of necessity, then truly there would be little place for historical contingency and human liberty. But, as we shall see at the end of this chapter, this is by no means the Christian position.

These Absolutes are false because they result from the misplaced concretion of abstractions. Each restricts the basic philosophic experience in some way. Naturalism reduces being to a universe of things governed by an impersonal causality; intellectualism reduces it to a dialectic. Metaphysics is betrayed by each. To the philosopher who speaks in terms of historicity, the idea of a necessary Being (in the rationalist sense just mentioned) as well as that of 'eternal matter' or of the "whole man" will "appear prosaic when it comes to dealing with the upsurge of phenomena at all levels of the world or the continuous coming-to-be with which he must occupy himself."[18] The mystery of being, seen in the light of our historical position within it, must be approached in terms of historicity and intersubjectivity. It is not impossible that one might, in this way reach a view of being similar to the scholastic description of it in terms of "act." "Act" would here imply that "the metaphysical nature of being" is to be "essentially participable, communicable, generous."[19]

B. Historicity in Contemporary Epistemology

To say that being is not a thing nor an idea, but "the upsurge of phenomena," "presence," "generosity," "communication," a "gift," implies that one must speak of being in terms of its appearance. Defining being as "presence" clearly supposes that it is of the essence of being to show itself, to make itself present to someone. Every doctrine of being immediately involves a certain notion of truth and this is particularly true in this case. Temporality and historicity are highly relevant to contemporary epistemology, not just in the sense that all human truth has a historical aspect, but also in the more fundamental sense that truth is itself ontologically somehow an "event" within being and furthermore that being—in the strong sense in which we have been using the term—is not being except through this "event." Epistemology has thus gained a historical, dramatic, even poetic, conception of truth.

Truth. This means that the classic definition of truth as an "adequation of intellect and thing according to which the intellect judges that to be which is and not to be which is not" becomes of somewhat less than primary importance. It holds for the predicative statement (*die*

---

[18]Merleau-Ponty, *Eloge de la philosophie*, p. 62.
[19]J. de Finance, "La négation de la puissance chez J. P. Sartre," in *Sapientia Aquinatis*, Rome, 1955, p. 481. See also R. Johann, *The Meaning of Love*, Westminster (Md.), 1955.

vorstellende Aussage) and is adequate for handling the truth of the ordinary proposition (*Satzwahrheit*). A proposition is said to be "true" when the person asserting or denying the predicate of the subject allows himself to be guided solely by the real as it appears. In this sense, Heidegger is correct in saying that true judgment already implies a moment of liberty since it involves submission to a norm, specifically as a norm.

All this presupposes, however, that some reality has already been present to consciousness, has shown itself as it is, in such a way that the question "what is it?" has become meaningful to the questioner. Every proposition is based on, and guides us towards, a more fundamental kind of truth, therefore. This truth Heidegger calls "αλήθεια"; it is a sort of unveiling, a coming forth from obscurity. This fundamental truth is not to be regarded as the presence in our minds of a more or less adequate copy of the object known. To suppose this would be a crude over-simplification, an assumption that the relation of truth is necessarily like that between an object and its mirror image. What we may call "truth by unveiling" is an "event" (*Geschehen*); it is, in fact, the fundamental "event," the one which ensures that in the world something "*happens*" (in the strong sense), that there is "history." As we have seen, this "event" appears at the level of phenomenological description as the encounter between the intention and the given, or, as Merleau-Ponty puts it, as the upsurge of meaning "which manifests itself spontaneously in that interlacing of actions by means of which man organizes his relations with nature and his fellow-man."[20]

At the level of the ontology of knowledge,[21] one can still speak of truth as an "event." It recalls the ontological history of a presence which realizes itself through encounter. "The presence of man with regard to Being and the presence of Being with regard to man"—this is more or less what *Dasein* means to Heidegger.[22] It indicates a "simultaneity" of sorts between man, taken as a historical existent, and Being, taken as a Presence which gives itself by making itself the light for man. In Heidegger's phrase: "*Sein und Zeit*," "*und*" expresses not just the juxtaposition of two philosophical themes, but rather the dialectical relation that is found between them. He does not mean to imply that the two terms are on the same level. Being is still the basic theme for him; it is that "which gives itself, is at once giver and gift."[23]

To express the characteristic of "event-ness" which truth by un-

---

[20]Merleau-Ponty, *Éloge*, p. 69.
[21]See Chapter 1, Section 3 B.
[22]H. Birault, "Existence et verité d'après Heidegger," *Rev. Mét. Mor.*, Vol. 56, 1951, pp. 35-87.
[23]*Ibid.*, p. 82.

veiling possesses, Claudel's pun about truth's being a *"co-naissance"* before it is *"connaissance"* may be recalled. If it be taken as an encounter which aims to unveil something, it can be likened to an "event" on whose account things begin to "be" for man at the same time that he becomes conscious of himself and begins to exist for himself. This is why we likened this earlier to a poetic or dramatic conception of truth; the poet, the artist, the philosopher, each in his own way must make us see things, make them "exist" for us. Indeed, perceptive life is itself already a kind of *"poesis,"* a putting in order of the world, thanks to which the world becomes a world-for-me.

Human truth is, in consequence, essentially finite, incomplete, and, in a certain sense, provisory. If all human affirmation is dependent upon the antepredicative or perceptive life of consciousness, as the existentialists maintain, and if at this level man, far from being an impartial spectator, is really a subject engaged in a particular historical situation, it follows that the insight into the world thus obtained must inevitably manifest an empirical, slanted, historical character. The meaning which the world takes up for me depends, to some extent at least, on my attitude, on the project I am proposing. And this project, in turn, is inseparably connected with my corporeal, social and historical vantage-point in the world. Since I am absolutely incapable of becoming "disembodied," of surveying my body and my world in a non-temporal, non-spatial, all-embracing way which would synthesize all points of view in one sweep, it would seem that my knowledge of the world must permanently reflect the oriented and historical characteristics of antepredicative conscious life. Thus human truth can never be definitive, can never give the last word. "There is certitude about the world in general but not about any object in particular," according to Merleau-Ponty.[24]

Despite what idealists have said, reflection, no matter how radical, cannot completely prescind from prereflective life. If it is not to lose itself in a vacuum, it must recognize its "essential dependence upon the pre-reflective life that provides its initial, constant and final situation."[25]

Evidence. It is clear, then, that existential phenomenology with its doctrine of encounter between intention and given is basically a view of the nature of evidence. It opposes the intellectualist approach by rejecting the possibility of man's ever finding *completely* adequate evidence for his assertions. By obeying Husserl's call to return to "things themselves," it wishes to emphasize the importance of "evidence," which

---

[24]*Phénoménologie*, p. 344.
[25]*Ibid.*, p. IX.

Husserl defined as "the quality which knowledge gains from the actual presence of the thing itself."[26] This quality is found where the intentional horizon is completely filled, as it were, by the actual presence of the reality which is viewed. In this privileged moment of evidence, things "give" themselves, "appear," to consciousness and make well-founded affirmation about the real possible. Thus, the primary significant intuition whose prototype is perception (*Wahrnehmung*) provides the evidence which justifies our knowledge of the real.

But human evidence is always inadequate, because the encounter of the intention and the reality presented can never give rise to the perfect identity which would make of the reality an object spread out in front of us, without mystery. This is what is meant by saying that the intentional consciousness, because of the encounter within it of intention and given, is a paradox of immanence and transcendence. "Neither in external or internal perception, nor in judicative or discursive thought does the thing ever 'give' itself totally or adequately. It is encountered only in the single aspect under which it is taken up."[27] External perception, in fact, is concerned only with aspects or "profiles" of things. Internal perception is always preceded by some external perception and is bound up in various ways with temporal processes which prevent its ever fully possessing itself. For this reason, we cannot form an exact and adequate idea of our own interior life. Can I truly say, for example, that I love someone? Only the future can tell whether I do, because love to be true must also be faithful; perhaps not even the future can tell this, because present fidelity does not absolutely determine my future course of conduct. The same is true of judgment and discursive reasoning; it can never attain a complete identification of subject and object because reflection is bound up with the pre-reflective (which it can never fully circumscribe) in such a way as to transform it into something which is completely grasped. "In reflection just as in perception, human consciousness cannot quite gain full possession of its operations."[28]

C. The Absolute Factor

From this, many phenomenologists conclude that since no human evidence is completely adequate, no human truth can be taken as definitive either.

---

[26]G. Van Riet, "L'évidence (dans la phénoménologie)," *Sapientia Aquinatis*, p. 573.

[27]G. Van Riet, *op. cit.*, p. 574.

[28]Merleau-Ponty, *Phénoménologie*, p. 62.

A piece of evidence is irresistible in one way yet is always revisable . . . It is irresistible because I take for granted some fact of experience, some feat of thought. This appears to me as evidence for the thinking nature I possess, a nature which, however, appears as contingent and given. The consistency of a perceived thing, of a geometrical relation or an idea can be shown only if I stop looking everywhere for an explanation for them and take them as given. Once I have actually begun the search in a particular direction, within a particular notional framework (say, that of Euclidean space or of a determinate social situation), I begin to find evidence, but this evidence is not beyond challenge since this space or this society is not the only one possible.[29]

Every human truth is thus regarded by Merleau-Ponty as provisory and revisable.[30] To this general rule he admits, however, one exception, namely, the primitive and undeniably given fact of my own presence in the world. Although I may always re-examine my perceptions and question my philosophical or my scientific positions in order to reach clearer truth or deeper certitude, this revision must always be carried out within the world, using the world as a starting-point. The ultimate condition of possibility of all particular human experiences is that we should be together in the same world. The indefinite series of events which mark the lives of all men past, present and future, is not a disorderly chaos but a complex articulation which goes to form history. This is the first given fact and this is what Merleau-Ponty means by saying that we are certain about the world in general, but not about anything within it in particular.

This exception is more important than might appear at first sight because it may indicate a way to answer the fundamental question raised by this theme of historicity. How can we hold fast to a historicity of human existence without falling into some sort of relativism? We have seen that within historical existence, the relative always presupposes a permanent and absolute factor. This existence is, then, a unique combination of the mutable and the immutable, whose features we may expect to find reflected in our knowledge.

---

[29]Merleau-Ponty, *op. cit.*, p. 454.

[30]It is worth noting at this stage that the alternatives "definitive" and "provisory" are not necessarily strictly disjunctive in this context. A middle term is possible, namely, valid though incomplete knowledge. One does not need to know everything about Peter nor about the essence of man to be able to say "Peter is a man" without fear of contradiction or later revision. The abstract concept, in general, provides middle terms of this kind. It expresses the concrete *totum sed non totaliter* in a way which is at once stable and yet is capable of being later supplemented.

4. Historicity and Relativism

This discussion of the historical dimension of our knowledge and of the question it raised about our ability to reach an absolute is closely connected with the traditional problems of the universality of truth and the finitude of the human mind. Human knowledge does not create the real. The real is "invariably already there" when we turn towards it to grasp it. For us, to know does not mean to invent, to build a scaffolding of concepts, to develop an *a priori* dialectic. To be true, our knowledge must be judged by the real. It must always begin, then, in perceptive experience. It might seem, at first sight, that the human mind is primarily *receptive* in the acquisition of truth and that our knowledge is true only insofar as it is passive with regard to the real. If this were so, then the important thing would be to leave consciousness wide-open to receive the images of things as accurately as possible.

This, the empiricist conception of knowledge, is defective for several reasons. One we have already seen. An impersonal process cannot give rise to a personal one. All knowledge, no matter how elementary, implies a conscious act, a lived interiority, what the scholastics would call an immanent activity. It cannot be treated as a transitive activity; nothing is explained by the metaphor of consciousness as a camera or of memory as a scrapbook. There is another difficulty also. Empiricism, if carried through consistently, would actually destroy the very notion of truth itself.

A. The Universality of Truth

Truth has an aspect of universality which empiricism cannot explain, try as it may. This universality may be approached either from the side of the subject or of the object. A truth must be true for all and must be capable of being recognized as such. Anything which is true for me alone, or for just this moment alone, is not really a truth; it is, at most, an "impression" of some kind. A consistent empiricism cannot claim to produce truths which are valid for all since it recognizes only sense-impressions passively received here and now in private events within the narrow confines of the individual subjectivity.

Universality from the Side of the Object. True knowledge is not just a collection of unrelated data; it always implies some comprehension. If one merely registers data, they remain exterior to one another; each is new in comparison with the preceding ones because each comes in an *a posteriori* manner to add to the others from the outside. But by comprehension, on the other hand, particular data are grasped as related to one another, as interior to a whole which contains them *a priori*. The diversity of the data is unified by a single concept or system of concepts. The concept of a triangle, for instance, is such that I can derive the properties of all individual triangles from an understanding of it. In physics, I must go out and gather the facts and then start organizing them with the aid of some hypothesis. In other words, I begin to unify the data in a certain light provided by the mind. Kant would call it an *a priori* of the understanding; Heidegger would speak of a natural and pre-ontological comprehension of the real (*natürliches Seinsverständnis*). If this "universality" from the side of the object were lacking, if the universe of experience were nothing but a chaotic flow of events, there would be no "things" as we know them and the world would be radically unintelligible. We could not recognize anything, name anything. There would be no universality from the side of the subject either because we would not be able to understand one another. There would be no way of reaching judgments that all could accept. In short, the known intersubjectivity of the human community implies a universality of truth which empiricism cannot provide.

Universality from the Side of the Subject. Besides this universality of truth here and now within the community, there is, as we have seen in the second section of this chapter, an aspect of universality within the history of thought also. We are constantly taking up again, or "reactivating" (to use Merleau-Ponty's phrase), the thoughts and acts of past generations. We may, if we wish, reject them, modify them, accept them. This weighing-up of the past implies, however, a *continuity* in the intellectual life of the community. It implies also a set of value-judgments. Now this continuity and this sort of estimation seems to be out of the question for a consistent empiricist. If there is nothing but the simple succession of events, how are we to introduce norms? Insofar as the data are regarded simply as "positive" empirical facts, all of them have the same value, all have the same degree of reality. They are unaffected by the distinction between good and evil, authentic and inauthentic. Radical empiricism cannot speak of a "progress" of science or of the "advance" of culture.

But history *has* a meaning and a direction. It is not true that everything is neutral. The history of mankind is the product of a dialogue between man and the world, which is carried on in a living, continuing community. This dialogue is animated by man's most deep-seated desire, a basic drive to express himself with the aid of the world, to liberate himself in order to emerge from the anonymity of the crowd and grope his way towards light and liberty.

B. An Exaggeration of this Universality

From this analysis, it follows that there are within truth the germs of universality and permanence. Must we, therefore, conclude that the source of truth is the mind rather than the world? It would seem to be an ideal that we project ahead of us, an intentional grasping-towards which proceeds from within us; it both underlies and illuminates our relations with the world. It may be called an "adequation of intellect and object," but the emphasis seems to have shifted; it is the real, it would appear, that is being regulated by the mind rather than the mind by the real. This is the "Copernican revolution" of which Kant spoke, which has had such a deep influence on modern philosophy.

Impersonal Universalism. But when we hold the desire for a universally acceptable and valid knowledge to be an integral part of man's historical existence, the universality we have in mind is of a very different kind to one which preaches a completely featureless set of universal principles. Such intellectualism, whether Cartesian or post-Kantian, depends entirely on its assumption that a "total reflection" is possible. In such a reflection, thought would turn back completely on itself and attain to a vision of things in which thought and being would coincide in a perfect identity. This vision would naturally be independent of any particular point of view, and would enable one to know things as they are in themselves, quite independently of any reference to one's own mode of existence. It would, in short, be the sort of vision which characterizes an infinite Divine consciousness. Any truth which cannot be derived from this vision of absolute truth would then be regarded as provisory and unstable.[31]

Its Illusion. As we have already noted in the previous chapter, however, this impersonal universalism is an illusion. It completely misrepresents the human condition. Because we are embodied spirits, and

---

[31]In scholastic terminology, this would be regarded as a confusion between the *prius quoad nos* and the *prius quoad se*. It amounts to asserting that authentic knowledge is possible only when the *rationes cognoscendi* on which our knowledge of things is based coincide with the *rationes essendi* of the ontological order. St. Thomas makes the world of which we form a part the ultimate ground on which all our knowledge is based. It is the *prius quoad nos* in all our affirmations, even the affirmation of God.

remain thus even in our most exalted reflections, our knowledge of the real is conditioned by our corporeal situation within the world, by the physiological *a priori* of our biological constitution, and by our cultural milieu (by the type of language we speak, for instance). If, for example, I see something as an ashtray, it is only because I belong to an era when tobacco is smoked. The world of utility-values is a genuine one, but it is relative to man and to a determinate civilization.

It may be objected that besides utility-values, there are always sensible qualities which present a more objective and unchanging aspect. The ashtray is solid, made of copper, brown-colored. The phenomenologist would be the last to deny this; like anyone else, he insists that things are as they appear to me. But he will add that their manner of appearing may well be conditioned by the make-up of my body, for instance. If my eyes had the magnification power of the electron microscope, the solid ashtray would take on a very different appearance to me. Can science restore our faith in a wide-ranging universalism? Though it may tell us something of the copper of which the ashtray is composed, it does so in cautious tones. Modern science is careful not to give the impression of being a definitive knowledge of things in themselves. Its theoretical systems are adequate to account for known facts but are not to be taken to mirror ontological structures; its concepts are constantly subject to revision.

The Limitation of Philosophy. What of philosophy? Surely it will provide us with a universalist framework? Here again a disappointment is in store. Even philosophic knowing has a finite and slanted character. The aim of the metaphysician is to seek the beginning and the end, as Jaspers says, that is, to attain to the roots of experience and to the ultimate meaning of the real. Nevertheless, he has no privileged insight into the Absolute; he is not himself either at the absolute beginning nor the absolute end. What is most fundamental in being (*prius quoad se*) is by no means necessarily what is most evident to him (*prius quoad nos*). We catch a glimpse of the mystery of being only insofar as our own mode of participation in being allows.

It would seem, therefore, that there is a sort of dilemma here, part of the dialectic between empiricism and intellectualism we have already noted. On the one hand, empiricism makes knowledge a private affair, thus excluding the universality we find in our direct experience; on the other hand, intellectualism emphasizes universality so much that there is no room left for different approaches or for the concrete richness of history. Existential phenomenology claims to be able to mediate successfully between these extremes.

C. The Notion of Historicity Provides a Via Media

Existentialists have developed the notion of historicity in an attempt to work out a theory of truth which will safeguard the empirical origin and incomplete character of our knowledge and at the same time give it a form of universality which is existential rather than purely notional.

Historicity, as we have seen, is a consequence of intentionality; it results from the combination of temporality and intersubjectivity. Less abstractly, human existence is historical because of the fact that we find ourselves as a community, thrown together in a world. The unity of this "world" which we have called the "horizon of horizons," is not that of a sum of *a posteriori* data, nor is it a purely notional one. It is an *a priori* unity but material or "real" rather than purely formal. It is the unity of "a whole which is anterior to its parts, a totality which is open to a boundless horizon of different perspectives."[32]

This unity is the noematic correlate of the character of "ubiquity" which, as we have seen, characterizes our experience of presence and allows human consciousness, though always embodied in some determinate situation, to range at will over the whole universe and over the entire history of mankind. Within such a unity there is room for an intersubjectivity of different consciousnesses; the hallmark of universality is to be found on even our most rudimentary efforts to reveal the world. This universality is an existential one; when the world is regarded as the unique noematic correlate of all human endeavor, man is placed in a community of intention and of situation and yet retains the individuality of his own individual existence.

It is absolutely necessary to find some germ of universality within historicity; it is equally necessary to find some element of permanence within the flux of history. The existentialists are, on the whole, well aware of this. They do not admit to being relativist, in the traditional sense of this term.

> We do not despair of attaining a truth which would transcend particular points of view ... Once it is understood that truth and value can only be presented to us in the verifications or evaluations we carry out when faced with concrete cognitive or practical situations the world recovers its accustomed diversity ... There is, both in knowledge and in action, something that cannot be gainsaid, something which is either true or false, good or evil.[33]

---

[32]Merleau-Ponty, "Le primat," p. 124.
[33]Merleau-Ponty, *Sens*, pp. 126, 191.

They are quite consciously "searching for a middle term between traditional relativism—that of Dilthey, for example—and the impersonal universalism of the classical rationalists, such as Spinoza."[34] Historicity is, for them, something more than mere succession; it must somehow contain what Marcel calls "an indubitable existential factor" which will serve as the "primitive fact" we have already mentioned so many times. But in what precisely does this factor consist? What is its content and ontological significance? For Merleau-Ponty, as we saw at the end of the last section, it is a vague "absolute certitude about the world in general." Is this a sufficient answer? We shall see that the philosophers of historicity diverge in two quite different directions at this point.

5. Divergent Trends

The primitive indubitable factor is taken to be our "being-towards-the-world." Thus the question we have just posed is equivalent to the old one about the essence of man. How deep does historicity go, so to speak? Does it affect the metaphysical depths of our being where the values of our existence ultimately find their ground? If it does, it would seem that nothing has value of itself and that man is simply what he makes himself by his "free" projects. This is relativism, not as marked as the traditional scepticism, but unmistakable nonetheless. Historicity would here become historicism.

The existentialists claim to be giving more than an introduction to philosophy; they intend to seek the *ultimate* value of human existence and of being-in-general. Having shown that existence is the "primitive fact," they go on to analyze the ontological status of this "new *Cogito*." What is the manner of being of the intentional consciousness or, as Sartre puts it,

> What is the synthetic relation we call "being-in-the-world"? What must man and the world be in order that this relation may exist between them? . . .
> What is the meaning of being in general such that it can include two regions so radically diverse (the in-itself and the for-itself)?[35]

To describe the historical structure of our familiar world of science and culture, even of philosophy, and to show that this historicity comes from the intentionality of consciousness, all this is but a beginning of philosophy. There are problems which cannot be eluded: What is the

---

[34]A. De Waelhens, "Phénoménologie et métaphysique," *Rev. Philos. Louvain*, *47*, 1949, p. 366.

[35]*L être et le néant*, Paris, 1943, pp. 38, 34.

ultimate meaning of human existence? Why should we stay alive? How can there be *any* being if all being is historical?

It is answered that history begins with man, but is founded in the last analysis, on something which is (in a sense) outside history and makes history possible, namely, the fact that there *is* a world in which man has arisen. The uninterrupted "arising" of a subjectivity within the real is an "ontological event" (Sartre), an *Urgeschehen* (Heidegger). Beyond the mobilities of our cultural life, there is a "metaphysic in man himself" (Merleau-Ponty).

If we press the matter further, divergences begin to appear. This should not surprise us. Existentialism is not really a philosophical "system"; it is rather a way of thinking inspired by the phenomenological theme of intentionality. On this issue, the important questions are: What sort of being is assigned to man? What is the meaning of the basic intentionality of consciousness? What kind of "openness to existence" is signified by the "ex-" of "exist"? Two different kinds of answer are usually given.

A. ATHEIST EXISTENTIALISM

Some make the human subjectivity the measure of being, the source, as well as the norm, of all value and intelligibility. According to the common interpretation of *Sein und Zeit* (1924), this would have been *Heidegger's* early position.

> At the time of writing *Sein und Zeit*, the thought of Heidegger seemed quite clear-cut. He held that things acquire meaning only through the appearance of man within the real. This meaning is given them by the projects man sets before himself. The real must be conceived as a sort of brute facticity which man, because of the transcendence his power of comprehension affords him, forms and constitutes as a world. This view appears to reduce to an idealism of meaning based on a realism of brute existence.[36]

Sartre seems to say much the same thing, though in a different way and for different reasons. According to him, the originality of consciousness, when the latter is taken as a source of spontaneity (*aus sich sein*), resides in an act of negation (*néantisation*) "by which consciousness determines itself not to be that which is in-itself." The "in-itself" here

---

[36]A. de Waelhens, "De la phénoménologie à l'existentialisme," in *Le choix, le monde, l'existence*, Paris, 1947, pp. 61-2. A somewhat less idealist interpretation of *Sein und Zeit* is put forward by W. Biemel in *Le concept de monde chez Heidegger*, Louvain, 1950.

means "the transphenomenal being of that which appears." This transphenomenal being is somehow "pointed out" within the phenomenon as a factor which is "invariably already there," that is, as "existing also in-itself and not solely insofar as it appears." The transphenomenal "in-itself" is nothing but an "undifferentiated identity." It is and it is what it is; these are about the only things one can say about it.[37] Life takes on a meaning only through man's own intervention, therefore; it is through him that all meaning comes into the world. "Man is the inventor of man"—this is the phrase Sartre uses to summarize his views on humanism and moral philosophy.[38]

Merleau-Ponty puts forward yet another version of this theme. He does not admit Sartre's radical division between the "in-itself" and the "for-itself." He relies greatly upon his analysis of "embodiment." He is first and foremost a phenomenologist and a psychologist; he has no intention of straying into the hazardous domain of metaphysics which he takes to be a search for the ultimate conditions of possibility. There is a metaphysics "in man," it is true, but "that which is metaphysical in man cannot be referred to something above and beyond his empirical being, a God, a Consciousness. He is metaphysical in his own very being, in his loves and hates, in his individual and collective history."[39] There is little that one can say about this "metaphysics in man"; it is far beyond intelligibility and reasoning, a source of paradoxes which arouse our sense of wonder. It would be silly to try to define conditions of possibility in such a domain. Even the most profound reflection must be content with merely revealing the temporality and liberty which go to make up the structure of the human *Cogito*.[40] When this is accomplished, there is no more to be done. "If we find the subject to be temporal and if we add to this paradox those of the body, of the world, of the thing, of the other, there is nothing more to be understood beyond this."[41]

Metaphysical Relativism of these Views. This group of existentialists defends a position which is (from one point of view, at least) a "closed" one, leading to some form of metaphysical agnosticism (taking "meta-

---

[37] *L'être et le néant*, pp. 29-33. In the section, "Aperçus métaphysiques," which closes the book, the author makes some suggestions about the manner of being of the transphenomenal in-itself; see pp. 713ff.

[38] *L'existentialisme est un humanisme*, p. 38.

[39] *Sens*, p. 55. Cf. p. 195.

[40] See Chapters 2 and 3 of the third part of *Phénoménologie*.

[41] *Phénoménologie*, p. 419. For a thorough discussion of Merleau-Ponty's metaphysics, see A. De Waelhens, *Une philosophie de l'ambiguïté*, Louvain, 1951, chap. 18. See also R. Bayer, *Merleau-Ponty's Existentialism*, Buffalo, 1951.

physical" in its traditional sense) or even of atheism. Historicity takes on for them a rather extreme aspect, since man is the only measure of intelligibility and value. Man's historical character is so strongly emphasized that it eventually swamps him altogether. Because of this, it would seem that the mystery of man automatically loses its profundity, its properly metaphysical dimension. The only way in which we can still speak of man's unchanging "essence" is as a sort of pure "possibility-in-general" of bestowing meaning. "Man exists only insofar he realizes himself; he is nothing more than the series of acts that make up his life." Man "chooses on his own"; "life has no *a priori* meaning"; "it is up to the individual to give a meaning to things, and value is simply the meaning that is chosen"; "no universal moral philosophy can really tell one what to do. There are no signs to be seen in the world. Catholics say, 'but there *are* signs!' Even if we admit this, it is I who interpret them in the last analysis."[42] This anthropocentric position is, from the metaphysical point of view, radically relativistic.[43]

B. "Open" Existentialism

There is, however, another way of developing the existentialist theme, an "open" way. It refuses to take man as the measure of all things and recalls the time-honored philosophical tradition which founds truth and value on being. The essence of truth is no longer taken to be man's capacity for attaching meanings to things by means of his free projects. This latter explanation would suffice when one is dealing with the world of utility-values, of things constructed by man, whose "truth" is man-made. But apart from this secondary realm, truth is dependent upon man's capacity to open himself to the mystery which underlies all beings, that which "lets them be."[44] This docility of man towards being, what Heidegger calls "*offen-sein*," or Forest "consent to being," is not just a pure receptivity but an act of liberty; it is, in fact, the foundation of all true liberty. To recognize the real for what it is, to

---

[42]*L'existentialisme est un humanisme*, pp. 55, 89, 47.

[43]It is only fair to add that it is not as relativistic from the moral point of view as it appears. He does not hold that *all* choices are equivalent; to choose "liberty" or "authenticity" in any moral situation is the "better" course. Thus, he says that "though the content of morality is variable, a certain form of it is universal" (see *op. cit.*, pp. 82-85). Though it is man who decides what is "authentic" (just as it is he who decides what is artistic), this does not mean that there are *no* norms to guide him in his moral or aesthetic decisions (p. 73). However, the difficulty of this position needs no emphasis. See M. Grene, *Dreadful Freedom*, Chicago, 1948.

[44]M. Heidegger, *De l'essence de la vérité*, tr. by A. De Waelhens and W. Biemel, Louvain, 1948, p. 19.

recognize the other in his dignity as other, above all, to accept the mystery of being, all these demand a respect and a fidelity which must be proof against temptation.

We may, perhaps, see this "open" existentialism in the Heidegger of the *Vom Wesen der Wahrheit* and the *Brief an Beaufret*. There is an inkling of it in the work of Le Senne who in 1938 described his philosophy as "an ideo-existential spiritualism."[45] One may find it, too, in the work of Jaspers and Marcel. The latter sees human existence taking the form of a living dialogue, and oscillating between the twin poles of "being" and "having," the two fundamental alignments of man's being. "Having" means that we withdraw within ourselves into our possessions so as to "become," in some sense, these possessions. By our attachment to them, we even seem to surrender our rights over ourselves and to become possessed by our own possessions, *our* wealth, *our* careers, *our* ideas. In order to *be* truly, in order to realize the potentialities that slumber within us, we must accept the mystery that surrounds us. By our fidelity and love, we must open ourselves to the reality of the other; by contemplation and by faith, we must grope towards the mystery of the absolute Other, the living God. Thibon, in a perceptive study, has called Marcel's approach "a philosophy of participation"[46]; it would certainly appear that there is a strong bond of kinship between this wing of the existentialist movement and the traditional Christian philosophy of Aristotelian or Augustinian inspiration. The two ought, therefore, have much to gain from one another.

"Open" Existentialism and Historicity. There exists, then, a theist existentialism for which man is *not* the sole foundation and norm of intelligibility and value. Such a philosophy will still tend to emphasize the notion of historicity. Man *is* a historical being, and this historicity is not simply a superficial layer covering an inert and unchanging core. Every philosophy must allow for this, and a Christian philosophy more, perhaps, than most others. For the Christian, too, it is true to say with Canon Mouroux that "man perfects himself in perfecting the universe."[47] In doing this, he accepts the responsibility of deciding upon the meaning his life will take on; this he must do in a way which is anything but superficial. Not only does he mold his environment, construct a science, create new techniques, choose his profession; as a

---

[45] *Introduction à la philosophie*, Paris, 1938, p. 89.
[46] "L'existentialisme de Gabriel Marcel," in *L'existentialisme*, special volume of the *Revue de Philosophie*, 1946, p. 155.
[47] *Le sens chrétien de l'homme*, Paris, 1945, p. 12.

Christian, he is also aware that his choice has a much deeper significance. In the last analysis, it is *his* acceptance or refusal of God which counts and which lights up his life with meaning. The historicity of his being must be viewed in the light of the "capacity for being" which he possesses. But this "capacity for being" is, in his view, a gift from God, a talent he must set to work and use, a pledge of the goodwill of the Creator for his creature. Human existence, the "invariably-already-there" that we have dwelt on so much in earlier sections, now is seen to possess a meaning in advance because, as a gift of the Creator, it becomes the special object of His intention, so to speak. Our existence is thus justified in its very roots and is given a fundamental meaning: God loves us.

There is, therefore, a meaning within our being which does not come from us alone, which holds universally for *all* men who come into the world, and which no human choice can alter. Man's duty is to accept this meaning freely, to realize it in his acts, to further it in his own life and that of others. He must, in short, co-operate with and enter into God's plan for mankind. It may well be that for one who accepts an idealist position, moral consciousness would "shrivel up" at the touch of the Absolute. But this is certainly not true for someone who accepts a personal transcendent God Who gives human life a meaning; for such a one, to choose with God is to find one's true destiny. In this way, we can come to see that each man has an essence shared by all, and that this essence receives in this view a depth, a consistency, a density of being and of "capacity for being" which is afforded it by no other metaphysical approach. Far from excluding one another, then, universality and historicity on this view finally appear as mutually dependent.

C. Conclusion

It may be well to conclude this long chapter by a rapid glance over the ground we have covered. The historical character of human existence raises the question of whether or not historicity is reconcilable with the presence of some unchanging factor in history. A brief phenomenological analysis sufficed to show that historicity is itself unthinkable without some *permanent* and *universal* element, an "existential indubitable" which would underlie and orient history. This element is the experience of my existence as an "I-with-others-oriented-towards-a-world." However, this is still too vague and easily leaves the way open to an exaggerated historicism. If man's essence is—as some hold—simply the pure possibility of giving meaning to life and of making meanings appear in the world, man becomes the sole source of intelligibility and value. There is a nondescript "absolute certitude of the world in general" but it is of such a shadowy character that it really tells us nothing of the mystery of being that surrounds us. In later chapters (four and five), we shall try to trace the genesis of this metaphysical agnosticism and see in more detail how it can be transcended. It would seem fair to say at this stage, first, that there is within what we have called the "atheist" wing of existentialism more than a trace of Cartesian intellectualism or idealism, and, second, that the theory of historicity does not necessarily lead to agnosticism. The description of the intentional consciousness as an "encounter" is acceptable as far as it goes, but it must be pushed further if any kind of ontology of knowledge or of being-towards-the-world is to be elaborated. As we shall see, a philosophy of act and participation, such as that of Aquinas, can prove of tremendous worth in this connection.

Besides this epistemological question, the doctrine of historicity also raises a problem about God and His relation to us. If God is, then our life takes on a meaning in His sight. Our historical existence becomes completely consistent when it is seen as the object of God's love, while our freedom takes on a new dignity and an unsuspected weight of responsibility because of the power we are given to hearken or not to hearken to His appeal. It is possible to reconcile historical existence with the presence of an eternal Being who transcends history, on condition that this Being be not categorized in concepts drawn from naturalism or intellectualism.

> When we think of a Creator God, we tend to assimilate Him as a rule to a superior craftsman . . . . Thus the concept of man in the mind of such a God can be compared with the concept of a paper-knife in the mind of a manufacturer.[48]

Now, it is evident that beginning from such a notion of God, one would be almost inevitably led to deny any historicity to human existence and to view man, as Sartre's disciple, Jeanson, puts it, as "dispossessed of all liberty," "his existence transformed into destiny."[49]

When writers like Sartre or Merleau-Ponty declare that the existence of God is irreconcilable with the contingency of history and the autonomy of human freedom, what they have to say has nothing to do with the God of Abraham, Isaac and Jacob, the God of love preached by St. John. They are attacking an notion of their own making, conceived

---

[48]Sartre, *L'existentialisme est un humanisme*, p. 19.
[49]F. Jeanson, "Athéisme et liberté," in *Lumière et Vie*, 1954, p. 95.

in the likeness of a manufacturer of paper-knives, or an Absolute Knower reached on the basis of notional evidence or of an immanent dialectic. If God be revered as Word and Love, His co-existence with human liberty ceases to be an insoluble antinomy. For the function of the Word is to bring a message which will waken us to true liberty, and the function of the Spirit is to liberate us for love since He cannot love without inspiring us to love in return.

CHAPTER THREE

REASON AND THE IRRATIONAL IN
CONTEMPORARY THOUGHT

1. Introduction

"The task of our age," according to Merleau-Ponty is "to explore the irrational and to integrate it in a broader conception of reason."[1] If contemporary philosophy is stamped with an often violent antipathy to rationalism, it is nonetheless anxious to avoid at all costs the appearance of romanticism. Just because it is a severe (to our mind excessively severe) critic of the concept and of discourse, and introduces subjectivity, freedom, sentiment and even faith into its treatment of knowledge, it does not follow that it abandons the ideal which is common to all philosophy, of clear, rigorous, communicable thought, in favor of an easy acceptance of the facile tenets of subjectivism, voluntarism and fideism. In a sense, one can say that contemporary philosophy, because of its anxiety to get back to the concrete beyond conceptual representation and discursive thought, is only linking up with the tradition of philosophy which preceded Descartes. There is, therefore, an element of exaggeration in the claim that the attempt to bring thought to bear on the irrational and to broaden the idea of reason is the exclusive "task of our age." It would be truer to say that it is a task for every philosophy which retains a respect for the concrete and refuses to reduce reality to a palace made of concepts. Cartesian rationalism with its double issue, idealism and positivism, has, however, ruled over Western thought for so long and exercised such prestige within it that it has become for most moderns the "classical" ontology, as if scholastic metaphysics had never been classical or had never even merited the name of ontology.

This does not mean that we ought to regard the contemporary preoccupation with the concrete simply as a return to the Middle Ages. No great philosophy is satisfied to go on repeating the past. If it claims to take up again the eternal problems, it does so within an historical framework of which it is fully conscious and in regard to which it takes up a definite position. Let us, then, try to form an exact idea of the historical situation with which contemporary thought must come to

---

[1]*Sens*, p. 125.

terms. This must be our starting point if we wish to grasp the precise implications of present day irrationalism and pass judgment on it in all truth and sincerity.

Reason and the Irrational. Before entering into the subject proper, the ambiguous character of the term "irrational" must be noted. There are two reasons for this ambiguity. The first is that the term "reason," which enters into the definition of the irrational, is itself open to different interpretations. Each science is characterized by the type of rationality or intelligibility which is proper to it and which constitutes its logical structure. Broadly speaking, there are two principal meanings of the word *"reason,"* corresponding to two very different types of rationality. In the first place, there is the narrow, rationalist or "Cartesian" sense of the word, which leaves no room for mystery. By "reason," Descartes understands the faculty and seat of clear and distinct ideas as well as of logical deductions that they contain in germ. Geometry is the model and ideal form of this type of thought. Modern positive science, especially mathematical physics, its crowning achievement, is akin in spirit to Cartesian rationalism. It seeks clear precise facts and tries to establish mathematically formulated relations between them. The Kantian term "understanding" seems very close to this first sense of the word "reason."

The second sense of "reason" is the broad and existential one which is characterized by a much wider and more supple comprehensiveness. As Merleau-Ponty has justly remarked, "this reason is more comprehensive than the understanding . . . it is able to respect the variety and individuality of minds, civilizations, ways of thought and historical contingency," without however giving up "the task of mastering them in order to guide them to their proper truth."[2] It is this "reason" which makes freedom possible. To act freely is to take responsibility for one's actions. In order that there should be freedom, then, we must be able to give a reason for our actions, we must justify them before "reason." And clearly it must be before "reason" in the wider sense, for a justification *more geometrico* would be of no use here. Far from eliminating mystery and paradox, reason in the broader sense proclaims that they are unavoidable, because they enter into the structure of every human meaning. According to Marcel, mystery is at the heart of human thought like "an ontological exigency," the admittedly paradoxical conviction that it is thinkable that there are

---

[2]*Sens*, p. 126.

things inexpressible in thought constitutes, according to Jaspers, the metaphysical dimension of human existence.[3]

It is the opposite of the narrow Cartesian sense of the word "reason" that contemporary writers mean by "irrational." By it they intend to designate those realities or aspects of existence which are not entirely conceptualizable. However, these realities are of many different kinds, for there are many ways of escaping from the net of the clear concept and Cartesian reasoning. This becomes another source of ambiguity in the word, "irrational." There is the irrationality that lies at a level beneath that of the clear concept. To this level belong brute facts, experienced contact, sensible qualities, instinct and all that unconscious life which psychoanalysis has tried to bring to light. These might be called "infra-rational" realities. There is the irrational that lies, so to speak, on the same level as the understanding and forms with it the total concrete existence of man as, for example, in sentiment, in value-judgment and in adherence to value. Finally there is the supra-rational, that which is incomprehensible because of an *excess* of intelligibility, such as human existence considered as a whole, the intersubjective character of our existence, the mystery of the being which surrounds us and sustains us, and, above all, the supreme ineffable God, Who is the transcendent, *par excellence.*

These considerations about the meaning of the word "irrational" open the way to a clearer definition of the object of our inquiry. The opposition to Cartesian rationalism which is characteristic of our age, extends to every sector of philosophical thought, affecting psychology, the philosophy of history, ethics, the theory of truth, metaphysics and the philosophy of religion. In other words, the term "irrational" can be used to designate in a general way all those realities that have been so unjustifiably neglected in the Cartesian tradition. Because of our general purpose in these pages of confronting Christian faith with contemporary thought, our inquiry will be concerned principally with the presence of the irrational in the metaphysical and the religious thought of our times.

In doing this we shall again encounter the existentialists, though the authors with whom we shall have to deal will be mainly those of the group who profess what we have called "open" existentialism. Existence is not for them solely or even principally defined as "being-towards-the-world," but rather as an organic link with the Divine transcendence. Among the representatives of this group, two have a special claim on our attention, namely Gabriel Marcel and Karl Jaspers.

---

[3]*Philosophie*, Berlin, 1932, vol. III, p. 38.

Occasionally we shall mention Blondel, for whom moral choice has an epistemological value of the highest importance, and Newman, whom some consider, not without reason indeed, to be the Catholic Kierkegaard.[4]

2. The Historical Situation of Contemporary Philosophy

Anyone who undertakes to philosophize in these hard days runs up against a disconcerting but undeniable fact right from the beginning. Whereas positive science has no difficulty in rallying around it the world of scientists, philosophical reflection is becoming increasingly powerless to create agreement in spite of the never-ending efforts that have been made to establish philosophy on apodictic evidence. The history of phenomenology is significant in this regard. Dismayed by the never-ending disagreement between philosophers and the disorder of philosophical congresses, Husserl proposed, like so many others before him, to base philosophy once and for all on solid foundations. "To free philosophy from every possible prejudice, to make of it a really autonomous science built on ultimate evidences drawn from the subject himself and finding its absolute justification in these evidences,"[5] such was the ambitious program that, in a manner reminiscent of Descartes, he wished to carry through. Although the founder of phenomenology enjoyed an immense authority, one which has gone on increasing, the agreement he sought on the great problems of life has not come about. Within the phenomenological school itself, the most diverse tendencies had already appeared while the master was still alive, and they have multiplied further since his death. The precarious position of philosophy when compared with the success of empirical science is not only something of a scandal to the uninitiated, but also a fact which the metaphysician must take into account and for which he must have an explanation. In our discussion of philosophy, it constitutes a preliminary objection that must be answered.

A. The Prestige of Science

The Triple Demand of Scientific Intelligibility. The enormous prestige of science is easily explained. It springs from the very nature of scientific intelligibility. Implicit in the desire for truth and certainty which haunts

---

[4]The idea of comparing Newman to Kierkegaard owes its vogue chiefly to Przywara. See his *A Newman synthesis*, New York, 1945.

[5]*Méditations Cartésiennes*, Tr. by G. Peiffer and E. Levinas. Paris, 1947, p. 5.

our minds, there is, as it were, a triple necessity, a threefold demand, which positive science succeeds in fulfilling to a surprising degree. There is a necessity, in the first place, for *objectivity*. What we need is a knowledge which gets to the things "in person," as they really are, and not as we would like them to be. True knowledge, according to Heidegger, consists in "allowing beings to be," or as the well-worn formula puts it, in letting the facts "speak for themselves." In other words, true knowledge gets beyond mere opinion. This means that it tries to be *universal* or inter-subjectively acceptable; this is the second of the necessities we are speaking of. We need a universally valid knowledge capable of bringing about agreement among minds, and susceptible of verification and control by others. In the third place, there is the necessity for *clarity* or rationality. The human mind cannot be content with merely recording facts and storing them up in a heap. Its ultimate purpose is to see its way among the facts and to grasp their why and wherefore, to *understand* them. Understanding involves the bringing together of different data under the unity of an idea, or of a law, or of a system of logically coherent ideas and laws. In a word, the mind wishes to introduce order, unity and intelligible clarity into the infinite complex of events which make up the universe.

Positive Science and this Demand. Now modern science, which is based on methodically organized experiments that are verifiable at will, answers perfectly this threefold demand for objectivity, universality and clarity. This follows from the structure of scientific intelligibility and of scientific method; it is worth recalling that in any science there is a close correlation between the intelligibility sought by the science and the method used to reveal it. As Claude Bernard puts it in a passage we have already quoted:

> When using the experimental method one performs experiments solely to see or to prove something, that is to say, to control or to verify it. The experimental method, in so far as it is scientific, is based entirely upon the experimental *verification of a scientific hypothesis.*[6]

It is characteristic of science, therefore, to verify hypotheses on the basis of the data. It is true that the hypothesis is in the first place a construction of the mind which has a meaning for the mind; it is the light which is indispensable to it if it is to see its way among the facts. But it is not just a construction in the air. The mind goes to meet the facts "armed with hypotheses," so to speak, in order that

---

[6]*Introduction . . .,* p. 409.

it may understand the language that the facts speak. Thanks to experimental verification of the hypothesis, the objectivity, universality
and clarity which constitute the ideal of all knowledge, support one
another and tend to coincide.[7] Intelligible clarity (answering the how
and why, exhibiting regularity and obedience to law) bears in itself
the mark of objectivity; it springs in a sense from the data since it
can be verified in the data. Thus it is that positive science is today
adorned with the imposing, though somewhat ambiguous, title of
"objective" knowledge, as if all the other forms of knowledge ought
to be relegated to the domain of dreams and myths. And this, of course,
is just what positivism maintains. This latter is nothing other than
a dictatorship of scientific method, extended first to epistemology and
then to ontology. Taken as a theory of truth, it has as its motto: "the
only truth and intelligibility are those present in science." Understood
as a theory of being, it becomes a sort of materialism. "Reality is as
positive science shows it to be, and it is nothing other than that." As
we shall see later, the almost complete fusion of objectivity, universality
and clarity manifested in experimental verification, is achieved only
at the price of a considerable impoverishment of reality as a whole.
The world of objective science, and *a fortiori*, that of positivism, is a
world emptied of man and of the values that make it a world-for-man,
or as contemporary writers would say, a world from which "existence"
has been eliminated.

B. The Disunity of Metaphysicians

While the unity of scientists about science is easy to understand,
the same cannot be said of the disunity of metaphysicians when faced
with the ultimate problems of existence. This disunity is all the more
disconcerting when it is recalled that a characteristic of metaphysics
is to claim for itself a universal validity because of its being based on
ultimate and unshakeable evidence. We must not, however, fall into
exaggeration, by taking for granted that the failure is complete. For
the man who knows how to read the secret intentions of creative thought
hidden beneath the linguistic differences between philosophers, philosophy appears much less disunited than it would seem to be at first sight.
The more one makes oneself familiar with the philosophic past of mankind, the more one gets the impression that the great philosophers
are very near each other, that in the long run they are concerned

---

[7]See A. de Waelhens, "Science, Phenomenology, Ontology," *Cross Currents*,
Vol. 7, 1957, pp. 167-174.

with the same eternal problems, and that their general view of the universe shows a basic and profound unity. Some, like Lagneau, for example, would even go so far as to say that in spite of appearances, there are no true "atheist" philosophers.

> There are only "practical" atheists whose atheism consists not so much in denying the truth of God's existence as in not realizing God in their actions ... Outside this "practical" atheism, there is really no atheism. Wherever a thinker discusses with himself the reasons for believing in the existence of God, there is already present an affirmation of an absolute truth against which all particular beliefs must be measured. Such an affirmation implies in a more or less obscure way the affirmation of God.[8]

However this may be, the philosopher cannot simply be satisfied to say that systems which are apparently in opposition to each other really have the same philosophical intention, though only in an implicit and confused way. Philosophy exists in order to make explicit what is implicit, and to reflect on the pre-reflective. On the plane of explicit reflective thought the divergence still remains immense, above all on the essential questions, and notably on the question of the existence of God. This divergence is rightly held to be a scandal, and the metaphysician must give an honest explanation of it. There are two main reasons for this "scandalous position"[9] which have long been recognized by philosophers.

Trancendence of Metaphysical Truths. In the first place, there is the fact that metaphysical truths in general, and in particular "truths concerning God and the relations of God with man, absolutely transcend the sensible order." It is for this reason that the mind cannot successfully engage in the work of metaphysics "unless it has first received the appropriate training."[10] It is a well-known fact that prolonged familiarity with the positive sciences and with a culture like ours which is dominated by technology, may well deaden within us all feeling for truths which escape experimental verification. However, the background of an unfavorable culture is not sufficient as an explanation. For the scandal of philosophy lies not so much in the fact that men of science so often

---

[8] J. Lagneau, *Célèbres leçons et fragments*, Paris, 1950, p. 229. This theme has recently been developed by F. Van Steenberghen, "Y a-t-il un 'problème' de l'existence de Dieu?," *Bull. Ingén. Louvain*, 1957, n. 4.

[9] G. Marcel, *Du refus à l'invocation*, Paris, 1940, p. 229.

[10] Both quotations from Pope Pius XII, Encyclical letter: *Humani generis*, 1950. Several English versions of this letter are available, for example, one done by the late Mgr. Knox for the Catholic Truth Society (London).

fail to understand the discussion of metaphysicians as in the fact that even metaphysicians themselves, who pass their whole lives in cultivating metaphysical reflection, agree so little among themselves. Is it not true that the more the serious philosopher advances in age and experience the more he is struck by the complexity of truth and the difficulty of philosophical problems?

Influence of the Affective Life. There is a second reason for disagreement among metaphysicians. It is the influence of activity, of affective life and of the will on our grasp of the truth. This influence has always been underlined by the great thinkers. Plato said that man must approach the truth "with his whole soul." "Non intratur in veritatem nisi per caritatem," as St. Augustice said.[11] This idea, which is so profoundly Augustinian, became a central theme in the thought of Pascal.

> From this it follows that, whereas in speaking of human things it is said that they must be known before they are loved—as the proverb has it—the saints on the contrary tell us that in speaking of things divine, it is necessary to love them in order to know them, and that we come to the truth only by charity.[12]

But it is not sufficient to remark that, in a general way, the dispositions of the soul may easily influence our conception of the world and our view of life. This influence is open to many interpretations and the question is how to make precise the nature and bearing of the relationship that holds between action, will and affectivity on the one hand, and knowledge on the other.

C. Affectivity and Knowledge

Bad Faith. A first hypothesis might be that our grasp of the higher truths is measured simply by the degree of good will we each possess, so that, to take a very concrete example, the disagreement that divides thinkers into theists, pantheists, agnostics and materialists, is in the long run a simple question of good or bad faith. But who would dare maintain this thesis? Have we not all met sincere and intelligent unbelievers who, in spite of their honesty and their hunger for the truth, remain unconvinced by even the best proofs for the existence of God?[13] The latest studies on the psychology of conversion are very revealing in this regard. They are unanimous in telling us that conversions

---

[11]*Contra Faustum*, bk. 32, chap. 18.
[12]*Pensées et Opuscules*, Paris, 1920, (Brunschvicg edn.), p. 185.
[13]See Van Steenberghen, *op. cit.*

following purely rational demonstration are rather rare, and that the living witness of a sincere and radiant faith has a power of persuasion beyond the best treatises of philosophy and apologetics. Not that the convert looks upon his faith as a blind urge or as an arbitrary choice which cannot be objectively justified. In most cases what actually seems to happen is that before conversion the rational proofs have no "bite" in them, whereas, when they are taken up again in the light of faith, they acquire at once an unquestioned probative force.

Pascal saw this long ago and made it, as we have said, the central idea of his work. The same might be said of Blondel and Marcel. It is a well known fact that the disturbing realization of the obvious good faith of some of Newman's Protestant and atheist friends determined the vocation of this great thinker and apostle, and was the source of his best work.[14] It is always rash to claim the power of judging the interior state of one's neighbor, just as it is rash to pass judgment on oneself. The "judge not" of the gospel is also a philosophical truth. However, one thing seems certain. The philosopher who consecrates his entire life to the search for truth is almost necessarily a sincere being for whom the discovery of the truth is the most sacred thing in the world. Thus it would be simply dishonest to accuse him of bad faith just because his meditations do not give rise to the same conclusions as our own. The hypothesis of bad faith cannot, then, be considered satisfactory. Not that bad faith is never present in the hearts of philosophers, but it is not a sufficiently general explanation of the disagreement among them.

Fideism. Another popular hypothesis is that of voluntarist subjectivism or fideism. *Voluntarist subjectivism* consists in claiming that the truth is in the long run a matter of free choice. What is true is what man chooses as the truth. This is to go against the very essence of truth and to make philosophy useless as a search for truth. As for fideism, it is, when all is said and done, only a hidden form of subjectivism. For if it wants to be consistent, it must maintain that belief in God is entirely outside the scope of our common reasoning capacity, and consequently that it is supported and justified in the last resort only by the personal attitude of the individual believer. Voluntarism and fideism are, therefore, irreconcilable with the demands of philos-

---

[14]The essentials of *The Grammar of Assent* are already implicitly contained in Newman's correspondence with his friend Froude who was an agnostic. See M. Olive, "Le problème de la 'Grammaire de l'assentiment' d'après la correspondance entre Newman et Froude," *Bull. Lit. Eccles. Toulouse*, 1936, pp. 217-40.

ophy. They are, of course, even more at odds with the demands of faith and of sane theology.

> It is one thing to recognize the power that affective dispositions of the will have in helping reason to attain a more certain and more assured knowledge in moral matters, but it is quite another thing to attribute to the affective and appetitive faculties a power of intuition, and to maintain that man is incapable of discerning the truth by his reason and must turn to the will to choose by his free decision between contradictory opinions.[15]

Are we then at an impasse? Must we conclude that our highest affirmations—those concerning God, the ultimate sense of existence, our moral and religious convictions—are irrational, indeed quite beyond the grasp of reason, even in the widest sense of that word? Are we forced to rest content with a metaphysical agnosticism after the manner of Kant, admitting that the only universally valid method of arriving at truth is that given by empirical science?

Fideists? At first sight one might think that this is more or less the position of Blondel, Newman, Marcel and Jaspers. In reality this is not the case; indeed it is rather the contrary. Not that their thought is always impeccably precise, or that the accusation of fideism often made against them is completely groundless. Nevertheless one thing is certain. The constant intention of all these writers was to work out a philosophy of the transcendent which would, on the one hand, take account of and account for the historical situation we have just described, and, on the other hand, avoid the twin dangers of subjectivism and fideism. It is true that Blondel and Newman were for a time suspected of these latter errors, but history has gradually done justice to them. As far as Marcel is concerned, this is the judgment that he passes in retrospect on his own thought:

> The whole of the first part of the *Journal Métaphysique* is a reflection on the act of faith, considered in its purity, as well as on the conditions that allow it to remain an act of faith even though it is also an act of thought; it is at the same time a rather desperate attempt to escape from subjectivism and fideism in all their forms.[16]

Jaspers' position is basically the same, as Ricoeur has shown with great penetration. It is true, as Ricoeur remarks, that "the peril of subjectivism or of incommunicable conviction is more obvious in the

---

[15] *Humani generis*, Part II.
[16] *Du refus . . .*, p. 193. An excellent synthetic account of Marcel's thought is given by R. Troisfontaines, *De l'existence à l'être*, Louvain, 1953.

case of Jaspers than in that of Marcel," because Jaspers tends to lay more emphasis on the radically unique character of personal free existence and considers Kierkegaard and Nietzsche as the "inimitable exceptions" that "invite each one of us to tread an exceptional path, namely his own."[17] Yet it has been said that "Jaspers, more than Marcel, has, because of his critical temperament, the desire for a positive existential methodology."[18] "We approach the task of philosophizing without being the exception, but with our eyes fixed on the exception" is a phrase which occurs often in Jaspers' work.[19] It is a good summing up of the intention underlying his philosophy. If he calls free existence "the unique" (*der Einzige*), he is careful to add that "the reflection that throws light on existence involves an objective kind of thinking."[20] For Jaspers, as for the others, philosophy is not simply an account of a personal journey, a sort of "journal intime."

As Nédoncelle very justly remarks, one finds two types of philosophy all through history, "those which begin by eliminating mystery, and those which accept it, bear it with them, and neither can nor want to rid themselves of it. The thought of Newman is clearly an example of this second kind of philosophy."[21] The same holds for Blondel, Marcel, and Jaspers; to work out a philosophy of mystery and of transcendence that goes beyond rationalist thought without falling into "a new romanticism, lost in the sentiment of the ineffable,"[22] is certainly the ultimate purpose that animates the work of the thinkers we have just named. It goes without saying that the first task of a philosophy of this kind is to reflect on the rationalist tradition and to bring out its shortcomings.

3. Rationalism on Trial

The criticism of rationalism that is so important an element in the background of contemporary thought is governed by a certain conception of rationalism, which, though it is not exactly contrary to the facts of history, still constitutes a particular interpretation of them. This interpretation has immense importance for the understanding of the place that the irrational occupies in the new philosophy. It may be summarized under three heads. In the first place, great insistence is placed, and rightly placed, on the close connection between idealist

---

[17]*Gabriel Marcel et Karl Jaspers*, Paris, 1947, pp. 84-5.
[18]P. Ricoeur, *loc. cit.*
[19]*Vernunft und Existenz*, Groningen, 1935, pp. 22, 94.
[20]*Philosophie*, vol. II, p. 9.
[21]M. Nédoncelle, Preface to *Oeuvres philosophiques de Newman*, Paris, 1945, p. 19.
[22]P. Ricoeur, *op. cit.*, p. 86.

intellectualism and positivism. At the same time, it is emphasized that rationalism, whether of the idealist or of the positivist variety, is at once "a particular conception of what it is to be objective, and an interpretation of the subject of knowledge."[23] Objectivity is reduced to the Kantian *Gegenständlichkeit*, while the subject of knowledge is regarded as a *Bewusstsein überhaupt*, anonymous and disembodied. The third theme lays bare the deepest root of rationalism. It consists in identifying cognitive life, and ultimately the whole of human existence, with abstract concepts, or more precisely with an organized system of concepts. The rationalist tradition has, then, failed to take account of the concrete, and for this reason must be abandoned and superseded.

A. The Rationalist Notion of "Objectivity"

It may appear strange that two types of thought which differ as much from one another as idealism and positivism do, can be brought together under the same head and submitted to the same criticism. However, this classification is not a mere fancy. There is, in fact, a close connection between these two currents of thought, not only from the point of view of their logical structure but even historically. The principal strand in this connection lies in the idea of *objectivity*, which is substantially the same in both and which goes back to Kant. What is the nature and the role of the other-than-myself or of the object in post-Kantian idealism? The first point to note is that the expression "other-than-the-self" is here to be taken in the strict sense. It means the "other-than-the-subjectivity," that is, the physical object in general, and not just the selves which are other than myself. (Thus the problem of other persons and of intersubjectivity has no place in the idealist ontology). The other-than-myself exists by and for the self, so that its appearance exercises a function within and for the benefit of the self. To grasp the nature of this function, it is necessary to recall that the characteristic of objects is to appear to the subject as a *Gegenstand*, in the Kantian sense of the word, that is to say, as something that stands before the subject, in opposition to the subject as a *norm*, and consequently as an *a priori* which is universally valid for each individual consciousness. For Kant, "objectivity"—which he identifies with scientific objectivity—and "universality," are synonymous.

When interpreted in the context of idealist ontology, the formation of the *Gegenstand*, which is commonly called objectifying, is one of the most important moments in the living dialectic of the mind. This

---

[23]Ricoeur, *op. cit.*, p. 14.

dialectic, in virtue of a process which is at once necessary and historical, brings the mind of humanity to the stage of being fully conscious of itself. It takes place between two poles. First, there is the sensible empirical consciousness, which is characterized by its passivity and by the absence within it of clearly defined borders between subject and object. The sensible impression is here taken to be a sort of modification of the subjectivity, in which the quality sensed and the subject sensing it are mixed up together in the unity of a pure act of sensation. At this stage, consciousness has not yet come to the full possession of itself since it considers itself passive and determined from outside, whereas in reality it spontaneously creates its object. This revelation of the mind to itself is accomplished in a definitive way only by philosophical reflection, the other pole of the process. The aim that every idealist thinker sets himself is to suppress the distance which in prereflective life separates the mind from itself. Once arrived at the perfect identify of the self with the self, the self finally appears for what it is, namely the ultimate foundation and last end of all things.

The Objectivity of Empirical Science. It is somewhere between these two extremes, empirical sensibility on one hand and philosophical understanding on the other, that the stage of "objectivity," in practice, of objective empirical science, occurs. In the hypothetico-deductive science developed by Galileo, Newton, and their successors, human consciousness is not purely passive. Science was born, as Kant says in the preface to the second edition of the *Critique of Pure Reason*, when man first had the happy idea of putting questions to the world in a methodical, intelligent way. Instead of being content with collecting facts "as a school boy who takes in whatever his master cares to say," the post-Galilean scientist takes his stand before nature "as a judge who forces the witnesses to reply to the questions he puts to them."[24] He sizes up things with his logical constructions, his intellectual *a priori* or, as we should say today, with his hypotheses. At one stroke, the *blosse Mannigfaltigkeit* (bare multiplicity) of sensible impression is transcended and systematized in a scientific and objective way by means of a network of laws characterized by "universality" and giving rise to "objectivity." The next step in the process of "objectifying" is that on the noematic side, the "object" appears. It is there before the consciousness as a norm, which for Kant and his followers means as a group of universal and necessary laws. On the noetic side, this means that the subject shows itself to itself as a universal non-temporal, imper-

---

[24]*Critique of Pure Reason*, tr. by J. Meiklejohn, London, 1908, p. xxvii.

sonal consciousness, the *a priori* source of the laws that science sets out
to discover. Thus it is that scientific knowledge appears to the idealist
as an indispensable stage in the long and difficult road that leads the
mind from the limbo of sensibility to the full consciousness of self.

Similarity Between Idealism and Positivism. It is true that positivism is
not at all well disposed to these airy speculations of idealist ontology.
Nevertheless, it is not as far removed from them as might be supposed.
For example, *"objectivity"* for the positivist, too, becomes synonymous
with subjection to law, and in the long run it reduces to little more
than a network of logical relations which have their origin in the
structure of the understanding. As for *matter*, considered as a pure datum
or as a "form of exteriority," to use Brunschvicg's phrase, it is beneath
all intelligibility. It is of even less interest to the positivist scientist than
to the idealist philosopher. There is much in common between positivism
and idealism regarding the *subject* of knowledge also. For both, the
knowing subject is an anonymous and interchangeable consciousness,
a sort of universal logical structure common to all men. Indeed, it
does not seem that the subject is exempt in any way from the subjection to law which is the characteristic of the scientific object itself.
In the long run, human consciousness is only a sector of cosmic determinism, an integral part of the equation that is the universe. Without
noticing it, we can pass from the most exaggerated spiritualism to the
most absolute materialism. As frequently happens, the two extremes
meet and end up by being indistinguishable from one another.

We must keep all this in mind when following the accusations
brought by our contemporaries against rationalist thought. The difficulty in understanding these accusations arises from the fact that they
are couched in part in the terminology of the thinkers who are under
attack. Hence there arise obvious exaggerations and regrettable ambiguities. The *abuse* of conceptual thought, of systematization and
language, and more generally the identification of the scientific object
with the whole of human reality, are the real object of criticism, but
the impression is often given that all conceptual and discursive thought
is being condemned, as if human thought could get by without concepts,
especially when it is dwelling on existence itself and trying to decipher
the mystery of being.[25]

---

[25]Ricoeur, for example, entitles the attack on rationalist thought led by Marcel
and Jaspers "The Critique of Knowledge" (*op. cit.*, p. 48). There is obviously a
tendency here to identify knowledge itself with the rationalist conception of it.

For the moment, let us leave this misunderstanding aside. On careful examination it will prove to be mainly a question of words, as we shall see later in our critical discussion. One thing is already clear and that is that the description of rationalism we have just given is a sufficient condemnation in itself. Rationalism falls short of the concrete, or as Ricoeur puts it, "impersonal, objective, systematic knowledge allows the essentials to escape."[26]

B. The Rationalist Diminution of the "World"

The essentials that are neglected in rationalist thought can be looked at in the first place from the point of view of the *world*, that is, of the object known. When reduced to a simple system of laws, an impersonal net of mathematical or logical relations, the world appears devoid of all human interest, stripped of the meanings and values which make it a world for man, that is to say, a place where men live, where they go about the pursuit of their personal destiny accompanied by other men and aided by material things. Rationalism takes no account of these ideas of destiny and of the value, because it has no place for the idea of a subject in a body or of liberty involved in the world.

Example. Let us give a very simple illustration of this point. A man takes his revolver and kills someone. As far as objective science is concerned, all that happens is merely a succession of physico-chemical processes, which physics and physiology are perfectly well able to explain by their laws. The act of firing the shot is treated as a contraction and release of muscular movement or as an expending of energy. The trajectory of the bullet is calculated according to the position of the gun, the amount of energy released by the explosion and so on. The death of the victim is a sudden change brought about by the projectile in an organic structure, or merely a reversal of the direction of change in entropy. These details are all that concern the biologist or the physicist. But the action in question did have a meaning too, for it was bound up with a value or a negative value. It could have been an act of heroism in a soldier who risked his life to defend his country. It could also have been a murder committed out of hate or greed or ill-will. Biology knows nothing of all this for it takes no account of value-judgments. It is true that psychology and sociology can go further; they tell us, for example, that we must take account of motives. But these motives are in the eyes of the scientist mere events, objective

---

[26]Ricoeur, *op. cit.*, p. 49.

facts like any others. The value of the motive as such, what makes and gives value to heroism as a value or to ill-will as a negative value, is something for which "objective" science has no place. Strictly speaking, it cannot even say that someone was the victim of an assault! For these words necessarily imply a twofold value-judgment. To speak of a "victim" is to consider the organism as *someone's* body, as a good, a value belonging to someone. To speak of an "assault" is to take another organism to be the author of the action, someone who in certain circumstances is capable of acting freely and deliberately.

In short, objective science—and the same may be said, *mutatis mutandis*, of the idealist ontology—by reducing the universe to a network of abstract logical relations, deprives it of its connection with man. Thus the world becomes a spectacle unfolded before the consciousness, logically coherent perhaps, but devoid of charm, poetry, color, warmth and consistency. The world of rationalism, as Marcel says, is one of "stifling sadness."[27]

C. The Rationalist Diminution of the Subject

This diminution of the "world" goes hand in hand with a reduction in the stature of the subject, who is left as an impartial spectator, anonymous and interchangeable with any other. This impoverishment of the subject affects not only the phenomenological description of "existence," but also and above all the metaphysical interpretation of it.

The Historical Character of Human Existence is Neglected. At the level of phenomenological description, rationalist intellectualism does not reach the real state of man since it takes no account of such phenomena as embodiment, being-in-history and intersubjectivity. It goes without saying that the idea of embodiment, *"incarnation,"* "a body of my own," has no meaning if the character of being a body is something belonging only to the external object. Corporeity cannot be simply identified with a *Gegenstand* opposed to consciousness. To speak of a body of my own is to imply a character of being corporeal that belongs to the *subject*, is bound up with its subjectivity and helps to constitute it. In other words, it means thinking of consciousness as something which cannot be defined in terms of pure translucid interiority, or, as Merleau-Ponty says, it is "to substitute for the consciousness as sole subject of perception

---

[27]*Le monde cassé*, Paris, 1933, p. 258. See the whole appendix to this book: "Position et approches concrètes du mystère ontologique".

the existent, a being-towards-the-world through a body."[28] This body of mine causes my point of view on the world to have an empirical and strictly individual character. Moreover, to suppress the fact of being in a body is to make the community of individual consciousnesses unthinkable. We must not confuse the mere coexistence of a number of egos with the phenomenon of intersubjectivity. In order to speak of intersubjectivity, it is not enough for us to be

> this one and that one for God, it is necessary for us to appear as this one and that one to each other. It is necessary that both the other person and myself have an exterior, so that, over and above the perspective of for-self, there is also a perspective of for-the-other-person.[29]

Materialism, by emptying man of his interior life, and intellectualism, by stripping the interior life of its bodily exteriority, make intersubjectivity something incomprehensible. Because of this, the true historical character of human existence evaporates, as it were, since, as we showed in the preceding chapter, historicity is a consequence of the slanted and intersubjective character of our basic relationship with the world.

Disastrous Influence on the Ontology of Man. This is not all. The neglect of man's embodiment in a world brings in its train even more serious consequences than these. It exercises a disastrous influence on the *ontological* interpretation of our existence. Thinkers like Newman, Marcel and Jaspers have shown that by eliminating from man's inheritance corporeity as well as the intersubjectivity and the being-in-history that follow from it, rationalism must end up by emptying human reality of its ontological content and of its intrinsic reference to the Transcendent. To reduce the human person to a bloodless and anonymous spectator is to destroy the very idea of a "person" and make man a being without soul or destiny, for whom life has neither rhyme nor reason, since there is really nothing he can *do*. Hence the importance in metaphysics of Blondel's theme, action. The character of having an exterior, which I possess in virtue of the body that is mine, is not merely an imperfection or a limitation for the interior life, as the intellectualists believed, it also gives us our grip on reality and allows us to realize ourselves as concrete individuals in a real world. Embodiment contributes to our insertion in being, towards making us participate in (in the sense of having a part in and also of taking part in) the mystery of being. Because it is

---

[28] *Phénoménologie*, p. 357.
[29] Merleau-Ponty, *op. cit.*, pp. vi-vii.

"incarnate," embodied, life takes on the sense of being a trial. But the idea of a trial or a test is inseparable from that of destiny and of value. Hence the idea, dear to Marcel, of considering "embodied being" as "the central point of reference of metaphysical reflection."[30] There is, then, every reason for believing that the theme of "incarnation" or embodiment possesses an ontological as well as a phenomenological value. This is a point to which we must return.

We pass now to the positive side of our case. Rationalism cannot be transcended simply by pointing out its defects. Having shown how deficient it is on the essentials, we must now try to do justice to these essentials ourselves. Let us see, then, how contemporary philosophy believes it can re-discover the ontological dimensions of our being by taking as its starting point concrete human existence, and in particular the phenomena of incarnate liberty, intersubjectivity and being-in-history.[31]

4. Getting Beyond Rationalism:

Existence and its Link with the Transcendent

With this third point we touch the heart of the problem that is the object of this chapter, namely the investigation of the nature and bearing of the irrational (perhaps better, the extra-"rational") in contemporary philosophy, and especially in contemporary epistemology. But why bring in epistemology? The reason is that the problem of the irrational is twofold: it has both a noematic and a noetic aspect. It is not sufficient to show that being, taken in its inexhaustible concrete realization, cannot be reduced to a scaffolding of concepts, or that at the heart of existence and of our existential situation there are realities and existential components which escape the grasp of clear and distinct ideas, and yet are meaningful. That is what we may call the noematic side of the problem. It is also necessary to throw light on the nature

---

[30]*Du refus* . . ., p. 19. This idea of the body as our "anchor" to the real is, of course, an old one. For Aquinas, matter is the individualizing factor. In recent writing, the thought has also been developed by Sartre and Merleau-Ponty. These latter, because of their hostile attitude towards metaphysics, are unable to explore its depths; they cannot avail of it in defining the ontological dimension of human existence or the link between this existence and the Divine Transcendence. See Chapter 4.

[31]Being-in-history, which occupies an important place in the work of Marcel and Jaspers, takes on for them a somewhat different significance from that which it possesses for Heidegger and Merleau-Ponty. The latter take it to be primarily an existential structure having great importance for the elaboration of truth and value. Marcel and Jaspers prefer to describe it as a dramatic situation from which some notion of our ontological status may be derived.

of the noetic activity that reveals this new *noema* to us and disposes us to grasp its true sense in such a way as to bring it within the range of a "reason" at once broadened and communicable. In more concrete terms, what precisely is the noetic behavior by which we succeed in assuring ourselves of the solidity of the values to which we hold, of the embodied character of our liberty, of the paradox of intersubjectivity, of our insertion into being, of the sense of the mystery of being, and finally of our link with God? Such is the crucial question that faces every philosophy which claims to escape from the impasse of rationalism by abandoning the primacy of the concept or, as some contemporaries would put it, by denying the "primacy of knowledge."

This last expression is ambiguous and rather misleading; one may well see in it a useless and dangerous concession to the rationalist adversary. The main fault of rationalism consists in identifying knowledge with the abstract concept, whereas, as the ancients had correctly noted, the concept is really only an instrument, a *medium quo*, in the midst of and at the service of knowledge, which is first and last a looking at the concrete. But let us once again pass over this question of terminology, even though it is not just a question of words. Our criticism will keep for later on. Let us remember, however, that the crucial point of the problem we are concerned with is basically an epistomological one. In their anxiety to enlarge the scope of truth and knowledge, many contemporary thinkers challenge the primacy of the conceptual order and insist upon the relevance in grasping reality, firstly, of affective elements, such as *Befindlichkeit* (Heidegger), anguish (Jaspers), hope (Marcel), secondly, of free choice, especially moral choice (Blondel and Marcel), and lastly, of attitudes of a more or less religious character such as recollection and faith. This program undeniably runs the risk of falling into romantic sentimentalism or into a new form of fideist voluntarism. But this is not the intention of the authors mentioned above, as has already been pointed out. This very difficult and delicate problem will be the next object of our inquiry.

It is our desire to pursue this inquiry as objectively as possible. This is the more important since the dilemma which engages the attention of contemporary thought is not peculiar to it alone. It is central to any philosophy which respects the concrete and does not attempt to reduce the world of intelligibility to an organized system of abstract concepts or to a logical chain of self-evident predicative judgments, in the manner of Spinoza or of Leibniz. We will try, then, to follow the progress of our contemporaries in their attempt to get beyond rationalism. It is not our intention to enter into the details of their work but rather to disengage from the tangle of their descriptions (which are often ambiguous and unclear) the deeper intention and the movement of living thought that animates them.

A. TURNING BACK TO THE CONCRETE

Two Meanings of the "Concrete." Since the chief fault of rationalism is its inadequate handling of the concrete, there is really only one way of refuting it, namely by making a detailed analysis of the concrete and of our experience of the concrete. What is meant here by "concrete" and "experience of the concrete?" There is, as Hegel clearly saw, a concrete which is really the most formidable of all abstractions, the *hic et nunc* of sensible experience, the localization of things in space and time. If visual perception allows me to distinguish Peter from Paul by localizing them here and now in space-time, it still does not give me the ontological dimension of human existence. The same applies to the "concrete facts" which empirical science produces in ever-increasing numbers in the course of its increasingly refined investigations. As we have already shown, objective science impoverishes reality, and, in this sense, its object is an abstraction.

But there is another meaning of the word "concrete," the one we have in mind here, which might be called its richer or philosophical meaning. By "concrete" we understand now *reality in all its concreteness.* This authentic "concrete" is, in the first place, the single existent thing in so far as it embraces in an indissoluble unity an inexhaustible multiplicity of aspects and of meanings, an infinity of ways of showing itself. From another point of view, the "concrete" is also this same singular being with its infinity of links anchoring it to reality itself, when it refers to the ensemble of beings and goes to make up with them being in its totality. These two words "ensemble" and "totality" are inadequate, since they might seem to imply that being in its totality can be arrived at by a process of addition, whereas it is rather the "ultimate enveloping reality" that embraces and underlies the diversity of individual beings and makes them possible as such.[32]

---

[32]The idea of the "enveloping" or the "encompassing" (*das Umgreifende*) plays a very important role in the philosophy of Jaspers. It is bound up with the notion of "horizon" but is not synonymous with it. "The enveloping is what envelops every particular horizon, or better, it is simply that which is no longer visible as a horizon because it is enveloping." There is even a double way in which reality may "envelop." There is "being itself, which is everything and in which, and by which, we exist"; there is also "the enveloping reality that we ourselves are, and within which we encounter each definite kind of being." Jaspers' essay on "The Enveloping" is translated in the Kaufman anthology, p. 184. It originally appeared in *Vernunft und Existenz*, 1935. See also his *Descartes et la philosophie*, Paris, 1938, p. 17, n.l.; and J. Collins, *The Existentialists*, p. 100.

Concrete and "Being." This richer sense of the word "concrete" is proper to philosophy, since it is the primitive and deepest intention of philosophy to rediscover this genuine concrete which human thought is always looking at, but which empirical science is forced to leave aside.

In the preface to his translation of Hegel's *Phenomenology of the Mind*, Jean Hyppolite rightly notes that "it is the conquest of the concrete that our time—and probable every age—seeks in philosophy."[33] Similarly Aimé Forest sees in the conquest of the concrete "the originality of metaphysical thought," and (with Bergson) defines the concrete as "that infinite which is open to both an indivisible appreciation and an inexhaustible enumeration."[34] To designate this philosophical meaning of the word "concrete," the ancients preferred to use the word "being," and for this reason defined metaphysics as the inquiring into being, understanding thereby the being both of singular beings and of being as a whole.

The Two Meanings of Experience. What we have just said about the concrete is also true of its noetic correlative, that is, of the act by which we grasp the concrete as such. The term "experience" has always been used to designate this act. There is first a narrow sense of the word. Empiricism consists precisely in recognizing no other experience than that of the sensible or scientific orders. But there is also an "open" sense of the word; indeed it may be said that the history of philosophy since Bergson is dominated by a progressive broadening of the idea of experience. At the present time, this idea has become synonymous with "existence," in its contemporary meaning. It serves to designate in a general way the awareness of our existence as an embodied and personal liberty, which is involved in the world and is called to realize itself in inter-subjectivity. In this sense Le Senne could write that "philosophy is the description of experience . . . knowledge is itself contained within experience."[35] Knowledge is not the whole of our existence but simply one of its manifestations, one which proceeds from existence, terminates in it, and thus contributes towards its accomplishment. Marcel, too, could say of his own philosophy that it is one long and difficult attempt to "arrive at a higher form of empiricism, and to do justice to the individual and the concrete that I bear within me. In other words, experience, far from being a springboard, was for me

---

[33]Introduction to *La phénoménologie de l'Esprit*, Paris, 1939, vol. 1, p. vii.
[34]*Du consentement à l'être*, Paris, 1936, p. 18.
[35]*Obstacle et valeur*, pp. 5 and 9.

in fact the promised land."[36] This opening of self to the concrete, the recognition of its inexhaustible density thanks to a certain assent to it, is what Newman calls *real* (as opposed to notional) assent.

B. EXISTENCE AS A MEANS OF ACCESS TO THE CONCRETE

Contemporary philosophy, more perhaps than any other, is haunted by this fidelity towards the concrete. This has been said in every possible tone before, but it is by no means clear that its bearing has always been properly noted. If, in order to elaborate a theory of being and truth, our contemporaries emphasize the unique character of freedom (*das Charakter der Jemeinigkeit* for Heidegger, *der Einzige* for Jaspers), and if they appeal to sentiment, choice or even faith, it is because they see in them aspects, constitutive elements or fundamental possibilities of concrete existence as such. In other words, and this is the capital point, if contemporary thought abandons the primacy of the concept and of knowledge, it is not in order to substitute for it a primacy of sentiment or of will or of faith, but rather a primacy of "existence." In this it sets itself apart both from romantic sentimentalism and voluntarist or fideist subjectivism. Its primary intention is to bring forward an existential philosophy for which the basic significant datum is existence itself, the means of access to the concrete. What precisely does this mean? Under what conditions can existence take on this role?

Human Existence. In the first place, it is not simply a question of reducing philosophical reflection to the dimensions of a *journal intime* or a phenomenological analysis of the condition of man. To throw light on existence is not the *ultimate* purpose of philosophy, as we have seen in Chapter I; it is rather the starting-point. As Jaspers put it, existence is the medium "because of which whatever is being becomes in the long run being-for-us."[37] In this sense, existence is in its turn an enveloping reality. But philosophy is not caged up within this "enveloping reality that we ourselves are," since our existence itself inclines us towards transcending ourselves in virtue of what Marcel calls its "ontological weight." It tends to open us towards the "transcendent,"[38] that is to say, towards the Being who is self-sufficient and to allow us find

---

[36] In his "Regard en arrière," *Existentialisme chrétien, Gabriel Marcel*, Paris, 1947, p. 296.
[37] *Vernunft und Existenz*, p. 29.
[38] The term "transcendent" has two related meanings in contemporary philosophy. It may mean the act of transcending or going beyond oneself in some way, or it may mean that towards which human consciousness goes in its attempt to transcend itself.

in Him peace, genuine joy and unity, in a word, true being. Even though it has existence as its reference point, says Jaspers, "the philosophy that sets out from possible existence has not existence for its ultimate purpose."[39]

Authentic Existence. However, if concrete human existence is the philosopher's way of arriving at being, it cannot duly fulfil this role unless the philosopher considers it in the concrete, unless he consents to "realize" it in all its concreteness by undergoing himself the trial of existence. Existence is not a ready-made thing that can be contemplated at will. It is not a *Gegenstand*, something set over against us, a sort of spectacle that passes before our eyes. Nor is it "a problem" to be solved without any involvement on our part. It is not an abstract idea worked out in us by an impersonal Logos. Its being is fundamentally a power of being, a call to being, an invitation to make ourselves something. It is, as Jaspers would say, *mögliche Existenz*. It is "a liberty which is first and foremost the power to affirm itself or deny itself."[40] In Heidegger's terminology, the *sein* of man is a *zu sein*, or, as Sartre translates it, "*l'homme a à être.*" Not that this power we have of making or unmaking ourselves, of following the path of bogus and decadent existence, or of rising to authenticity, is without its limits. Human liberty is a liberty bound up with a situation, conditioned by participation, that is to say, by the necessity of being part of and taking part in the world.

A Compound of Passivity and Action. In other words, existence is a compound, not simply a mixture, of passivity and activity. It manifests itself in the form of a dialectical tension between the situation and the free being, which are not to be thought of as two entities placed side by side, but rather as two significant phases which clarify and constitute one other, in virtue of an opposition that is at the same time the bond that unites them. Indeed, this is quite a traditional idea in philosophy. A limit is not apprehended as a limit nor an obstacle as an obstacle except in the attempt to get beyond them. Conversely, if there were no obstacle to be overcome, the movement towards an indefinite "going beyond ourselves" that haunts mankind and confers on our being an ontological dimension, could never appear to us for what it is.[41] But if we are a compound of passivity and activity, a living dialectic between the situation and the free being, it is understandable

[39]*Philosophie*, vol. I, p. 27.
[40]Marcel, *Du refus* . . ., p. 40.
[41]This is one of the fundamental themes in the philosophy of Le Senne, notably in his *Obstacle et valeur*.

that among the existential factors that make up our existence and help us to understand its meaning, there are some that belong to the side of passivity and the situation, while others belong rather to that of action. Among the former are ranged the sentiments and passions, which Heidegger groups together under the heading of *Befindlichkeit* or *Stimmung*. These include anguish and joy, despair and hope. Among the latter, we find such things as moral choice, respect for others, fidelity, love, and lastly, faith. This point had best be illustrated by example, since it would take too long to treat it in detail.

C. REVELATORY ROLE OF THE SENTIMENTS AND OF ACTION

"Befindlichkeit." It is difficult to find an English word which will give a reasonably exact sense of what Heidegger means by *Befindlichkeit*. The word "sentiment" brings to mind a distinct affective faculty or a determinate affective behavior towards a particular object, such as a soldier's fear of an enemy or the sadness of a student faced by failure. *"Befindlichkeit,"* however, takes us beyond determination and stands for a general and profound sentiment concerning existence as a whole. It is an "existentialistic factor,"[42] that is to say, a constitutive element of existence, not in the form of a succession of determinate ways of behaving towards particular objects, but an enveloping and primary unity, situated in and wrapped up in being-in-its-totality. It is this that makes man appear to himself as a "metaphysics-making animal," open to being, and able to investigate the meaning of „being in general." It is this too that allows man to grasp himself as situated (*sich befinden*) in being in general. It is the very awareness of my presence in the midst of being, since in this *Stimmung* I feel determined or affected (*bestimmt*) by reality as a whole, while at the same time I have the experience of being in league with it, as if I had come to an agreement with it (*gestimmt*),[43] This *Befindlichkeit* can take on many modalities, some negative (anguish, boredom, despair), others positive (joy, hope, peace).

Anguish. The importance given to "anguish" in contemporary philosophy is well known. Heidegger, in fact, considers it to be the basic manifestation of "sentiment." It is, above all, in anguish that man comes to realize that the intercourse with particular beings of which his daily life is made up, is not the sum-total of his life. When everything

---

[42]Heidegger uses the word *"existentiale"* ("existentialistic") to distinguish his position from that of Jaspers' *"existentielle"* ("existential"). See J. Collins, *op. cit.*, p. 154.

[43]See W. Biemel, *Le concept de monde chez Heidegger*, pp. 96ff.

crumbles about him, when particular beings lose all meaning and value, man can awaken to himself and dispose himself to ask "the fundamental question of philosophy," namely "whether or not life is worth living."[44] It has, of course, always been recognized that the approach of death has the power to shake us and stir up in us the sense of the seriousness of life. Faced with death, I begin to realize my own responsibility; all of a sudden, I see that worldly happenings like my successes or failures do not in the long run decide the sense of my life. What counts is rather what I myself have done (or will do) with it. I am now alone with myself, and in this solitude I perceive myself as a whole. This isolation, which opens my eyes to my uniqueness, is not the kind of smug self-contemplation that would shut me up in myself by its vain complacency and self-sufficiency. Anguish forces me to look at the mystery of my existence and of my bond with being. Solitude in the face of death makes me understand, or at least have a presentiment of, the fact that I am neither the foundation not the ultimate measure of value and that a genuine life does not consist in doing whatever I please. As Dostoievski said, "not everything is allowed"; my existence has a sense which dwells in me, but does not come only or finally from me.

Despair. Anguish in the face of death has a lesser role to play in the philosophy of Marcel. Its equivalent in his work is the despair of modern man condemned to live in a super-mechanized world, "centered around function." "A life in a world that centers around function is open to despair, since such a world is empty, it has a hollow ring."[45] If despair is accepted, it atrophies the power of wonder and causes us to forget the ontological exigency. But if we do not allow ourselves to be crushed by it, we find that it has also a tonic and purifying effect. There is a sort of despair that contains a seed of hope for it makes us refuse to accept the desperate situation and leads us to recognize that a mechanized and functionalized life cannot satisfy us, since we have more than that within us. "The greatest obstacle to the development of faith is not misfortune but satisfaction."[46] Despair makes us break through the circle of self-satisfied immanence and take a first step along the path towards the Transcendent.

Failure. The same idea is found in Jaspers' treatment of the theme of failure. Failure is the living witness to the fact that nothing here

[44]A. Camus, *Le mythe de Sisyphe*, Paris, 1942, p. 15.
[45]*Le monde cassé*, p. 259.
[46]*Être et avoir*, Paris, 1935, p. 317.

below can satisfy us, that man is, in the long run, not a being-towards-the-world but towards God and for God. In failure, he writes, "we make a test of being ... The non-being of all beings accessible to us is revealed by failure, and is itself the Being of the Transcendent."[47] This according of so much importance to negative affectivity, notably to anguish and despair, to the dramatic situation, to the historical character of reality looked upon as "the universal limit-situation of every empirical being,"[48] has been the source of many misunderstandings. There has been talk of a new nihilism, of a philosophy of nothingness or of pessimism. But this is to take a superficial view of things. In the existentialist philosophy, anguish is the starting-point, not the termination. It is, indeed, a sort of equivalent of the Cartesian methodic doubt. Whether it be speculative or existential, doubt is the main obstacle to be surmounted; consequently, it has the power of opening our eyes to ourselves and revealing to us the meaning of existence.

Consent. If the point of departure of the existential dialectic is in "negative" sentiment, its termination is a "positive" sentiment, such as hope, joy or peace. What the former expressed by defect, the latter brings forward into bold relief, for it constitutes the experience of the full flowering of existence. By giving us an intimate assurance that we are really in the path of truth and of light, these "positive" sentiments bring with them the living testimony of Being, re-found and possessed anew. They constitute a sort of answer from Being-in-person to the call we sent out from the depth of anguish to Him. They are the reply, existential rather than speculative, to the confidence that we placed in Him in giving our consent to the ontological demand on us. In this sense Lagneau wrote: "the proof for the existence of God lies in the happiness that makes moral living possible and that results from it."[49]

We have just spoken of a giving of consent. The passage from the crushed existence that manifests itself in anguish to the existential plenitude of recovered Being which reveals itself in joy and peace, cannot take place without a giving of consent on our part. As Marcel has written, "a philosophy that refuses to take account of the ontological exigency is indeed possible," but it "strikes at the spiritual life in its

[47]*Philosophie*, vol. 3, pp. 237, 234.
[48]See M. Dufrenne and P. Ricoeur, *K. Jaspers et la philosophie de l'existence*, Paris 1947, p. 193. As already noted, the historical character of our existence is taken by Jaspers to be an indication of our metaphysical dimension and of our link with something permanent in the ontological order.
[49]*Célèbres leçons*, p. 293.

deepest roots."[50] It is here that action, moral choice, and faith have their place. Undoubtedly free consent was already at work in the recognition of anguish as a call to "authenticity"; it remains present in the joy of glowing existence, since this too is no mere passive state of mind but rather the definitive setting free of our liberty. However, this liberation is itself the work of our liberty, not indeed of a liberty turned in on itself and acting on whim, but of a liberty which wholly consents to values, a docility and fidelity to the Being which bears us within itself.

Participation. Indeed all this is already contained in the very idea of participation. To participate is not simply to have a part in but also to take part in. If man is not just a thing, and if the being that surrounds us is not just a collection of things, it follows that our link with being and our growth in being cannot be expressed in categories borrowed from the world of physical causality. Rather does it belong to the order of dialogue, of giving in exchange, and of communion. This participation, understood as a communion, is not a particular manifestation of our existence but constitutes its general structure and its fundamental situation. It is to be found wherever we are effectively present in being. It is already at work in sensation, which is, as it were, the first form of participation.[51] It becomes manifest, above all, in those types of behavior which constitute intersubjectivity (fidelity, love, creative affirmation).[52] It is also the essence of the faith that unites us to the absolute *Thou*, God.

Fidelity. This dialectical link between "having part in" and "taking part in" constitutes the central idea of Marcel's thought, and is common in contemporary philosophy.[53] In Marcel's work, it is most clearly expressed by the theme of "creative fidelity." Man creates himself in fidelity. To "ex-sist" for ourselves does not consist in proclaiming our autonomy from the roof-tops nor in shutting ourselves up in self-love nor in a "having," no matter of how spiritual a kind. "The idea of autonomy . . . is bound up with a sort of reduction or particularization of the subject."[54] Autonomy is a kind of self-centeredness. As such,

---

[50]Marcel, *Le monde cassé*, pp. 262f.

[51]This is the theme of "Existence et objectivité," an appendix to Marcel's *Journal métaphysique*, p. 309.

[52]*Du refus . . .*, pp. 192ff.

[53]This idea of participation is shared by Lavelle and Le Senne. It had already been adumbrated in the work of Blondel and Lagneau.

[54]*Être et avoir*, p. 253.

it is the opposite of true liberty which helps to free us, to create us, to open our hearts to fidelity and love "to the depths of the being in which and by which we are."[55] "Having" hardens us, cuts us off from our true roots. It makes us "impermeable," so to speak. It is a kind of alienation, since in having, I am, in a way, possessed by my possessions.[56] To exist authentically means above all to make ourselves aware with unflagging fidelity of the world of values and the mystery of being which supports and nourishes us. It is fidelity to his inspiration that makes the genius pursue his vocation and contribute to transforming men and the world. It is in the fidelity of love that we discover the unique character of the "thou" and the personal dignity that is his and ours. In a word, we come to recognize that man is not a thing nor an instrument but an end in himself. Intersubjectivity then appears almost as a mystery of creative exchange; this helps to explain the power of living witness and of creative affirmation. Finally, it is in the fidelity of faith that man comes to recognize and discover the Transcendent by whom and for whom he ultimately exists.

D. The Theme of Faith

Meaning of the Term. What has gone before gives us a basis for understanding the importance of the theme of faith in contemporary philosophy. It must be noted that the word "faith" means something much wider than religious belief, which is the highest form of faith. Even if faith is understood (as it is by Marcel) in the sense of Christian faith—which takes us into the strictly supernatural order—it still remains a manifestation of our existence, and must, in consequence, be prefigured and prepared within this existence. Otherwise it would appear to be an accident or an anomaly and could never claim to be the ultimate plenitude of existence. There is, then, a broad usage of the word "faith" in which it is an analogous term and it is this which allows us to discuss religious faith and to elaborate a philosophy (and ultimately a theology) of religion. If Christian faith has a meaning for us, it is because our existence is permeated through and through by faith in the broad and existential sense of the word. Faith in this sense is a genetal and fundamental constituent of human existence, like participation, or giving in exchange, or the communion we spoke of earlier. By "faith" we understand the power that lies in us of recognizing "something that is beyond doubt, though existential rather than logical

---

[55]*Du refus* . . ., p. 89.
[56]*Être et avoir*, especially, pp. 252ff.

or rational."[57] This indubitable something lies beyond objective or scientific verification, but appears to reflection as a significant datum, at once primitive and central. It goes without saying that this something is nothing other than existence itself, recognized as a mystery in which we find ourselves involved.

But why use the word "faith" here at all? It is used in order to emphasize that the noetic behavior which leads to the assurance of this existential indubitable reality cannot be described in purely passive terms nor in terms of Cartesian rationalism. Existence, insofar as it is taken to be an embodied subjectivity bound up with a situation, is neither a *Gegenstand* nor an idea. It is a call to being, a sort of participation that must be undertaken. It is a trial or test, and every trial is an "invitation to betrayal," as Ricoeur puts it.[58] Hence full recognition cannot be given to this indubitable reality without our giving a certain consent, without our freely accepting an "opening" of some kind, something like an act of confidence or of faith in the mystery of being which bears us within it and is always there, prior to all reflection. Materialism, which reduces existence to a tangle of objective impersonal processes, and idealism, which makes of it an impersonal dialectic that goes on in us but without us, both spring in the long run from a refusal, a lack of confidence in the being that is offered to us as a gift.

But if it is true that faith in this wide sense is some sort of an "existential component," we ought to be able to find traces of it at every level of our existence, everywhere that existence manifests and realizes its presence in being. This is just what Marcel maintains. Recognition of embodiment already implies a prior phase of faith. The union of body and soul, of universal reason and individual experience, will always remain a mystery beyond our comprehension. But to accept the mystery is to refuse to obliterate ourselves; it is to sustain ourselves in a life full of trials by the hope that suffering and death will turn out to be of some value. In a word, we affirm implicitly that the mystery of being in which we find ourselves is ultimately a mystery of goodness. Existence has, therefore, a sense which does not come from us, which is not a mere datum or brute fact, but rather a grace. From this it would seem to be only a step to the affirmation of a God Who is both Creator and Providence.

The Affirmation of God. This is what Marcel maintains in the first part of his *Journal Métaphysique*, though in a language that is still strongly

---

[57]*Du refus . . .*, p. 25.
[58]*Gabriel Marcel et Karl Jaspers*, p. 113.

influenced by idealism. Faith in God the Creator, he writes, alone can fill the void between "myself as thought and will" and "myself as something empirical."[59] We find faith at work within intersubjectivity also. If they are to be authentic and reveal to us the "thou," our relations with other people must be sustained by faith in the other, as we have already seen when speaking of fidelity and love. In general, no value can be accepted without a certain prior confidence in what it stands for. We can esteem something as a value only if we expect from it an increase in existence. This is true even for *things* that appear as values (Things will acquire values for embodied subjects, for free beings faced with situations). It is true *a fortiori* of the recognition of the supreme value, God. It is in our invocation of the absolute Thou, that is to say, in faith in the religious sense of the term, which Marcel considers the "absolute form of fidelity." "I become truly a subject," finding the plenitude of life and freedom at the same time as I find the certainty of God's existence. God is the supreme mystery; for this reason, He can be recognized only in the very act of invoking Him. He can never be thought of as "an objective datum whose nature is to be determined by rational investigation." The formula that expresses faith is "I believe in Thee my only refuge." Furthermore, this faith must be constantly renewed. Of its very nature it is "in no way like a possession which can be taken for granted." Its witness is the peace and plenitude which its possession confers: "peace and faith are inseparable."

Faith and Mystery. Marcel points out that what is true of faith is equally true of its noematic correlate, *mystery.* The Christian mystery can have a meaning for us only because existence itself is already in the order of mystery (in the broad sense). Rationalism rejects religious mystery because rationalism has already restricted existence to the existence of a scientific object or of a clear idea. In reply to the objection that he is secularizing the content of the term, "mystery," Marcel writes: "A revelation, no matter of what sort, can be made, after all, only to a being who is *involved*, to a being, then, who participates in a reality that cannot simply be treated as a problem . . ."[60] What applies to mystery in general, is true above all of the supreme mystery which is at the back of all the others and towards which they all converge.

---

[59] *Journal métaphysique*, p. 6.

[60] *Le monde cassé*, p. 300. See *The philosophy of existence*, tr. by M. Harari, New York, 1949, pp. 8-12; Collins, *op. cit.*, pp. 130-8, for the distinction between a "problem" (in the order of manipulable things) and a "mystery" (in the order of being in its generality).

This reality (the mystery of God) gives me to myself in the proportion in which I give myself to it. It is through the mediation of the act by which I concentrate myself around it that I truly become a subject.[61]

The importance of faith is just as great for Jaspers as for Marcel. Faith in "the hidden transcendence" (God) is for Jaspers the supreme act of human existence, the act that confers on us ultimate authenticity and establishes us in genuine peace, joy and unity. "Existence tries out true-being in faith."[62] However, in the case of Jaspers, faith has not the same religious and Christian ring as it has for Marcel. It is a "philosophical faith." The expression is ambiguous, since it calls to mind, among other things, the "God of the philosophers and scientists" which Pascal contrasted with the "God of Abraham, Isaac and Jacob" and the "God of Jesus Christ." It is not Pascal's "God of the philosophers" that Jaspers has in mind when speaking of "philosophical faith," but rather the hidden God of Kierkegaard. For Jaspers, philosophical faith is not something this side of religious faith; it is something beyond it, its ultimate essence. He claims that religion, by bringing in the idea of revelation and proposing a God who is near to us and Whom we can address as "Thou," lessens the mystery of the divine transcendence. All formal religions constitute in his mind a danger to genuine faith, even though they are necessary for maintaining the spirit of faith in mankind. In his eyes, religion has the value of a sort of sign or myth. It is a channel of faith, which helps us to rise towards true (philosophical) faith, provided that we do not stop short at the sign itself but rather learn to interpret it with the eyes of faith.

The anguished experience of a shattered existence, the choice in faith, the joy and peace of an existence brought to fulfilment thanks to the rediscovery of being, these are the three principal phases of the living and personal dialectic which alone can lead us to the reconquest of the concrete, that is to say, to the recognition of the mystery of being.

One last point remains to be examined. Does a process of this sort fulfil the requirements of reason, even in the broad sense of the word? Can it claim the title of philosophy? Is not philosophy by definition an effort of thought attempting to give a foundation for a *universal* knowledge concerning the ultimate meaning of existence?

---

[61] *Du refus . . .*, pp. 234f.
[62] *Existenzphilosophie*, Berlin, 1938, p. 8.

E. The Demands of Reason

This has certainly been the ideal of human thought in every age; it is the very well-spring of philosophy. We must get beyond opinion and individual conviction to elaborate a knowledge about man and the universe which will be universally valid and based on a critical foundation. In every age, men have considered that this ideal can be pursued only through reflection, that is, through "reason," "reason" being taken here to be the summit of human thought, the supreme effort of the mind in search of truth and of being.[63]

The ideal of a universal and established knowledge is indeed present in contemporary thought; as we have already noted, the philosophy of our times still remains a work of reflection. The goal that Marcel sets before himself is to "think faith philosophically," and Jaspers tells us that "the sort of reflection that throws light on existence demands an objective thinking."[64] It goes without saying, however, that the terms "reflection," "critical foundation," and "universality" bear a meaning in this context quite different from that which they possessed in the rationalist tradition.

"Critical foundation." Like every other philosophy, existentialism claims to be a search for something beyond doubt, but this "indubitable" is here not a logical evidence (or "first principle"), nor a rationally demonstrable conclusion drawn from evident premises, nor a scientifically controlled reality. Being an "irrefragable element of existence," it can be encountered only in and through the experience of existence. Not that one records it like a brute fact. It is the result of sincere reflection, what Marcel calls "a reflection of the second order." Far from leading us away from concrete experience, philosophical reflection brings us back towards it, allowing us to recapture the essential structure that rationalist thought unfortunately allowed to escape. "Whereas primary reflection (in this context, scientific analysis) tends to dissolve the unity with which it begins, secondary reflection is essentially an effort of recovery and reconquest."[65] It brings us to understand that we cannot "resolve" the mystery of being by analysis, since "being is what resists the analysis that is brought to bear on the data of experience when the attempt is made to reduce them to elements more and more

---

[63]The noematic correlate of the supreme effort of the mind is also called "reason." We use our "reason" to find the ultimate "reasons" of things.

[64]*Philosophie*, vol. 2, p. 9.

[65]Marcel, *Le mystère de l'être*, Paris, 1951, vol. 1, p. 98. See also *Du refus . . .*, p. 34.

lacking in intrinsic or significant value."[66] In a word, secondary re-flection leads us to the inescapable affirmation "that I am more than I can say."[67]

But if it is maintained that the discovery of this irrefutable existential element involves a measure of personal assent, and that it is only in solitude that I attain an assurance of "the hidden Transcendence," does not this undermine all possibility of a universal and communicable philosophical knowledge? This would be the case if human choice were the foundation (and hence the standard) of truth and of value, or if the aspect of uniqueness or personality that is characteristic of freedom were in some way in contradiction with the idea of inter-subjectivity. But this is not admitted by the authors we have considered, as is clear from the analyses made above. The option of fidelity, or of faith, is an *assent* to being, a way of making ourselves receptive to the mystery of being that bears us within it. "Affirmation can never claim to be the source of the reality that it asserts," says Marcel.[68] The knowledge we get as a result of the existential dialectic is rather a *recognition* than a cognition; it is a rediscovery of the affirmation "I exist."

The apparent contradiction between the uniqueness of the person and the communication between persons will always remain a paradox, but a paradox contained in, and constitutive of, the primitive significant datum we call existence. Human existence has a primitive sense, namely, to appear to itself as an embodied liberty which has to realize itself intersubjectively by showing fidelity to the ontological demand. To say that "the essence of man is to exist" is to assign three characteristics to men: first, presence in the same condition or situation, second, the character of uniqueness, which is, above all, a call to take charge personally of their own existence, and third, the possibility of making themselves aware as a group of the mystery that envelops them. Far from excluding each other, uniqueness and intersubjectivity are com-plementary terms. The individual owes his recognition of the mystery of being to his communion with other persons, a communion which is helped by fidelity, by love, by the testimony of creative affirmation and by dialogue.

Universality. Truth is, then, *de jure* universal and communicable. But this universality is something to be achieved, in the sense that we ought by testimony and discourse to help one another find the

---

[66] *Le monde cassé*, p. 262.
[67] *Ibid.*, p. 266.
[68] *Du refus* . . ., p. 93.

truth, or, more precisely, to enter into the truth. This shared discovery
of ontological truth is the result neither of scientific verification nor
of logical deduction from abstract evident principles. It calls for a
personal assent from each of us. Philosophical discourse has the office
of *"speaking for all,"*[69] and is first and foremost an invitation asking each
of us to tread the existential road that leads to the recognition of being.
But it is more than that. Philosophy (taken here as a systematic and
objective knowledge rather than as creative "open" thinking) has always
been considered indispensable to our reaching a common possession
of the truth. "Existence," says Jaspers, "is only reached by knowledge
that throws light on it."[70]

It may help here to consider mystery for a moment from the noematic
rather than the noetic aspect, on which we have been concentrating.
In this sense, it reveals itself in the experience of the existential dialectic
with something like an internal objective dialectical structure. If, in
Marcel's phraseology, experience is like a "promised land" to be
"explored" and "penetrated", then it cannot be treated as a site to
be dug up. It is like a concentric ensemble of mysteries that converge
towards an all-enveloping yet central mystery, God. Embodiment,
intersubjectivity and the Divine Transcendence are not simply juxtaposed; one leads naturally to the next. Hence the fidelity which creative
thought manifests towards the dialectic that lies at the very heart of the
mystery cannot help being reflected in the body of thought that is its
objective expression.

For this reason, Jaspers considers that objective philosophical
knowledge is a necessary instrument in the common discovery of truth.
It is "the speculative cipher" of the Transcendence.[71] As Ricoeur
remarks, Jaspers has, "by means of this idea of a speculative cipher,
tried to rehabilitate everything that he at first condemned."[72] Marcel
shows himself to be extremely reserved with regard to all objective
thought, all rational dialectic, even though he constantly makes use of it.
His intricate analyses of fidelity, participation, having and being-in-a-
situation are not psychological descriptions but elucidations of a meaning.
If by "rational dialectic" one means logical reasoning cut off from
reality and separated from experienced existence, something like a
scaffolding of *a Priori* concepts, it obviously has no place in Marcel's
work. But to make a meaning explicit by means of a second-order

[69]Ricoeur, *Gabriel Marcel et Karl Jaspers*, p. 78.
[70]*Philosophie*, vol. 2, p. 16.
[71]M. Dufrenne et P. Ricoeur, *Karl Jaspers...*, pp. 313ff.
[72]*Op. cit.*, p. 382.

reflection is definitely a work of reason in the wider sense of the term. Who would deny that Marcel is a philosopher? But what does this mean if not that he pursues in a reflective and rational way the search for being which had haunted mankind? Thus he "speaks for all."

Newman and Blondel. We are nearing the end of this inquiry which has concerned itself mostly with the work of Marcel and Jaspers. The main contribution of Newman and the Blondel of the early *Action* was surely to prepare the way for the philosophical preoccupations of today. If they have been less often mentioned, it was mainly from a fear of unduly lengthening these pages which are intended not as a systematic exposition but rather as an attempt to discover beneath the divergences of the thought explored, a common inspiration and rhythm. Such a community clearly exists between Marcel and Jaspers. What of the other two?

Most of the themes that we have encountered in Marcel were touched upon by Newman too, sometimes in the very same words. There is the same severity towards "objective and systematic knowledge," with the same tendency to identify conceptual knowledge in general with its rationalist interpretation. There is the same preoccupation with the existential concrete, betraying itself in the priority given to "personal thought" and "concrete reasoning" in opposition to "notional" dialectic. The same way, too, of getting beyond rationalism by a philosophy centred around subjectivity, personality and community, being-in-history and mystery. Finally, there is the same conception of formal philosophical or apologetic thought, understood not so much as a rational demonstration of the truth than as an invitation to render oneself receptive to the same experiences and to enter personally into the truth.[73]

Blondel, too, is above all a philosopher of the concrete. His dialectic of action has no more than the appearance of voluntarism and pragmatism. The role of action is not to *make* the truth but to contribute towards *uncovering* it. It is action that anchors us in reality and brings about our presence in being. "The real will not become subject to our knowledge unless we voluntarily accept the truth and the light which it brings."[74] Action manifests the meaning of our participation in the real. The supreme form of action is faith. "The action that envelops and

---

[73]This kinship between Newman and contemporary philosophy is admirably brought out by C. Keogh, *Introduction to the Philosophy of Cardinal Newman*, unpub. doctoral dissertation, Louvain, 1950.

[74]F. Taymans D'Eypernon, S. J., *Le Blondelisme*, Louvain, 1933, p. 66.

crowns all others is our thought of God," he writes, following St. John of the Cross.[75] Faith gives God to us at the same time as it brings us the intimate assurance of His existence. "In the free choice (of faith) the absolute makes itself known, and we come face to face with the infinity of a will which gives being to phenomena and makes of them a subsistent and indestructible reality."[76]

5. Concluding Critical Reflections

The Merits of "Open" Existentialism. The great merit of the thinkers we have been studying is that they have recalled the necessity of getting back to the concrete in the richest sense of the word, and to a genuine experience of the concrete. By broadening the meaning both of the word "concrete" and of the word "experience," they have showed a way out of the dilemma of empiricism and intellectualism, one which avoids the dangers of subjectivism of sentiment, of will or of faith. It is clear that the introduction of subjectivity and communion, of the concrete historical situation, of affectivity and choice, makes the defence of a universally valid and critically based knowledge more difficult in some ways, but this is inevitable if we are to respect the concrete. Furthermore, it is to the credit of the philosophy of the present day that it has, if not demonstrated, at least indicated that this danger can be overcome, and that it is possible to integrate the irrational into a wider ideal of reason. This reason is equivalent to existence in the modern sense of the word. Existence is the primitive significant datum, and hence includes a "natural light" (*lumen naturale*) which is not logical or abstract, but existential and enveloping.

Does this mean that existentialism of the "open" kind, whose principal forms we have outlined, is to be considered wholly satisfactory? Without wishing to deny its very great merits or to diminish the importance that it must henceforth hold for any philosophy that wishes to undertake the eternal "reconquest of the concrete," we nevertheless believe that there are in it certain regrettable deficiencies, all springing from the same source, namely, an excessive distrust of concepts and of discourse. It is true that existential philosophy has not yet given us a systematic doctrine of the concept. If this were merely a simple matter of omission, it might easily be repaired. But it is more than that: there exists within the anti-rationalist reaction that characterizes contemporary thought a positive tendency to underestimate the intelligence and

---

[75]See D'Eypernon, *op. cit.*, p. 146.
[76]*L'action*, Paris, 1893, p. 370.

conceptual thought. We can see it in the works of existential philosophy of both the "open" and "closed" kinds. To this point we must now turn our attention.

A. EXCESSIVE MISTRUST OF THE CONCEPT

An Erroneous Identification. This mistrust of concepts and of reasoning shows itself in the first place in the fact that these thinkers adopt the rationalist terminology concerning knowledge without attempting to make the necessary corrections to it. As we noted earlier, they appear to identify objective knowledge in general with the idealist or positivist conception of knowledge. The criticism they make of the rationalists thus automatically takes on the appearance of a condemnation of all conceptual thought. They speak as if the concept did nothing but rigidify our infinitely mobile apprehension of reality and shut us off from the concrete. In a word, they seem to think of the concept as an entity in itself, a sort of representation or copy which has the effect of arresting the gaze of the consciousness which contemplates it. Now is not this an unconscious concession to the "illusion of immanence," which is just what these authors want to combat? The concept is, as the medievals put it, a *medium quo*, an *intentio*, that is to say, an instrument within and at the service of the cognitive intention that bears us towards reality in all its concreteness. Far from separating us from being, it helps us to come to grips with it, to bring us closer to it. At least this is what we are going to try to justify in our next chapter, thus forging a link with the Aristotelian tradition prior to Descartes.

Danger of Subjectivism. The mistrust of the concept shows itself, too, in the way in which existentialist epistemology tries to rid itself of the primacy of the concept and of knowledge in order to substitute for it the primacy of existence. It is true that the concept is not the whole of knowledge and that knowledge is not the whole of man, and in this sense there is, of course, a primacy of existence. It is obviously equivocal and dangerous, however, to reject the primacy of knowledge out of hand when one is trying to elaborate a theory of knowledge and of truth. It is equivocal because knowledge becomes identified from the outset with the conceptual and discursive aspect of knowledge alone, even though the broadening of the field of knowledge is supposed to be our main concern. It is dangerous, too, since the foundations of knowledge are sought among certain types of "revealing behavior" such as sentiment and activity, and yet these are placed right from the beginning outside the borders of knowledge. In this way, they are placed in a very ambiguous initial position and on a path that leads all too easily to one or other form of that subjectivism they are trying so hard to avoid.

The Accusation of Fideism or Voluntarism. This is the explanation of the accusation of fideism or voluntarism so often made against Newman and Blondel, Jaspers and Marcel. We have tried to show that this accusation is unjustified if one takes into account the basic intention animating these writers. It must be remembered that it is not really a primacy of sentiment, action or faith, that they are trying to establish, but rather a primacy of concrete existence, considered as the primitive significant datum. Action, sentiment and faith are only existential factors in this primary datum. However, the fact remains that it has been—and still is—possible to give a voluntarist or fideist interpretation of the works in question, and this sort of interpretation seems to some extent justified. The reason is very simple. Among the factors which go to make up existence as the primary significant datum, knowledge is treated as a poor relation, since it is considered not as an originating existential factor but as a derivative manifestation of existence, a manifestation which, far from bringing us close to being, tends rather to take us away from it. This conception would be correct if it were permissible to identify knowledge with the concept, taken as a static "frozen" entity. But it is false if predicative knowledge is carried forward by an originating primitive cognitive intention that helps to constitute existence as such.

Truth and Value Encompass Each Other. In this latter case, we must admit a certain primacy of knowledge, in the broader sense of that word. Our next task is to try to define this factor and then to reconcile it with the primacy of existence and of being. It seems to us that the older philosophers can help us in carrying through this difficult enterprise. Did they not maintain that a distinction should be made within being as a whole, insofar as it reveals itself to us and takes on a meaning for us, between the spheres of truth and of goodness, a distinction which did not, however, oblige us to separate being—or, for that matter, existence—into two sectors, juxtaposed and mutually exclusive. In the eyes of these philosophers, the domain of truth and the domain of value are mutually "encompassing" and "encompassed," since the behavior that reveals being as true and that which reveals it as good are equally primitive, and together make up the synthetic unity of human existence as an openness towards being. Such is, in our opinion, the meaning of the old phrase "*ens, unum, verum, bonum convertuntur.*" This formula deserves to be thought over anew.

B. Latent Empiricism?

Intuitive Grasp of God. There is a third way in which the new philosophy shows a tendence to discredit the concept. Existentialism, as we have said, claims to be a philosophy of the concrete. It is not content with merely preaching our return to experience, in the widest sense of the term; it also argues that this experience is the only way of getting to reality, thus excluding (or so it would seem) conceptual and discursive thought. We recall Marcel's words: "The rational proof for the existence of God is a phase in an interior journey of discovery."[77] Is not this perilously close to a new empiricism which would destroy the very foundations of any metaphysics of the Transcendent? A consistent empiricism, even "a higher empiricism" based on experience in the widest sense, can scarcely conclude to an affirmation of God unless it accepts with Malebranche some sort of intuition of God. Such an intuition may be described as "blinded" or "blinding" but it still remains an intuitive grasping, that is to say, an apprehending of a reality that is present-in-person.

The Intuitionist' Dilemma. Now it is well known that any consistent intuitionism leads to unacceptable conclusions. There are two possibilities. The intuition may be a natural one, springing from the *lumen naturale* given to us with existence itself, in which case God loses His Transcendence and is no longer "that which is beyond," that which is entirely different from everything else. He is no longer distinguishable from being-as-a-whole. Or the intuition in question may be supernatural.

In this case, we are faced at the outset with the thorny problem of the nature and probative value of mystical experience, thus reaching a new impasse. For even if we admit that mystical intuition can in certain privileged cases bring with it an unshakeable assurance of the existence and presence of a transcendent God, we are then faced with an experience of significant presence which gives us God in person. It goes without saying that this experience must in some measure admit of expression in an authentic affirmation of God. Such an affirmation would not be possible without the mediation of an authentic and universally valid *idea* of God. Otherwise mystical intuition falls back to the level of interior, singular, inexpressible grasping, which is without meaning for mankind as a whole and without value for philosophy. But then the question arises, how can this affirmation have a meaning

---

[77]*Du refus . . .*, p. 231.

that is universally valid, if it concerns a transcendent reality which the majority of mankind has never experienced? It may also be questioned whether the mystical experience would have a meaning for the mystic himself if he had not *some* prior authentic idea of God. This experience manifests itself as an encounter and a response which somehow complements a prior expectation and question, though it does so in a way which surpasses all expectation.

Marcel's "Second Reflection." This lack of a solid doctrine about the concept, about affirmation and about discourse constitutes in our view the weak point in Marcel's work. Since he makes no appeal to mystical experience in his metaphysics of Transcendence, he is in a particularly difficult position. There is, of course, his theory of "second reflection." According to him, it is by an existential dialectical procedure, a sort of negation of negation, that we retrieve the concrete which analysis began by negating. This is the "second reflection" which allows us to recognize mystery as an undeniable existential component. It would seem, however, that the mystery thus attained cannot be anything more than that *in us* which "resists all analysis." But this is not God. If the return to the concrete is to lead us (as Marcel claims) not only "to the recognition of something irreducible (the embodied being that we ourselves are), but also to something over and beyond this irreducible (God),"[78] reflection on embodied being must in some way lead us to an affirmation of this something beyond experience. This reality no longer belongs to the order of experience but to the order of the conception that affirms it. In other words, if God is really "the hidden Transcendent," "the entirely different One," the "supreme absent One" (even though this absence be indicated in the very heart of our existence and constitute its ultimate meaning), we must admit that there lies in us the power of attaining Him intentionally, not as a reality present in person, but as Someone whose existence must be affirmed on the basis of our experience.[79] An affirmation of this kind cannot be treated as "an affirmation that I am" unless we are content to play with words, for it is concerned with something beyond what I am. This something beyond me is conceived and affirmed as such; it is also affirmed through

---

[78] *Être et avoir*, p. 255.

[79] It is in this sense that St. Thomas interprets the affirmation "God exists." This proposition does not, he says, mean that we understand the being or the essence of God — *non possumus scire esse Dei nec ejus essentiam* — but we understand that the proposition "God exists", which we formulate from a consideration of creatures, must be affirmed: *"scimus quod haec propositio quam formamus de Deo, cum dicimus 'Deus est', vera est."* *Summa Theol.*, I, q. 3, a. 4, ad 2.

the mediation of a conceptual attitude, or, as the medievals put it, by means of a *conceptio mentis*.

The Central Problem of Existentialism. What we have just been developing with regard to Marcel is true generally, though in different degrees, of all the existentialist phenomenology so far produced. By affirming the primacy of experience, it exposes itself to the danger of leading to a new empiricism, very different no doubt from classical empiricism, but still empiricism.[80] In other words, the central problem raised by the new philosophy is, as becomes clearer every day, that of the passing from the phenomenon to its trans-phenomenal foundation, being, or, what comes to the same thing, passing from phenomenology to metaphysics.[81] This problem is in the long run the problem of reflection and of the relationship between reflective or speculative knowledge and the pro-reflective or ante-predicative life of consciousness.

Its Importance for Theology. The problem of passing from phenomena to the being of phenomena is important not only for metaphysics but also for theology, which sets out to reflect on the mystery of the faith, on the basis of revelation about this mystery. Theological reflection cannot be satisfied with collecting revealed data. These data refer to all-enveloping mystery, the mystery of God and of His redemptive love, commonly called the mystery of grace or the supernatural order. It is incumbent on theology to work out, as far as it can, the synthetic unity of this mystery, beginning from the partial and convergent data of Revelation, and relying upon the *analogia fidei*. For this reason, theology is a task for reason in the wide sense, enlightened by faith: *fides quaerens intellectum*. This explains the apprehensiveness of the Church in the face of every attempt on the part of philosophy to diminish the range of human reason or to restrict the field of truth. It also explains (as we shall see in a later chapter) the attachment of the Church to the philosophy of St. Thomas.

---

[80]This is especially true for Merleau-Ponty, in view of the fact that perceptive experience is for him "what constitutes the foundation of our idea of truth." It is less true for Jaspers because of his theory of "ciphers" (which recalls, to some extent, the medieval theory of analogy) and less still for the Heidegger of *Vom Wesen der Wahrheit*.

[81]See Collins, *op. cit.*, pp. 104-111.

CHAPTER FOUR

EXISTENTIAL PHENOMENOLOGY:
CREDIT AND DEBIT

In the last two chapters, we have examined the notions of historicity and the irrational in contemporary thought. Each chapter ended with some words of criticism; the reader may have noticed that the criticism in each case was more or less the same. This is not surprising, because the different problems raised so far are really only variants of a single one, perhaps the most fundamental one which any philosophy must face. Is it possible that, despite the empirical origin of our knowledge, we possess the ability to transcend experience by achieving a trans-historical and metempirical truth? On the answer to this question, the fate of philosophy—and, in a sense, of man—depends. In this chapter, we shall ask directly whether existential phenomenology measures up in the answer it gives to this problem, which is essentially the classical problem of the relation between experience and reason. Before seeing the shortcomings of this answer, it is important to summarize the positive contributions that this philosophy has made.

1. The Merits of Existential Phenomenology

A Critique of Empiricism and Intellectualism

It would be difficult to find anywhere else a similarly profound and perceptive critique of empiricism and intellectualism. By developing Husserl's notion of intentionality, the new philosophy succeeds in avoiding these extreme positions without losing the element of truth that is to be found in each of them. It retains the empiricist insistence on the primacy of perceptual experience, but broadens the notion of experience. Following Descartes, it maintains the original, irreducible character of the *Cogito* and the possibility of a reflective thought which, though bound up with our pre-reflective life, is not entirely hemmed in by it.[1] Thus, not only does the new philosophy get beyond classical empiricism and idealism, it also avoids the semi-empiricism and semi-idealism of Kant, Brunschvicg and Lachieze-Rey. Merleau-Ponty puts it as follows:

---

[1] Merleau-Ponty, "*Le primat . . .*," p. 150.

We cannot apply to perception the classical distinction of form and matter (Kant), nor conceive the perceiving subject as a consciousness which interprets, unravels or orders a sensible matter whose ideal law it is supposed to possess within itself (Brunschvicg and Lachieze-Rey). Matter is pregnant with its form: which amounts to saying that in the long run every perception takes place within a certain horizon, and finally within the world.[2]

The classical opposition between sensation and intellectual knowledge is thus bypassed, even at the perceptive or pre-analytical level of consciousness. "Perception is here understood as reference to a whole (namely the thing, and ultimately the world) which in principle can be grasped only through certain of its parts or aspects."[3] The unity of the perceived thing—and the same goes for the world as a whole—is not a sum of *a posteriori* data; nor is it "an ideal unity held in the mind, like that of a geometrical concept." It is that of "a whole which is prior to the parts, a whole which comprises an indefinitely large number of possible perspectives."[4] The unity of the human *Cogito* is thus reestablished, since there is no longer a noumenal world behind the world of phenomena, nor a *Cogito* which is purely spiritual, cut off from the world of sense experience and superimposed upon the empirical *Cogito*. Lastly, intersubjectivity comes into its own again. It is no longer something secondary and derivative. Thanks to intentionality we can exist together in the same world. "If I consider my perceptions as simple sensations, they are private, mine alone. If I treat them as acts of the understanding, . . . communication takes its rightful place once again," though, of course, "we have stepped into the order of ideal existence." The characteristic of intentionality is that "the thing imposes itself, not as true for every intelligence, but as real for everyone who shares my situation."[5]

Notion of truth. These conclusions are not to be despised. They incorporate not merely an improved psychological description of the concrete situation of man, but also include a general doctrine of truth which, though it has (in our opinion) some faults, deserves the attention of philosophers on several scores. In the first place, in trying to "integrate the irrational in a broadened notion of reason," it broadens the scope of human truth and brings back to philosophy the sense of mystery

---

[2]Merleau-Ponty, "*Le primat* . . .," p. 119.
[3]*Ibid.*, p. 123.
[4]*Ibid.*, p. 123.
[5]*Ibid.*, pp. 124f.

and paradox. Furthermore, without succumbing to the temptation of
a lazy relativism, it appreciates the historical aspect of cognitive life.
As we noted above with de Waelhens, it "tends to seek a middle way
between traditional relativism, that of Dilthey for example, and the
universalism without any definite context, dear to classical rationalism."[6] In the eyes of our contemporaries, historicity and historicism
are not synonymous. "We do not renounce the hope of a truth over
and above divergent standpoints," writes Merleau-Ponty. "There is
in human action and knowledge an element that cannot be gainsaid,
true and false, good and evil."[7] Together we look out upon the same
world, which is not just the sum of *a posteriori* aspects, but the noematic
correlate of our fundamental tendency, the sphere that envelops all
possible perspectives, both mine and those of others. A common intention,
with its correlate the "world," constitutes our *lumen naturale*, our source
of understanding. It explains the fact that we are conscious of speaking
about the same things, that by means of often-ambiguous linguistic
signs we can bring to life again our past, rethink the thoughts of others,
reject them or correct them. For this reason, truth is by rights universal.
True, this universality is mainly something to be achieved in the course
of history. But it always implies within history an existential factor which
cannot be rejected, one that is universal and outside history. Husserl
called it the *Urdoxa* or the *doxische Seinsglaube*.[8]

B. CRITIQUE OF IMMANENTISM

The last and not the least advantage of the new philosophy is
its firm denial of monist and immanentist conceptions of truth and
being. Undoubtedly the ways of speaking that these philosophers adopt
can give rise to misunderstanding. They reject "the idol of absolute
knowledge."[9] At first sight it might seem that we are back to complete
relativism and that the very idea of truth has been rejected. But in
reality, only the intellectualist and idealist conceptions of truth, which
make of it a world actually and fully understood in the depths of our
consciousness, are being questioned. According to the idealists, truth
is an organic system of necessary and immutable concepts or a perfect
identity of consciousness and being, which philosophical reflection is
supposed to attain deep down within ourselves. Because of its opposition

---

[6]"Phénoménologie et métaphysique," p. 366. See Chapter 2, Section 4.
[7]*Sens*, pp. 126, 191.
[8]See Merleau-Ponty, *Phénoménologie*, pp. 340, 395, 455ff.
[9]Merleau-Ponty, "*Le primat* . . .," p. 128.

to this, the existential doctrine of truth, even among those who claim to be atheists, has an important bearing on any metaphysics which wishes to keep alive the sense of mystery and defend a theist interpretation of things. In showing the emptiness of the immanentist conception of the Absolute, it has reopened the way to the affirmation of a transcendent God.

It is true that many contemporary phenomenologists are not content to reject rationalist or idealist monism; they reject the Christian idea of God as being equally irreconcilable with the historical character of human existence. This seems to reveal a confusion between the idealist interpretation of the Absolute and the traditional affirmation of a transcendent God. The confusion appears to be due in great part to the fact that in its reaction against idealism, the new philosophy has not always succeeded in escaping from the snares into which its idealist opponents have fallen.[10]

2. Defects of Existential Phenomenology

Merleau-Ponty. Rather than passing the existentialists in review, one after the other, we shall concentrate our attention mainly on the work of Merleau-Ponty. This may not really simplify our task very much. Merleau-Ponty has worked out better than anybody else a coherent doctrine of human embodiment, and for this reason is certainly further removed than any other of the atheistic existentialists from the Cartesian and idealist position. Take Sartre, for example. Although his phenomenological descriptions are usually poles apart from intellectualism, his ontology undeniably contains a number of ideas that are reminiscent of the philosophy he is combatting. The sharp opposition between the "in-itself" and the "for-itself" naturally brings to mind the Cartesian dichotomy of thought and extension,[11] just as the presentation of the "in-itself" as "undifferentiated identity," without the least sign of duality or differentiation or structure, is obviously reminiscent of an idealism of meaning. For Sartre, it is only through man that meanings come into the world. "The character of being a world, of being in space, quantity, purposiveness, time, belong to being only because I am the negation of being."[12]

---

[10]See Chapter 2, Sections 4 and 5.

[11]See, for example, *L'imagination*, p. 1: "My consciousness could not, in any case, be a thing, because its mode of being is that of being-for-itself. For the consciousness, to exist is to be conscious of existence. It appears as pure spontaneity against the world of things which is pure inertia." See also pp. 125f.

[12]*L'Etre et le Néant*, p. 269. The expression: "it is through man that meanings come into the world" is clearly ambiguous, as we shall see more fully later.

If we now claim to find traces of idealism even in the work of Merleau-Ponty, this must not be misunderstood. We are not trying to make him a disciple of Berkeley or Kant or Brunschvicg. His philosophy moves in an entirely different atmosphere. By defining perception as the original modality of consciousness, he immediately puts himself in opposition to idealism. For idealism, being only exists in-so-far as it is perceived or known; *esse est percipi*. For Merleau-Ponty, on the other hand, "the natural world stands before us, existing in itself beyond its existence for me, so that we find ourselves in presence of something which does not need to be perceived in order to exist."[13]

Even Kant's semi-idealism is finally rejected, as we have seen. "Matter is wrapped up in and deeply saturated with meaning."[14] In spite of all this, it is difficult to escape the impression that Merleau-Ponty's position in regard to idealism suffers from certain ambiguities. Not that we reproach him for insisting on the element of "definitive truth contained in the Cartesian turning away from things and ideas towards the self." As he says, "experience, even of transcendent things, is possible only if I find within myself a projection towards them."[15] St. Thomas had the same idea when he said that the human soul is "in a certain sense all things." The part assigned to man by Merleau-Ponty seems, however, to be equivocal; it concedes too much to idealism.

A. The Dangers of Pure Phenomenology

"Being" and „To-Be-forMan." It may well be asked whether a philosophy like that of the *Phénoménologie de la Perception*, which claims to use an exclusively phenomenological method, does not take us back inevitably to an idealism of meaning, if not on the descriptive level, at least on that of the ontological interpretation of knowledge. Such an interpretation is never completely absent when one is philosophizing, since philosophy is a search for ultimate foundations. To identify philosophy, a transcendental and basic mode of thought, with phenomenological description is possible only if one begins by setting up the phenomenon, that is to say being-for-us, as the supreme transcendental. The reduction of the whole of philosophy to phenomenology is an implicit acceptance of a more or less idealist interpretation of things, since one is claiming that "to-be-for-man" is the *only* meaning that the word „being" can have for us.

---

[13]*Phénoménologie*, p. 180.
[14]*Ibid.*, p. 374.
[15]*Ibid.*, p. 423.

Two Meanings. It is true that what we have just said can still be understood in two different ways. Either we identify "being" and "phenomenon," in which case the existing thing is reduced to the series of appearances which manifest it, or else we recognise the necessity of a trans-phenomenal foundation if the phenomenon is not to founder in the immanence of consciousness. The first position, that of Berkeley, involves the identification of *esse* and *percipi*: things exist only in their appearances. (Sartre sometimes insinuates that this was the final position of Husserl).[16] Sartre and Merleau-Ponty adopt the second alternative, and recognise the necessity of finding a being which escapes "the condition of being a phenomenon, that is to say, of existing only insofar as it is revealed."[17] This trans-phenomenal being must be understood not as a noumenal world standing behind phenomena, but as the *trans-phenomenal being of that which appears.* It is, they say, indicated within the phenomenon itself as something which is "always already there"; it exists not merely insofar as it appears, but also in itself. "The trans-phenomenal being of what is before our consciousness exists in-itself," writes Sartre.[18] And in the same sense Merleau-Ponty says: "The natural world stands before us as existing *in itself,* over and above its existence *for me.*"[19]

Trans-phenomenal Being is Meaningless. If it be granted, however, that the phenomenon (or "being in so far as it appears to human consciousness") is to be considered as the supreme transcendental, the absolute measure of all meaning, it follows that the trans-phenomenal being of the phenomenon is stripped of all meaning. "It is what it is," and this is just about all one can say of it, since it is through man that things acquire meaning.[20] Sartre maintains (as we have just seen) that the characteristics of „worldness," extension, temporality, and so on, belong to being "only because I am the negation of being." Merleau-Ponty likewise declares:

I am the absolute source of my existence. It does not come to me from my forbears nor from my physical and social environment; it goes out towards them and sustains them, since it is I who make them live for me and *so exist, in the only sense in which the word can have for me.* This tradition that I choose to take up would vanish if I ignored it; the distance from me to this horizon would shrink to nothing were I not there to look at it, since it does not belong to it as a property.[21]

---

[16]*L'Etre et le Néant,* p. 28.
[17]*Ibid.,* p. 16.
[18]*Ibid.,* p. 29; see also p. 16.
[19]*Phénoménologie,* p. 180.
[20]*L'Etre et le Néant,* pp. 30-4.
[21]*Phénoménologie,* p. III. Italics ours.

And a little further on he adds: "it is consciousness that first brings the world for me into being and disposes it around me." If this be so, then "being-for-man" would be the only meaning that the word "exist" could have for us, since human consciousness is said to bring my world into being. Is this so very different from what we usually call an "idealism of meaning?"

B. The Analysis of Embodiment

There is another consequence of the exclusive use of the phenomenological method that is apparent throughout the work of both Merleau-Ponty and Sartre. It is to be found in their explanation of human subjectivity as an embodied subjectivity. Phenomenology has, it is true, rendered a valuable service to philosophy both by drawing attention to the irreducible and primitive character of human existence as an embodied being, and by providing us with the appropriate method for clarifying the living experience of the body as my body. But it is questionable whether phenomenology is an adequate tool for a complete philosophical study of "embodiment." Is there not an element of truth in materialism which must be preserved and which the new philosophy seems to have neglected?

A Truth Element of Materialism. As we explained at length above (Chapter II), phenomenological analysis has clearly shown that the primitive or pre-analytic life of consciousness cannot be thought of in terms of cause and effect. The relation to the world which defines the kind of being characteristic of intentional consciousness takes on the form of a dialogue or a give-and-take that works itself out according to the dialectical relations of intention and motivation, involvement and historical situation. Is this all that experience teaches us for certain about the being of the embodied self and its "insertion" in the world? Obviously not. Besides the living experience of my body, there is external experience and scientific experimentation, or, as the phenomenologists put it, there is the body as it appears to other people, to observers. Only an objective study of the world can teach me that, in order to see, I need a nervous system of a particular kind, a beam of light to stimulate the retina by means of a photo-electric process, and so on. These objective data, which materialism has rightly stressed but wrongly claimed to be the only valid data, are not just a further projection of that living experience that phenomenology sets out to describe. In the actual experience of my being-in-the-world, I am not separated from the objects I perceive: my vision, so to speak, goes out to touch the things themselves. Objective experience cannot, of course, disqualify this basic datum—as materialism might lead one to believe—but it does teach me that my perceptive relations with the world imply physical relations, impersonal processes. If my eye is not ,,sensitive" in the physical sense of the term, it will not be "sensitive" in the psychological and phenomenological sense either. But if these physical data are not further projections of the living experience of my body, it follows that they are neither an elaboration of it nor a conceptual construction resting on it. Like the results of phenomenological analysis, they are primitive basic data drawn from the synthetic enveloping unity that is man. Our comprehensive grasp of man is through two different series of *Abschattungen* or cognitive elements, each irreducible to the other, namely, external or objective experience on the one hand, and living or phenomenological experience on the other.

Inadequacy of Phenomenology. All this is not exactly denied in the phenomenology of Merleau-Ponty and Sartre. It is granted that "to reconcile these two opposite aspects within the same being poses a difficult problem," as de Waelhens remarks.[22] But the question remains whether the new philosophy takes sufficient account of it. Our opinion is that it does not, and that this is a serious fault. It would not matter so much if these philosophers were content to say that the data of objective experience are not the province of phenomenology. But they go very much further. They claim to work out a philosophy of man, a rounded study of the whole real, which establishes the ontological status of the human being as an unique synthesis. But in performing this task, they act as though phenomenology were the only means available for the philosophical study of man. This way of going about the question necessarily leads into a blind alley. For if it is true that man can be reached in his completeness only through two irreducible series of cognitive elements, then obviously he cannot be grasped as a whole in terms of either series. His unity cannot be described in terms of physics nor of idealist psychology nor even of pure phenomenology.[23] Wider and more flexible categories than those of contemporary phenomenology are needed for an adequate philosophy of man; those the phenomenolo-

---

[22]"La phénoménologie du corps," *Rev. Philos. Louvain, 48,* 1950, p. 384, n. 2.
[23]It is clear that this overall synthetic unity which is the ground of the twofold series of experiential elements, will be transphenomenal and thinkable only in terms valid in the transphenomenal order. We must have a concept of a "subject" which is applicable to transphenomenal being. This suggests that it might be profitable to rework the scholastic notion of substance in this context; this notion has not been understood by Descartes and his successors.

gists offer us do not go beyond the order of living experience, that is to say, of being as being-for-me.

C. The Nature of Transcendence

Perhaps the most serious way in which the influence of idealism has misled the existential philosophers concerns the ontological inter- pretation of *transcendence,* that is to say, of the openness-towards-the- world which constitutes intentional consciousness. Here we touch on a very central point, namely, the relationship between consciousness and being, in other words, the essence of truth.

Idealism as an Ontology of Truth. Idealism is an *ontology* of truth, worked out in terms of the so-called "Copernican revolution." Kant main- tained that in interpreting the relation that constitutes knowledge, priority must be given to the subject over the object, to the active mind over the passive datum. Carried to its extreme conclusion, this revolu- tion ended by absorbing the object in the subject. What is other than the self loses all ontological autonomy, existing only by and for the self. It is a limit or obstacle brought forth unconsciously, which con- scious reflection must reintegrate in the genuine life of the real self. This real self is not, of course, the human self (with a small "s") but the unique infinite Self, of which the finite consciousness is only a passing manifestation.

This extreme form of idealism, of which Fichte is perhaps the most typical representative, is, in fact, rarely encountered. This is hardly surprising. For the finitude of human consciousness is irremediable. No philosophical reflection can ever change the basic exteriority of what is other than the self. Most idealists prefer, therefore, to look on human subjectivity as a mixture of spontaneity and receptivity (Kant) or, as Brunschvicg put it, of interiority and exteriority. But the Coper- nican revolution is not thereby abandoned. The priority of mental spontaneity over the datum remains the central theme of all idealism. We are still faced with an idealist doctrine of the rational and significant factors in knowledge, linked with the doctrine of an "experiential jolt" to explain what is completely other than the consciousness. As Brunsch- vicg writes, "it is because the mind recognizes that it is tied to some- thing other than itself" that it speaks of reality, and sees knowledge as „a relationship between thought and being."[24] According to this mitigated brand of idealism "the duality between thought and being is

----

[24]*La modalité du jugement,* Paris, 1934, p. 94.

definitely primitive and irreducible"; "in it, *being* means what is other than the mind's activity," that is to say, "being as impenetrable to the mind."[25] The fact that consciousness is from the start directed towards being, that is, to "being-other-than-consciousness" in a relation nowadays called "transcendence," is a sign of its finitude.[26] A pure, infinite consciousness would be pure interiority, closed in on its own immanence, completely unrelated to anything distinct from it. This is, of course, the Spinozist or monist conception of the Absolute. But the idealists we speak of do not accept the existence of Spinoza's God. They usually consider pure thought to be an ideal limit whose existence would involve contradiction. The dualism between thought and being is for them primitive and irreducible.

The Irreducibility of Consciousness and Being. What is important for our present purpose is not so much the phenomenological doctrine of the subjective origin of meaning as its inevitable correlate, the identification of the real with what is simply other than the consciousness or with being in so far as it is impenetrable to the mind. It is true that on this point the existentialism of Sartre and Merleau-Ponty differs from Brunschvicg's doctrine, since they do not subscribe to the empiricist description of the "experiential jolt" as a purely formless external factor. Matter is said to be "pregnant with its form"; that which is other than consciousness regains its existential consistency and is called the "in-itself"; it stands before the consciousness as something already there. But in spite of these differences, there are important resemblances too. In both doctrines, there is the irreducible duality between consciousness and being, understood as "that which is other than consciousness." Both retain the Spinozist conception of the Absolute as an ideal limit, a limit which is contradictory when it is postulated as a reality.

This is particularly clear in the case of Sartre. The opposition between what is "in-itself" and what is "for-itself" is just as irreducible for him as it is for Brunschvicg. The idea of God, that is to say, of the coincidence of what is in-itself and what is for-itself, "is contradictory."[27] Merleau-Ponty's position is not so very different from that of Sartre, as we have seen.

---

[25]*La modalité du jugements*, Paris, 1934, pp. 98, 90f.

[26]*Ibid.*, p. 143, ff. There is also a kind of "infinite" character about the possibility of knowing the other *as* other and of respecting it in its being. This "infinitude" or unboundedness shows itself in us as a deficient participation in the creative Thought of God, who makes things be for themselves. The significance of the non-self is not just to be a limit for the self, as the idealists since Fichte have argued.

[27]*L'Etre et le Néant*, See pp. 124, 133, 702, 714.

When I say that things are transcendent, that means that I do not possess them, I cannot compass them; *they are transcendent to the extent that I am ignorant of what they are, merely attributing to them bare existence.*

And again:

There is in perception a paradox of immanence and transcendence. Immanence, because the thing perceived cannot be foreign to the perceiver; transcendence, because it always implies something beyond what is actually given. [28]

It is true that knowledge, an immanent activity, always involves a process of *interiorizing* the thing known. However, according to Merleau-Ponty, this interiorization suppresses the autonomous existence of things; insofar as I interiorize them in knowledge they lose their transcendence.

If we were to attain the thing itself, it would be laid bare before us, and there would no longer be any mystery. It would cease to exist as a thing the moment I thought I possessed it. *The reality of the thing is what removes it from our grasp.* [29]

In this theory, than, "to be known" and "to be real" refer to two irreducible spheres. There is no longer a simple paradox of immanence and transcendence: the two tendencies are mutually exclusive. To the extent that knowledge interiorizes reality, producing in me a spiritual and intentional grasp of it, it banishes existence-in-itself from the real. Is not this exactly what the idealists have always maintained? Is it not true that just the opposite is really the case? Of course, as St. Thomas said, knowledge is an immanent operation in virtue of which the subject in a sense possesses, or spiritually assimilates, itself to the object known. But this possession is not at all like physical assimilation. Its characteristic is that it *respects* reality; it "affirms the other as other," as the scholastics put it; it "allows beings to be," as Heidegger says. The better I understand that which is other than myself, whether it be other things or other people, the more I respect it for what it is. This is why knowledge gives birth to the love, whose characteristic is to will the good of the other for its own sake. Knowledge is, in the long run, as Forest has it, "a consent given to being." The fact that friendship for example, allows me to penetrate the thoughts and intentions of a friend more effectively, does not necessarily involve any loss of autonomy for the friend.

If being known and being real are incompatible, it is evident that

---

[28] *Phénoménologie*, p. 423, and "Le primat . . .," p. 123.
[29] *Phénoménologie*, p. 270. Italics ours.

the idea of a perfect Thought, capable of perfect understanding, is contradictory. "I think that it is proper to man to have the thought of God," writes Merleau-Ponty, "but this does not mean that God exists."[30]

D. The Origin of Meaning

An Ambiguous Formula. Ultimately everything we have said is already implicit in the formula so often used by the existentialists: "it is through man that meanings come into the world." This formula is as ambiguous as the old idealist axiom: "What is beyond thought is unthinkable." What is completely foreign to thought is obviously unthinkable. But it would be wrong to conclude that thought can know only its own immanent states, or that thinking is synonymous with creating. Similarly, one can read true and false senses into the assertion that it is through man that meanings come into the world. To unravel them all with due precision would be a long and difficult task.

Its True Meanings. Let us begin with the senses in which it is true. In the first place, it goes without saying that in a world of inert matter, without a trace of consciousness, the idea of rationality and meaning could not even arise. Obviously, if things are to be known and understood there must be a consciousness. Secondly, this consciousness is never merely passive in grasping its object. If the meaning of an object is to be revealed, there must be a revelatory activity. There must also be, as we shall see in the next chapter, the application of a *lumen naturale*, a source of understanding, a fundamental meaningful intention, which is activated only by a living contact with the world. To discover numbers we must count; to lay bare the structure of the physical world, we must try it out with mathematico-physical hypotheses, "embodied," as it were, in laboratory apparatus. In general, it can be said, in Heidegger's phrase, that "to let beings be" is the most fundamental manifestation of our liberty. To know is "to give our consent to being."

There is a third sense in which the formula is true. Some meanings enter the world only because of man. These are the *res artificiosae*, whatever is due to human initiative insofar as it transforms the world of nature into a world of civilization and culture. A fountain-pen, a book, a scientific instrument—these have a sense only through man. Even our knowledge of natural things almost always involves an element of creative cultural activity. Hence, what we commonly call "natural"

---

[30]"Le primat . . .," p. 151.

things generally bear some imprint of culture. In this sense, Merleau-Ponty is not entirely wrong in considering the nebula of Laplace, not as an object that stands "behind us, at our origin," but as, in a way, "in front of us, in the world of culture."[31]

Inadmissible Meanings. Merleau-Ponty fails, however, to give sufficient attention to the relationship between the "natural" and the "cultural" within the object known. This makes his theory ambiguous, so that the formula we are discussing continually tends to take on meanings that are quite inadmissible. Though it may look plausible, it is, in fact, incorrect to define the "natural" simply as that which is completely untouched by the "cultural". The "natural" is very often known, or discussed, or elucidated, through the medium of concepts that are, in the broad sense, "cultural". The whole effort of physical science, for example, is to try to *understand* the world of nature with the aid of its constructs. These latter are the work of man, but they cannot on that account be said to be unrelated to the structure of the real. This relation has, it is true, been challenged in modern times by several philosophical groups. There are those who follow Mach in holding that physical science is nothing other than a set of convenient correlations between phenomena. There are others who hew nearer the Kantian line by arguing that the only structure revealed by science is that of the knowing subject. Still others maintain that science simply gives us a set of convenient rules which enable us to master Nature.

Among working scientists, however, these ideas cut little ice. Just try telling a chemist that his model of a complex molecule bears no relation to an actual structure but is merely a convenient way of pigeon-holing certain experimental data. The problem of the relation between scientific constructs and real structure is an exceedlingy complex one, but it can safely be said that as empirical science progresses, our knowledge of the real structure of the world will improve and our knowledge of the past become more precise.[32] It is incorrect, therefore, to suggest that scientific "meaning" comes entirely from man and is imposed by him on the real. Any experimenter who has a little experience of what we may call the "intractability" of the real, would smile at this suggestion. The Laplacean nebula, the Ice Age, the Cro-Magnon man, as

---

[31]*Phénoménologie*, p. 494.
[32]See, for example, M. Hesse, *Science and the Human Imagination*, London, 1954; E. McMullin, "Realism in Modern Cosmology," *Proc. Amer. Cath. Philos. Assoc.*, vol. *29*, 1955, pp. 137-50. The contrary case is presented e.g. by R. Braithwaite, *Scientific Explanation*, Cambridge, 1953; G. Bergman, *The philosophy of Science*, Madison, 1957.

well as being "in front of us, in the cultural world," are also in another sense just as definitely "behind us, at our origin."

Furthermore, underlying the meanings the world takes on through man's efforts or which man discovers as science progresses, there is a primary indubitable factor, an *Urdoxa* which does not come from ourselves, yet is by no means devoid of sense. The fact that I experience existence as myself-with-others-in-the-world constitutes a sense or meaning which I use in my dealings with the world, a sort of illuminating intention which does not take its origin from me. This fundamental meaning which enters into all particular meanings as a constituent, comes into the world *with* man but there is no sense in which it is true to say that it comes *by* man.[33]

3. The Significance of These Defects

The criticisms we have just been making might at first sight seem inconsistent with what we said at the end of the last chapter. Did we not say that existential phenomenology by affirming the primacy of perception runs the risk of falling into a new empiricism? There is, however, no contradiction. Having granted too much to the idealists, the phenomenologists may very well have rendered themselves incapable of winning complete victory over empiricism. In order to make a decisive step beyond empiricism and idealism, we must have categories that are supple enough and broad enough to retain the element of truth in each of these positions. They must render the mystery of man intelligible without distorting it. This is difficult mainly because the human situation constitutes a basic existential whole which can be attained only through two series of irreducible cognitive elements. Since phenomenology lacks categories of this sort, it is only to be expected that it will fail to get beyond empiricism.

Once again, let there be no mistake about what we mean. The empiricism of Merleau-Ponty is undoubtedly an improved and broadened impiricism. In a certain sense, it is the contrary of the classical empiricism of the "experiential jolt" or of the pure diversity of sensible qualities. Matter, remember, is "pregnant with its form." Nor do we agree with F. Alquié who claims that we are dealing with "a sort of corporeal metaphysics, a non-scientific and non-mechanist materialism."[34]

---

[33]Merleau-Ponty does not deny this, but this *Urdoxa* is for him quite empty, being nothing other than the certitude of the world in general. See chapter 2, Sections 3 B, 5.

[34]"Une philosophie de l'ambiguité," *Fontaine, 10,* 1946, p. 55.

There is, as Merleau-Ponty constantly reminds us, an element of truth in the Cartesian doctrine of the immanence of things and ideas in the self. A self implies projection, involvement, free initiative, and these cannot be reduced to what is usually called matter. Moreover, the affirmation of the primacy of perception "as the enduring foundation of our idea of truth"[35], does not mean that consciousness is restricted to the registering of natural data.[36] It is of the essence of perception, because of its intentional structure, to make possible, and in a way to encourage, reflection.[37] This reflection will never completely separate itself from pre-reflective life but it is certainly not hemmed in by it. Reflection, of its very nature, is a retreat from perception and the perceived world. It is in this way that it gives rise to a genuine *Cogito*. The question now is: what is the nature and significance of this *Cogito* and of the reflection that makes it possible? What is the bond between reflection and its pre-reflective roots?

A. The Nature of the "Cogito"

It must be noted in the first place that the word "reflection" (like "*Cogito*") is ambiguous. A turning back towards the thing perceived in order to analyze it more closely is simply a new perception. Much the same can be said of psychological reflection, which is something like an interior perception: I perceive myself perceiving. It does not yet give me a genuine "I think." The possibility of digging deeper into existence, of throwing light on its fundamental structures, or of working out a philosophy of existence, all this is contained in the genuine *Cogito*. It is, therefore, bound up with reflection in the strict philosophical sense, that is to say, reflection in order to *understand* better. This is the only sense we wish to keep for the moment. Reflection, then, is not just a turning back of the self on itself; it is rather *the intentional act par excellence*. To reflect is to sally forth to conquer the concrete; it is to make an effort to uncover the why and wherefore, the general structure of reality.

Looked at from the noetic aspect, the *Cogito* (according to Merleau-Ponty) is consciousness of the self: "All thought is at the same time consciousness of the self. Self-consciousness is the very being of the mind in its activity."[38] The "I" of the "I think" is personal and bound up with the body. It is not a "universal thinker," outside the world,

---

[35] *Phénoménologie*, p. 423.
[36] "Le primat . . .," p. 150.
[37] A. De Waelhens, *Une philosophie de l'ambiguité*, p. 400.
[38] *Phénoménologie*, p. 426.

separated from history, like the Kantian self or the transcendental self of the idealists. It is "an ego which expresses itself in and through the body, without being either separated from it or absorbed into it."[39] Merleau-Ponty undoubtedly deserves great credit for his fidelity to the theme of "embodiment" in his theory of the highest activities of man. But the question of how the personal and higher *Cogito*, which is revealed in reflection, takes its roots in perceptive or pre-reflective existence seems to go unanswered. For pre-reflective existence is anonymous, pre-personal. This is one of the perpetual themes of *La Phénoménologie de la Perception.*

> Perception is always a matter of the impersonal "someone" ("*On*"). It is not a personal act by which I give my life new meaning. What links up the past with the present in sense-experience and prepares the present for the future is not the self as an autonomous subject, but the self as possessing a body and knowing how to look at things properly. Perception bears witness to and renews in us a pre-history rather than being itself a genuine history.[40]

De Waelhens points out in his commentary on Merleau-Ponty that "there is an "I" that is individual, just as there are decisions which are mine. But these decisions can arise and take concrete shape only against the background of pre-personal existence."[41] Now the relationship between the personal autonomous *Cogito* on the one hand, and the pre-personal almost anonymous subjectivity on the other, has never been clearly explained by Merleau-Ponty. This is not surprising in view of what we have seen. Once one affirms the primacy of perception as categorically as he does, once one considers existence (that is, "being-in-the-world in and through a body") as the primitive significant fact, the primordial intention by which we make the world exist-for-us, one or other of two things must follow. Either the original character of a personal free *Cogito* is also asserted, or else the higher *Cogito* and the reflection that makes it possible are taken as epiphenomena of the anonymous perceptive life. In the first case, the difficulty arises that it is impossible to see how perceptual existence, which is prepersonal and anonymous, could give rise to this higher self. So it would seem that we are reduced to the unsatisfactory doctrine of a twofold subjectivity. In the second case, we cannot escape from empiricism and its insoluble question: how can empiricism be affirmed consistently if the doctrine of empiricism is true? To avoid this dilemma, it would

[39]A. De Waelhens, *op. cit.*, p. 165.
[40]P. 277. See p. 249.
[41]*Op. cit.*, p. 326.

be necessary to admit that we have the power to develop the primitive existential fact by means of the natural light or source of intelligibility that it contains; in this task, we would need more adequate categories than those of Merleau-Ponty's phenomenology. This brings us back to a former criticism.

B. THE OBJECT OF THE "COGITO"

What we have been saying about the noetic aspect of the *Cogito* is valid *a fortiori* of its object. The problem is to grasp how and in what sense perceptual life, which is said to be "the permanent foundation of our idea of truth," can supply a foundation for philosophical truth, whether it be phenomenological or metaphysical. Here we come across the main objection that critics have levelled at the work of Merleau-Ponty.[42] "This objection," writes de Waelhens, "questions the possibility of defining perception the way Merleau-Ponty does and at the same time undertaking to make a phenomenological study of it."[43] M. de Waelhens notes that the position of Merleau-Ponty on this point is unclear and unsatisfactory and that it must be superseded. He himself suggests a way out of the difficulty which remains in the line of existential phenomenology.[44]

What is necessary is to work out more profoundly the nature of the *doxische Seinsglaube* which results from any thoroughgoing phenomenological analysis, and develop its implications. Merleau-Ponty does not entirely neglect this primitive existential factor. There is for him an unquestionable trans-historic certitude which is, as it were, the ultimate source of light. Perceptive life, and in the long run all human knowledge, moves within this certitude. It comprises the twofold truth that there is a world and that I am in-and-towards-the-world. For Merleau-Ponty, as for Sartre, this primitive certitude is very meager indeed. This can hardly be helped, since man is for them the source of meaning. As soon as there is question of finding a definite content, or, in more concrete terms, of saying what the world is and whence it is, "we are referred to the origins of perception and to the history of human dialogue."[45] A text often mentioned in Chapter II is appropriate here: "There is absolute certitude about the world in general but not about any particular thing."[46]

---

[42]See, for example, the remarks made by E. Bréhier and J. Hyppolyte in the issue of the *Bull. Soc. Franç. Philos.*, vol. *41*, 1947, already quoted.

[43]*Op. cit.*, p. 399.

[44]*Ibid.*, pp. 400, ff.

[45]*Ibid.*, pp. 401-2.

[46]*Phénoménologie*, p. 344.

Even the widest human categories apply only within the limits of the world. This world itself, as the horizon of all horizons, is outside these categories. "The world is the reality of which the necessary and the possible are only portions."[47] In order to bring out the point that this basic certitude, though it is the foundation of all knowledge and the cradle of all meaning, is, properly speaking, beyond knowledge, Merleau-Ponty then goes on to speak of the "ontological contingency of the world." Sartre expresses the same idea when he says:

> Being which is "in-itself" *is*. This means that being can neither be derived from the possible nor reduced to what is necessary. This is what we call the contingence of being "in-itself." Uncreated, without *raison d'être*, without relation to anything else, being "in-itself" is eternally absurd.[48]

If the term "metaphysics" be taken in its traditional sense, it is evident that this is a sort of metaphysical agnosticism.

C. Conclusion

It is possible to get beyond this agnosticism only if human experience, faithfully described, allows us to broaden the significant content of the *doxische Seinsglaube*, the fundamental ground of all certainty. It is, then, necessary to show that our basic certainty of the world is not empty of meaning as Merleau-Ponty thinks, and also that its meaning helps to constitute the particular meanings which we meet throughout the world. Otherwise we fall back into the theory of the double *Cogito*, since we would be dealing with a world of being hidden behind the world of phenomena, as in Kant's system. The important thing, therefore, is to rethink the relationship between being and particular beings, between being and essence. We must examine the relationship between what is in-itself and what is for-itself, that is to say, between being and the consciousness that uncovers it. It is necessary to eliminate not only absolute idealism, but also all forms of mitigated "idealism of meaning," while at the same time avoiding a regress into the materialist realism of the empiricists.

In the next chapter, we shall try to show that the philosophy of Aquinas can be of very real help to us in this quest. We can conclude from this to the very great relevance of this philosophy to contemporary thought.

---

[47]*Phénoménologie*, p. 456.
[48]*L'Etre et le Néant*, p. 34.

PART TWO

CHRISTIAN FAITH

CHAPTER FIVE

THE RELEVANCE OF THOMISM

Christianity is not a philosophical system and Christian dogma does not impose a particular philosophy. It is admitted even by those who are most strongly attached to the scholastic tradition that one can be a Christian without being a Thomist! The Church cannot, however, be indifferent to philosophy. The encyclical, *Humani generis* (1950), devotes a lengthy passage to the importance of philosophical doctrines for the preservation of the faith.

It puts Christians on their guard against some of the novelties in contemporary thought, and underlines the appropriateness of the philosophy of St. Thomas for working out a philosophy "in conformity with the necessities of modern culture" as well as for theology, in view of the fact that "his doctrine harmonizes with divine revelation as if by previous agreement." It is obvious that an "agreement" of this kind, if emphasized, could raise difficulties for Thomism as a *philosophy*, properly so called.

1. The Problem of Thomism

A. CHRISTIANITY AND PHILOSOPHY

The Church's attitude towards philosophy might easily appear equivocal to a casual observer. On closer examination, it is found to be neither contradictory nor ambiguous. It does, however, manifest a profound paradox which arises from the very nature of the Faith and constitutes the clearest indication that Christianity, notwithstanding the supernatural character of its mission, also has a humanistic and historical character. It is characteristic of Christian belief that it is directed towards a transcendent God who, in His gratuitous mercy and without any abdication of His transcendence, makes Himself God-for-us, our last end, the ultimate meaning of our existence. For this reason, the Church has always maintained both the strictly gratuitous and supernatural character of the order of grace and its compatibility with the highest aspirations of mankind, particularly the demands of rationality (in the broad sense defined in previous chapters), liberty, and unity. These are the aspirations which haunt the human mind and are essential to man's personal existence. Theologians express this by saying that grace does not destroy nature nor does it merely stand on it like

an upper story. Rather does grace bring nature to its perfection, elevat-
ing it to a new dignity, the dignity of the children of God. This harmony
between nature and grace has always been defended by the Church
against all those who either exaggerated our natural impotence in the
intellectual and moral order (under the pretext of stressing God's
mercy), or exalted the powers of nature in a way that imperilled the
supernatural and transcendent character of grace.

Implication of the Harmony of Nature and Grace. It is important, however, to have a clear grasp of what is implied by the harmony of nature
and grace. Human nature is not something static and lifeless, nor is the
life of grace a closed circle; rather is it a call to open ourselves up more
and more towards God and His sanctifying love. Hence the working
out of a Christian humanism, that is, of a humanism illuminated by
faith and therefore propitious towards the flowering of the life of faith,
is a duty for every Christian. A so-called "simple" faith that is merely
accepted without being assimilated by the mind, is insufficient for the
task of building up God's kingdom in the world. Not that Christian
belief is first and foremost a kind of humanism or that only intellectuals
have a share in salvation. But the Faith would be betraying its mission
if it failed to give rise to a genuine humanism. God reveals Himself
as the ultimate meaning of our existence in the order of grace into which
we are incorporated by faith; He is the supernatural and unmerited
answer to the deepest of all questions: "what is life worth in the long
run?" It follows, therefore, that the Faith is a light *for man*, sent to
illuminate his mind and his activity and make fruitful the highest, most
human and most universal aspirations of human life, those of truth,
liberty and unity. Christianity calls on the Christian to take up his faith
personally, actively assimilate it and reflect upon it. Hence the importance for faith of reason, understood as the supreme effort of the mind
in search of the highest truths, of the ultimate and unquestionable values,
and of final unity.

The Necessity of Reason for the Growth of Faith. Reason in this sense is
doubly necessary for the growth of faith. In the first place, it is necessary in order that Christian belief take on in our minds the form of an
obsequium rationale, a homage given to God freely, with full knowledge,
as something worthy both of man and of God. Reason is also necessary
if one is to arrive at a better *understanding* of the mystery of faith. This is
indeed demanded by faith itself. The Christian is not a collector of
revealed data nor someone who wanders through life repeating me-
chanically the words of Christ to the apostles. The scattered data of

revelation refer to an all enveloping mystery called the order of grace, which is nothing less than the mystery of God and of His redemptive love, manifested by the Word Incarnate and the pouring forth of the Holy Spirit. Faith is our adherence to this mystery. It is, then, the constant duty of Christians to take the data of revelation, to think and rethink the synthetic unity of the Christian mystery in order to arrive at a fuller understanding of the mystery, of its repercussions on human life and of its meaning for human conduct. This is theology, properly so called, which is the work of reason enlightened by faith, or more exactly of faith using reason, *fides quaerens intellectum.*

B. PHILOSOPHICAL TRADITION

What we have just said makes it possible to understand the paradoxical attitude of the Church towards philosophy. For even though she does not wish to restrict freedom of research nor impose any particular philosophy, the Church cannot be indifferent to philosophical thought.[1] Because a genuine theology and a Christian humanism are both necessary for Christendom, the Church is obliged to condemn those doctrines which either exaggerate or minimize the powers of natural reason, that is to say, the two extremes of rationalism and fideism in all their forms. Both of these restrict the field of truth over which the human mind can range, either by making faith unthinkable or by denying the possibilities of a Christian humanism or of a solid theology. But the Church is not satisfied with simply denouncing what is incompatible with the demands of faith. That would be a rather negative approach. Reason has a positive role to play in safeguarding, developing and spreading the Faith; it is this that justifies the importance that the Church attaches to the scholastic tradition, particularly to the thought of St. Thomas Aquinas.

Regard for Medieval Christian Philosophy. It is important to understand the regard that the Church retains for medieval Christian philosophy. It would be a mistake to interpret this as a reliance upon dogmatism, as if the Church had asked us to base philosophical reasoning on authority or to take the thought of St. Thomas as the last word in philosophical reflection. Because it is a "radical" type of thinking, philosophy

---

[1]M. Labourdette, O.P. "Les enseignments de l'Encyclique (*Humani generis*)," *Rev. Thomiste*, Vol. *50*, 1950, p. 40: "Christian dogma does not impose any particular philosophy, though—contrary to what many think and say—not every philosophy is compatible with it."

will always be an invitation to begin over again, an effort of personal reflection. But this effort must be made in intersubjectivity, in the company of the masters of the past, or as Merleau-Ponty put it, we must be "conscious of the secret bond which makes Plato still live on among us."[2]

It is not surprising that the philosophy of the Middle Ages has a special interest for the Christian who has a proper regard for his faith and for Christian culture. For the oftmaligned Middle Ages were the cradle of western civilisation, and form the background of any authentically European thought. The characteristic traits of the West are: an emphasis on the human person as an end in himself, the affirmation of liberty as the basic constituent of personality, the importance given to the body, to incarnation and to the earthly mission of man, and lastly the spiritual and personal conception of the Absolute. But let us not forget that this way of looking at man and his links with the world is the legacy of medieval humanism, which was born from the union of Greco-Roman thought with Christian theism and personalism. It is historically unforgivable to make European thought begin with Descartes. Hence the philosopher who is preoccupied with that humanism which is the glory of the West would be making a grave mistake, particularly if he is a Christian, if he were to neglect the venerable patrimony which has been handed down to him.

C. Saint Thomas Aquinas

The work of St. Thomas is the richest part of this legacy. It was his great merit that he grasped with the sureness of genius the necessity of a Christian humanism, and with it of a Christian synthesis of human knowledge. As against those who feared that Christian piety would be corrupted by pagan philosophy, St. Thomas, urged on by a great respect for human reason and boundless confidence in the unity of truth, firmly held to the belief that the synthesis of faith and reason was not only possible but necessary for the survival of both. Both in the long run flow from the same source and lead to the same end, namely the fulness of truth which lies in God. Without wishing to diminish the gratuity of grace and the revealed character of our knowledge of it, St. Thomas always maintained that grace could only be a light and a perfection for us if there were *in us* some need for grace, a sort of natural desire to possess God supernaturally in His essence.[3] In his eyes, *Eros*

---

[2]*Sens*, p. 189.
[3]*Summa contra Gentiles*, bk. 3, c. 50; *Summa Theol.*, I, q. 12, a. 1.

and Agape could not stand in irreconcilable opposition. If the Charity that comes down from above can bring forth fruit in our souls, it is because it finds in us something on which it can build, a natural drive towards the Absolute, an existential openness that makes us capable of being perfected supernaturally. There is no exaggeration in the claim that no philosophy has ever been so generous towards natural reason ✓ while staying so far removed from rationalism as has Thomist intellectualism, at least if one takes it in its basic inspiration. Hence Pius XII has good reason for deploring "that this philosophy, received and recognised in the church, is today spurned by certain people who unwarrantedly say that it is outmoded in form and rationalist in method."[4] But this brings us to the problem which is the subject of our present chapter, the problem of the present philosophical value of Thomism.

D. Is Thomism Relevant to Contemporary Thought?

Nobody dreams of denying that the philosophy of St. Thomas has been of great service to the Faith, to Christian theology and to Christian humanism. The question is whether it is in a position to continue the work with equal success today.
One thing is certain: it can only do so if it presents itself as a living, contemporary philosophy, ready for discussion with contemporary thought, capable of supplying an answer to the problems of our times.[5] There are many people to-day who dispute the present philosophical value of the scholastic tradition. Of course,

> They admit that the philosophy taught in our schools ... can be of use as an introduction to scholastic theology, and that it was wonderfully fitted to the mentality of the men of the Middle Ages. But it no longer offers, so they think, a philosophical method that satisfies the needs of modern culture.[6]

According to M. Marrou,

> There is at the moment among young priests and religious (he is speaking of France) a polite indifference, to say the least, in regard to traditional theology and its conceptual armory ... This is something quite surprising for there is no seminary, scholasticate or house of studies where the rules laid down in Canon 1366 of the

---

[4]*Humani generis*, Part II.
[5]See L. De Raeymaeker, *Introduction à la philosophie*, Louvain, 4th edn., 1956: "Le choix d'une école," pp. 169-172; "L'autorité de Saint Thomas," pp. 172-181; "Le role de l'école," pp. 181-184. See also his article on "Thomism" in the Jan. 1958 issue of *The Review of Politics*.
[6]"Du bon usage d'une Encyclique," *Esprit*, no. *172*, 1950, p. 568.

Code of Canon Law are not observed. The young clerics both secular and religious are formed in the philosophical and theological sciences according to the method, doctrine and principles of the Angelic Doctor.[7]

It is true that the obsession with activity and the ardent desire to be in harmony with the spirit of their times, so characteristic of the present generation, count for a good deal in this polite indifference towards traditional speculation. But it would be unjust to throw all the responsibility on the young, or to be too quick to accuse them of ill will or of unthinking enthusiasms. Youth, and particularly clerical youth, generally asks for only one thing: to be able to pour out its enthusiasm on the true, the beautiful and the good, or at least on everything that appears to be such.

A Crisis for Thomism. Must we then speak of a failure of neo-Thomism, and grant that those who consider the scholastic tradition no longer in harmony with the needs of modern culture are correct? *A priori* this is unlikely, for, as *Humani generis* remarks, "truths which rest not only on an age-old wisdom, but also on their harmony with divine revelation, cannot change from day to day." Instead of speaking of failure, it would be more exact to speak of a crisis for Thomism. Looked at in the light of the great events which have been upsetting the philosophical world for some centuries past, this crisis need hardly surprise us; it is for this reason that we are inclined to see in it a crisis of growth.

The arrival of such an original and powerful philosophy as the phenomenology of Husserl cannot but have a profound impact on all those who at the present time wish to take their philosophy seriously. The mere fact that our time has seen the appearance of a philosophy about which it has been said that "it is identical with the very striving of modern thought," is an event which forces us to reflect. It invites the philosopher to give new thought to old problems. Such an event cannot be attributed to a mere taste for novelty. As we have seen, the new philosophy derives its prestige in the long run from the fact that it reflects the situation of man in today's world with extraordinary fidelity. Hence it contains a set of problems and views which every thinker, at least if he wishes to speak for his time, must be able to recognise and integrate into his philosophical synthesis. The Thomist, more than others, is bound to this task. For the mission of Thomism is less to create new things or to open up new fields than to carry out the work of synthesis.

---

[7]See L. De Raeymaeker, *op. cit.*, p. 175.

What has made the Thomist revival a success during the three-quarters of a century that have passed since the time of Leo XIII ought to assure its success in the future. The prestige of Thomism has grown in proportion as a better knowledge of the Middle Ages has been joined to a more sympathetic understanding of modern thought. As Mgr. De Raeymaeker notes in his INTRODUCTION TO PHILOSOPHY, "only real contact established in this way between traditional principles and the needs of contemporary thought can give birth to a living Thomism. This is the program proposed by Leo XIII in the encyclical *Aeterni Patris: vetera novis augere*."[8] The value and success of Thomism as a form of philosophical thought has always been dependent on its fidelity to this programme. What was true in the time of Mercier, Sertillanges, Roland-Gosselin and Maréchal, to name only a few of the more illustrious dead, remains true today.

2. The Foundations of Thomism

But here there arises a difficult and delicate question on which, in our opinion, the fate of the Thomism of tomorrow will largely depend. How are we to understand these *vetera*, these old and enduring truths, of which Pope Leo speaks? What are these truths in St. Thomas' work which are so sound and so illuminating as to resist the passage of time and stimulate thought even today? If Thomism cannot succeed in setting out certain fundamental principles, which are at the same time sources of originality and perennial fruitfulness, then the alleged value of St. Thomas for the present day is only an illusion. In other words, the crux of the problem is the question of the principles or foundations of Thomism.

This question has long preoccupied Thomist philosophers,[9] but it is particularly pressing today because contemporary thought has revived in striking fashion the ancient problem of the foundations of philosophy. In its desire to escape from the dilemma of empiricism *versus* Cartesian intellectualism, it maintains (not quite unreasonably) that the first indubitable data, the ultimate bases of philosophical reflection and truth, are neither empirical facts of sensation (in the classical sense of that term), nor abstract "self-evidences," such as self-evident concepts or unquestionable logical principles. Whatever be the value of

---

[8]A particularly acute discussion of it has been given by Bishop Fidel Martinez in a recent work: *De l'authenticité d'une philosophie à l'interieur de la pensée chrétienne*, Ona (Burgos), 1955.

[9]*Summa Theol.*, II, IIae, q. 8, a. 1.

this position, a Thomism which wants to be living and contemporary must take up again, in the context of this contemporary questioning, the eternal problem of the principles or foundations of philosophical truth.

A. ETERNAL PRINCIPLES?

The time has not yet come for giving a positive answer to this question. Still it is well to note from the start how *not* go about the problem, what are the traps to be avoided. In our opinion, it is supremely important to preserve oneself from what we should call a rationalist or Cartesian way of rethinking Thomism, which is unfortunately very widespread. If one were to believe certain manuals of scholastic philosophy, the true greatness of Thomism would seem to reside in the fact that it holds to certain principles which are self-evident and infinitely fruitful: the principle of identity or of non-contradiction, the principle of sufficient reason, said to include the principles of causality and finality, and lastly the affirmation of the transcendental and analogical character of the concept of being. These principles are suppose to constitute the very essence of Thomism. They are said to be the reason why it can claim to be an original philosophy and yet valid for all time. Their unquestionable and supra-temporal value is supposed to be evident simply because the principles themselves are intrinsically evident.

As will be plain from what follows, it is not our intention to throw doubt on these venerable principles or to play down their importance for thinking. On the contrary. However, there is a Cartesian, more accurately a Wolffian, way of looking at them which reduces the originality of Thomism to practically nothing. It consists in formulating and interpreting them quite apart from all reference to concrete reality, or more precisely, apart from all significant existential experience. They end up as logical rules, expressing nothing more than the absolutely universal logical structure of thought which is denied by practically nobody, except perhaps by a few of the ancient Sophists. Let us take some examples.

Non-contradiction. There is a way of understanding the principles of identity and non-contradiction which creates problems for no one. Who on earth would doubt that a thing cannot be affirmed and denied at the same time under the same aspect, who would question the supreme rule of all affirmation and reasoning, namely, not to contradict oneself? Someone will say: what about Hegel, Hamelin, Bergson? But none of these ever claimed that it was permissible to contradict oneself, to state that something is black and white at the same time. If they had, they would long ago have been struck off the roll of philosophers. To maintain with Hegel that the history of the world and of mankind is not a collection of static isolated events, that Thought arrives gradually at selfconsciousness through history by means of immanent process, and that all becoming implies a pair of terms which are at once opposed and bound up with each other in such a way as to call forth each other in the dialectic of thesis, antithesis and synthesis—all this may well be a poor interpretation of being as a whole. But is it *not* to deny the logical principle of non-contradiction. The same might be said about Hamelin's doctrine that dialectical relationship is the very life of the mind, or about Bergson when he maintained that the unity of *durée* (that is to say, of the kind of being which is characteristic of life and particularly of liberty as self-determination) is a unity of a very different order from that of numbers. This way of describing duration or lived time is perhaps open to criticism; but it would amount to a complete misunderstanding of Bergson's thought if someone held that he had fallen into the stupid error of rejecting the logical principle of non-contradiction. Bergson never maintained that his conception of time was true one day and false tomorrow; on the contrary, he makes it the constant theme of his writings.

Sufficient Reason. Similar considerations might be advanced concerning the principle of sufficient reason. There is a way of understanding this principle which is common to all philosophy, indeed to all intellectual activity whatever, whether scientific of philosophical. It is characteristic of the mind, as we have seen earlier, to be dissatisfied with the mere registering or amassing of data. Its basic intention is to see its way among the facts, to explain, understand, uncover the why and wherefore, or, in more technical terms, to discover relations and explanations. The postulate of every science and every philosophy is that the world is not just a simple sum of events or of perfectly distinct and self-sufficient entities, but an enveloping, synthetic unity in which everything hangs together and the parts support each other, so that they are explicable only within the whole. "Understand," "explain," "look for reasons and establish relations," are more or less synonymous expressions. The term "sufficient reason" is as vague and imprecise as the term "explanation." This is not all. If it is true that the unity of the whole is not just the unity of a heap, and if the form of the whole is in some way prior to and penetrates the parts that make it up, it follows that the parts do not simply exist *by* the whole, but also *for* the whole, contributing towards the unique character and sense of the whole.

Every philosophy, and perhaps every science, uses *some* sort of a notion, though a rather vague and imprecise one perhaps, not only of causality but also of finality.

Unity of Being. What we have said about the principles of non-contradiction and sufficient reason is also true, *mutatis mutandis*, of the transcendental and analogical character of the most fundamental concepts, notably those of being, unity, truth and goodness. Every philosophy, in proportion as it tries to attain what is fundamental and metaphysical, must claim that its concepts are transcendental and must make use of analogy. It is a commonplace that being is one and that this unity is not simply a sum. This basic conviction is the very condition of metaphysics as a search for being in general. If it is true that the purpose of metaphysical thought is to reconquer the concrete, to throw light on the meaning of particular beings from the viewpoint of being as a whole, then it must be said that metaphysics is essentially transcendental and that it necessarily makes use of transcendentals and analogical concepts. To construct one metaphysics applicable to only one part of being and another for another section, would be to reject the characteristic originality of metaphysical thought. The idea of the transcendental is, therefore, not proper to Thomism alone. It is true, however, that many of the "transcendentals" that are chosen elsewhere, are really only particular aspects of being, like self-consciousness, liberty, sentiment, or their noematic correlatives, being-for-me and value.

The idea that there is unity of being underlying the multiplicity of particular beings and their manifestations, is, as we have said, the key to all metaphysics as a transcendental type of thought. The task of the metaphysician is to determine more precisely what this unity is. The theism of St. Thomas, the monism of Spinoza, post-Kantian idealism, Schopenhauer's voluntarism, Nietzsche's doctrine of the eternal return, the Bergsonian creative evolution, are so many different ways of interpreting the unity of being as a whole. To state that every being is one insofar as it is "undivided in itself and divided from others" is to make a concept more explicit, but it is not yet an attempt to face up to the problem of being. The question to be resolved in metaphysics is: to what extent, and in what sense, is being in the long run one or many, and what is the basic structure of being as a whole, looked at in terms of the one and the many?

What we have said above is true not only of the concept of being but also those of unity, truth, goodness (or value). These concepts are central to every philosophy; there is a manner of interpreting each of them that would be accepted as valid in *any* philosophical system, and which consequently misses what is characteristic in the Thomist doctrine of the one and the many, of truth and of value.

Truth. The problem of truth is at the heart of every philosophy. They all presuppose a first general notion, what we might call a pre-philosophical idea of truth, which is bound up with the human existence of a subject open towards the world. For this reason, there is in any philosophy a general idea of truth, which amounts roughly to this: truth consists in coming to grips with being by means of thought. However, the questions that engage the attention of the metaphysician are: to what extent can man attain truth? What is the ultimate structure and meaning of being insofar as it can reveal itself to man, or as Sartre puts it, insofar as it embraces the twofold aspect of what is in-itself and what exists for-itself? Once again, the theism of St. Thomas, the rationalism of Spinoza, the pantheist idealism of Fichte or of Hegel, the existential philosophy of Heidegger or of Jaspers, all are all so many different ways of giving an answer to the question.

Value. The same applies to the idea of good or of value. It is possible to begin one's investigations into the nature of value with a general definition of the good, such as Aristotle's, for instance: "the good is what all men desire," and then to add that things are desirable only insofar as they exist. However, this does not get us far. The question to be resolved is this: in what sense and to what extent are things desirable or lovable? Is there a hierarchy of values, and if so, what is its basis? And, above all, what is the ultimate meaning of human existence and of being in general? This question has in the course of time received widely differing answers. For Hegel, for example, the ultimate sense of being—and consequently of man—is that through the history of the world Mind is progressively advancing by means of a dialectical movement which constitutes its very life. For Christianity, on the contrary, the ultimate sense of being is that there is at the beginning and the end of all things a transcendent God, Who, in His infinite love, has made man to His likeness. For Nietzsche, there is the conception of the eternal return. For communists and certain modern existentialists, the ultimate meaning of human life lies in making a better world, so as to make man free and bring about a more genuine recognition by men of the dignity of men.

These are all different replies to the question of the structure and meaning of being in general, looked at from the point of view of value. It goes without saying that to solve this all-important question even the most diligent reflection on the Aristotelian definition of "good" will

prove of little avail. Such a way of going about the investigation of the
basic concepts and principles of metaphysics has been called "rationalist" and "Wolffian." The characteristic of Wolff's philosophy is that it
reduces metaphysics to an *a priori* science, depending on simple concepts
and claiming to discover the most universal laws and properties of being
as being, whether it should be living or non-living, mind or matter,
finite or infinite, on a purely *a priori* basis. But it is questionable whether
this sort of ontology is anything more than a collection of nominal
definitions, or what amounts to the same thing, a sort of philosophical
dictionary. In any case, this way of looking at ontology is radically opposed to the mind of St Thomas. For him, the foundation of every human
truth lies in the *concrete real order* which surrounds us and sustains us.

B. THE ORIGINALITY OF ST. THOMAS

The original character of Thomism does not lie, therefore, in its
insistence upon the principles of identity, sufficient reason, and so on;
nor does it consist in taking the concepts of being, truth, and value in
their vaguest possible meaning in such a way as to arrive finally at a set
of logical axioms and nominal definitions. Rather does it lie in a special
way of justifying, elaborating and interpreting the content and meaning
of these principles. They are never considered in isolation, but only
in their intrinsic relationship with concrete reality, that is, with the
basic significant datum. St. Thomas does not slur over the question of
the basis of knowledge and of truth. He recognizes the necessity of a
"first-known-to-us," a *primum notum quoad nos*. For him, however, this
primary datum is not, as it was for Descartes, a group of abstract concepts and principles, self-evident and self-sufficient, but the created
universe in which we live and of which we ourselves form part. It is only
in their link with the concrete that concepts and principles have their
meaning. In themselves, they are not knowledge, properly speaking, but
rather means of knowledge, *principles* of knowledge drawn by abstraction and reflection from what is primary and indispensable for us,
namely our perception of the world, or more precisely, our "insertion"
into being, our human participation in being. The rest of this study will
give us the opportunity of elaborating on these few remarks. For the
moment, let us simply underline the importance of not falling into a
new kind of Cartesianism—and a pretty poor one, at that—on the
pretext of giving a critical foundation for Thomism and singling out its
fundamental principles.

After these preliminary considerations, mainly intended to clear the
ground, let us try to go to the heart of the problem. It is only possible

to claim a real importance for the thought of St. Thomas in our own day if one has first made careful comparison between Thomism and contemporary thought in its most relevant form, existential phenomenology. Can Thomism help throw light on the problems of today and work out a philosophy which responds to the needs of our time? In view of what has been said above, we cannot be content simply to take Thomism as it stands and set it up alongside modern systems. What we must do is to single out within Thomism whatever throws light on the problems of our time. We have, then, a twofold task: to make a selection within Thomism of the relevant doctrines and then to make a comparison with existential phenomenology.

3. Elements of St. Thomas' Theory of Knowledge

The part of Thomist philosophy which is most relevant for the problems we have been discussing is its theory of knowledge. It is true that the debate between intellectualism and empiricism in its modern form began only with Descartes. Thus we cannot expect St. Thomas to have dealt with all the epistemological questions that have arisen along the way. Nevertheless, there is one very good reason why his philosophy ought to be able to help us with some of these questions. This is precisely *because* his work preceded the Cartesian bifurcation of philosophy into the two opposing traditions mentioned. This bifurcation comes from taking a one-sided view of things, from a lack of fidelity to the real. It may be urged that medieval philosophy with its enthusiasm for distinctions and sub-distinctions could be equally remote from the real. But its elaborate logical superstructure should not prevent one from admitting that it begins from a common-sense basis, not unlike what is nowadays called "the ingenuous perception" of things. Though scholasticism is prior to the modern dilemma, it was not unaware of the basic point at issue, the problem of reconciling experience with conceptualization, pre-reflective life with reflection. This is particularly true of Aquinas who faced a very similar problem in making his synthesis between the traditional Augustinian Platonism and the new-found Aristotelianism.

At first sight it might seem that St. Thomas failed to solve this problem. He made human knowledge the result of the combined activities of two faculties, sense and intellect. Insofar as one can define their functions separately, one can say that by sense we attain only "the external sensible qualities of things," while the intellect, on the other hand, gives us entry into the "real essence" of things, as the scholastics put it, the "*quod quid est.*" St. Thomas writes:

The term 'intellect' connotes a certain intimate knowledge. It is said to 'understand,' *intelligere*, that is to say, 'read within,' *intus legere*. This is obvious if we consider the difference between intellect and sense. For sense knowledge is concerned with the exterior sensible qualities, while intellectual knowledge goes right to the essence of a thing. The object of the intellect is what the thing is.[9]

Not that we are faced with two separate knowings. It is *man* who knows by means of the two faculties. They perform their functions in a relationship of reciprocal subordination to each other. The intelligence illuminates, orients and guides the senses in their dealings with reality. Sense perception explores the world in an intelligent manner because it is at the service of the mind.

> Those powers of the mind which are prior in the order of perfection and of nature are principles for the others, both as ends and as activating principles. For we see that sense finds its purpose in the intellect and not vice versa. The sense is a sort of weak participation in the intellect.[10]

On the other hand, the senses are equally necessary for intellectual knowledge; they bring it the material for a knowledge of things. "There is nothing in the intellect which is not first in the senses." The human mind has no innate ideas. It *abstracts*, as the scholastics say, its concepts from sense experience, or more precisely, from the "phantasm," which is a sort of schematic image in the imagination, already having a certain element of universality. "Our intellect understands material things by a process of abstraction from phantasms."[11]

A. The Doctrine of Abstraction

This explanation of the origin of concepts by abstraction is the opposite of the associationist doctrine. Our ideas are not the product of a process of addition, but rather of an illuminating analysis of the perceived datum. This datum is potentially intelligible; it has structure, general significance, aspects common to other things; in a word, a form. By introducing the notion of form embodied in matter, Aristotle (as St. Thomas puts it) brought Plato's ideas back to earth. "Aristotle did not hold that the forms of things exist separated from matter. The natures or forms of the sensible things which we understand are not intelligible

---

[9]*Summa Theol.*, II IIae, q. 8, a. 1.
[10]*Op. Cit.*, I, q. 77, a. 7.
[11]*Op. Cit.*, I, q. 85, a. 1.

in act."[12] There is in man, however, not an *a priori* knowledge of the world, but a *lumen naturale*, a natural light or source of understanding capable of illuminating our perceptive experience. This factor, which is, as it were, a reflection of the divine intelligence, is called by St. Thomas the "active intellect." "Just as light is required for seeing, the active intellect is required for understanding."[13] "The active intellect makes the phantasm intelligible in act, as if by throwing light on it."[14]

The particular material thing, the "here and now" of sense experience, is, in its particularity, not subject to the human intelligence, whose characteristic act is to understand by grasping the common aspects of a number of individual things. Thus the illuminative activity of the intellect inevitably tends to strip the concrete perceptual data of their individual characteristics so as to give birth to abstract universal concepts. The active intellect "makes the phantasms received from the senses intelligible in act through a certain process of abstraction."[15] "The intellect abstracts the species of a natural thing from its individual sensible matter; it does not abstract from matter as a common property of sensible things."[16] But these concepts are not the end of knowledge: knowledge has for its object the concrete existing thing, though we cannot understand the concrete except by means of abstract concepts.

If this be so, then human knowledge has, as it were, two sources, and it is important to be able to say exactly how much is due to each. St. Thomas does not give a clear answer to this problem. It is as if his thought followed two different paths, one leading back to Aristotle, the other to St. Augustine. According as one takes one or the other, one arrives at rather different conceptions of the origin and ground of knowledge.

B. Transcending the Sensible: the "Natural Light"

Following the abstractionist path, one gets the impression that our concepts are in the long run derived from what is sensible. The role of the intellect is to uncover the intelligible characteristics contained in what is sensible, thanks to a process of abstraction which consists principally in eliminating particular characteristics. "To abstract the universal from the particular or the intelligible species from phantasms, that

---

[12]*Op. Cit.*, I, q. 79, a. 3.
[13]*Op. Cit.*, I, q. 79, a. 3, ad 2.
[14]*Op. Cit.*, I, q. 79, a. 4.
[15]*Op. Cit.*, I, q. 84, a. 6.
[16]*Op. Cit.*, I, q. 89, a. 1, ad 2; q. 86, a. 1.

is to say, to consider the nature of the species without taking account of the individual principles represented in the phantasm" is, it would seem at first sight, the characteristic function of the intellect.[17] This view would make it relatively easy to understand how we come to single out common aspects among things. Will this, however, enable us to go beyond the sensible exterior qualities and reach the essence of things? If intellectual abstraction is only an analysis of what is perceived through sensation, how can it provide a foundation for those items of knowledge which, as Kant puts it in the *Dissertation* of 1770, are "metasensible," not only "in regard to their logical form" (like the universal concepts of red, hardness or heat) but also "in their content," (like judgments of value, the affirmation of the ontological contingency of the world and of its dependence on a Creator)? Does not this become an open empiricism? Descartes expressed his amazement that the scholastics claimed to demonstrate the existence of God, and at the same time held it as a maxim that there is nothing in the understanding which was not first in the senses, "where it is certain that the ideas of God or of the soul have never been."[18]

The "Natural Light." Descartes would be right if this saying were to be taken literally. This St. Thomas never did. His doctrines of the *lumen naturale* and of the agent intellect represent an important qualification. The "natural light" is not just the power of abstraction or analysis; it is a light capable of somehow bringing with it a positive intelligible content, namely the "basic intelligibles," being, onenesss, truth and goodness, with their corresponding principles. It is true that in St. Thomas's eyes this "natural light" must not be understood as a kind of knowledge, properly speaking. There is no question here of innate ideas, but rather of a "virtual presence of the idea of being" and of the ideas which are necessarily connected with it.[19] This presence awakens to itself and becomes "knowledge" properly so called, only through contact with the matter of sensation. It seems, therefore, that the knowledge of the transcendental concepts and the first principles, so important for philosophy, does not come from sense experience. "To know the primary intelligibles is an action which follows from one's being a man . . . The power which is the principle of this action is the power of the active intellect."[20]

---

[17]*Op. Cit.*, I, q. 85, a. 1.
[18]*Discours de la méthode*, Part 4.
[19]G. Verbeke, "Le développement de la connaissance humaine d'après St. Thomas," *Rev. Philos. Louvain*, 47, 1949, pp. 445-56.
[20]*Summa Theol.*, I, q. 79, a. 5, ad 3.

These primary intelligibles are the imprints of the Divine Intellect on our knowing faculty.

> There are in the intellect, by its very nature, certain conceptions known to all, such as those of being, unity, goodness and the like ... And because natural knowledge is a certain likeness of the divine truth imprinted on our minds ... Augustine says that these dispositions are known in knowing the first truth.[21]

Thus thanks to the primary intelligibles, whose absolute and universal value is immediately evident, there is in us, as in a mirror, a reflection of the very transcendence of the First Truth. "The mind does not judge all things according to just any truth, but according to the first truth inasmuch as this is mirrored in it through the primary intelligibles."[22] We are now worlds away from empiricism but have we not landed in an intellectualist apriorism? Are we so far removed from Descartes, who takes the idea of the Perfect Being (which he claims to be natural to us) as "the imprint of God upon his work"?

C. St. Thomas and Descartes

In reality these ideas are very far removed from those of Descartes. In the first place, it must be noted that for St. Thomas the transcendental idea of being is not, as the Cartesian concept was alleged to be, an adequate idea of God. One cannot deduce the existence of God from it by mere analysis. For this reason, St. Thomas opposed the ontological argument of St. Anselm. Our idea of being does not allow us to grasp the essence of God. It helps us to understand the world, and it is our knowledge of the world that leads us to affirm the existence of a Creator.

If by *esse*, Aquinas says, we mean the Divine Being or Divine Essence, we must say that we do not know God's *Esse*. "We cannot know God's *Esse* nor His Essence." All we know is "that this proposition we make about God when we say 'God exists' is true. This we know from its effects."[23] Moreover, the fact that he refuses to consider the idea of being an innate idea and attributes to it only a "virtual presence," is not just a linguistic subtlety. The claim that our natural source of understanding wakens and gives rise to knowledge, properly so called, only by a living contact with the world, amounts to saying that the Thomist doctrine of knowledge is not in the last analysis a representationist one. Rather

[21]*Quodlibetum*, VIII, q. 2, a. 4.
[22]*Summa Theol.*, I, q. 16, a. 6, ad 1.
[23]*Op. cit.*, I, q. 3, a. 4, ad 2.

must it be formulated ultimately in terms of existence and action, or, as the scholastics put it, in terms of being and participation.

It must be noted that the brief summary of the Thomist noetic we have just given is incomplete. According to the scholastic classification of the parts of philosophy, what we have given is a *psychology* of knowledge, that is to say a theory of the faculties and conditions of knowledge, not a clarification of the foundations of knowledge as they concern us. But Cartesianism (and the same is true of Humean empiricism and existential phenomenology) is primarily a doctrine of the bases of *human truth*. It would be a serious mistake if, in order to get beyond these doctrines, we thought it sufficient to set up against them, as so many have done, the Thomist psychology of knowledge. The first rule of dialogue is that the parties must choose a common ground in order to talk about the same things. Let us then try to find what St. Thomas would regard as the *primum quoad nos*, the first indubitable datum which is the permanent foundation of our idea of truth. Only if we can do this will it be possible to bring out to best advantage the original character of St. Thomas' thought and its present philosophical value.

D. That Which is First Known to Us

What constitutes the *primum quoad nos* (or, as it would nowadays be put, "our path to truth"[24] and the ultimate basis of all our knowledge, is not the idea of God nor even the transcendental idea of being (which is only a means of understanding the concrete existent). Nor is it a *Cogito* separated from the world, nor the world taken apart from its relation to the thinking subject. It is not even being as a whole grasped in a confused way through the transcendental notion of being. It is *the concrete created order which surrounds us and of which we form part*. This is why St. Thomas always rejected any attempted demonstration of the existence of God which was grounded either on the idea of God or on the abstract idea of being. All the proofs for the existence of God start out from sensible things and form a "demonstration *quia,* that is a demonstration by means of what is more immediate to *us*."[25]

This created world which is the "first given" as far as we are concerned, is not a confused undifferentiated unity. It presents to us an undeniable diversity of qualities which are not just the result of our contact with the world. Although this contact is necessary if the world is to reveal its structure to us, and although the way the world looks

[24]Merleau-Ponty, *Phénoménologie*, p. XI.
[25]*Summa Theol.*, I, q. 2, a. 2.

to us is dependent on our biological situation in it, it is not we who make the world something with a structure, separating out the animal, for example, from the material and the community of men from among the animals. But if the world is not an undifferentiated unity, neither is it a collection of isolated self-sufficient beings. For St. Thomas, the unity of being is in a way more fundamental and more primitive than the diversity of particular beings; the unity may be said to underly the diversity. Just as on the one hand, differentiation ought not be regarded as a sort of varnish spread over an undifferentiated background called "being," so being understood as an enveloping and indeterminate unity ought not be taken as a world distinct from and behind the diversity of particular beings. Being is the being of beings; it is that which makes them be. To say with Heidegger that beings, looked at in their particular qualities, "show forth and yet hide the mystery of being" is in no way contrary to the spirit of Thomism. St. Thomas always opposed those who, in order to exalt the infinite perfection and omnipresence of God, tried to play down the existential autonomy of created being and deny it an *esse proprium*. "What I call *esse*," he says, "is the actuality of every act, and hence the perfection of perfections."[26] "*Esse* is more intimately present in a thing than the particular determinations it possesses."[27]

E. The Experience of Existence

Such is, in St. Thomas's eyes, the primary indubitable datum which human knowledge can never completely elucidate nor effectively escape in this life. In modern terms, one might say that this datum is nothing other than the experience of "existence" as inseparable from the existential orbit that is ours. It is the experience of my existence as myself-with-others-in-the-world. If we speak here of "experience", this is to be understood as a primordial, constant, and final experience which is implied in all particular experiences, in all the activities of our life. This is, indeed, why particular activities are called "manifestations" of our existence. They make our existence manifest while at the same time contributing towards bringing it about and making it actual, towards the assertion of ourselves by means of it. This existential experience constitutes our participation in being, our way of *having a part of* and *taking part in* the being that surrounds and bears us. It is at once the experience of our presence to being and of the presence of being to us.

---

[26]*De potentia*, q. 7, a. 2, ad 2.
[27]*Comm. Lib. Sent.*, II, d. 1, q. 1, a. 4, *solutio*.

It is not a neatly defined fact, nor is it a perfect possession of ourselves and of being; it is a power to be, a call to realize ourselves in realizing more and more our presence in being, particularly through a better understanding of being. Hence the elucidation of what is for St. Thomas the primary indubitable datum involves his whole theory of knowledge and this we must now examine more closely. This theory has important resemblances to contemporary doctrines, since like them it is based on an intentionalist conception of consciousness.[28] It also has the inestimable advantage of leaving room for those comprehensive categories which can remove, without simply suppressing, the antinomies we have so often met: between experience and idea, reflection and pre-reflective life, living experience of my own body and its being-for-others, between what is in-itself and what is for-itself, between the phenomenon and the being of the phenomenon.

4. Cognitive Life

It is one of the themes common to all philosophy that cognitive life is one of the most characteristic manifestations of human existence. Thanks to knowledge, man realizes himself and reveals himself to himself and to others as man, that is as someone-with-others-in-the-world. It is also a common theme that, within its living, organic unity, human knowledge includes an inexhaustible variety of phases, aspects, functions, movements and results. This is why the vocabulary of epistemology is so complex and so analogical. Truth is one, but there are many truths and regions of truth. The empirical sciences, phenomenology, metaphysics, all have their own type of intelligibility and rationality. The same can be said of the discovery of truth. The words "observation," "experience," "explanation," "understanding" and so on, are analogical terms denoting different aspects and activities of the life of knowledge looked at as a *noesis*.

This diversity, far from being destructive of the unity of knowledge, is rather that which makes this unity possible. The unity of knowledge is not the unity of a sum, nor is it simply due to the fact that this infinite series of activities takes place within the same subjectivity, for there are other activities of the same subject, (for example, willing and practical activity) that are not, as such, knowledge. The unity of the cognitive life can only come from the fact that each of its different phases shares

---

[28]This is not surprising when it is remembered that the idea of intentionality goes back, through Husserl and Brentano, to the Middle Ages. The modern meaning of the term is, of course, rather different.

in its own way in that life and springs from the same basic intention. It is because they participate in the life that is directed towards the realization of this unique intention that they have a meaning, which in turn presupposes that the basic cognitive intention itself has a meaning.

A. THE PRIMITIVE COGNITIVE INTENTION

Thus, the first task of any self-respecting noetic is to throw light on the primitive cognitive intention and the meaning it bears, or, as Husserl puts it, on "the operative intentionality" (*fungierende Intentionalität*).[29] Since this primary intentionality constitutes in a way the very essence of consciousness, it is clear that man, as soon as he awakens to cognitive life, immediately is in possession of a certain understanding of it. Every man knows the meaning of the verb "to know" and of the phrase "this is true." This prephilosophical understanding of cognitive life as a basic intention is not something the philosopher has to elaborate, but something he has to recognize and respect. The danger continually threatening us here is that of taking as our basic intention, primordial and all-embracing, some particular function of consciousness. Because it has constantly reduced cognitive life to one of its particular aspects, the theory of knowledge has, since the time of Descartes, fallen again and again into the errors we have been studying. What Gilson says of the metaphysics of being also holds good of the philosophy of truth:

> All the defeats of metaphysics come from the fact that metaphysicians have substituted for being, as the first principle of their science, one of the particular aspects of being studied by the different natural sciences.[30]

Similarly it may be said that the failures of the theory of knowledge come from its having substituted for the basic cognitive intention, one of its particular manifestations, for example, the experience of observing a fact, the judgment, reasoning, the *a priori* identity of the *Cogito*, and so on. The originality and fruitfulness of the Thomist theory of knowledge lies in its way of understanding the basic cognitive intention. Its originality is that it makes no pretence to "originality" in the ordinary sense of the word. Its sole preoccupation is to remain faithful to the primitive meaning of our cognitive life as an aiming for truth, as a desire to know

---

[29]See Merleau-Ponty, *Phénoménologie*, pp. XIII, 478. "Operative intentionality" is to be contrasted with "intentionality in act" which expresses itself in particular voluntary or cognitive acts. It corresponds to what the scholastics called a natural cognitive appetite.

[30]E. Gilson, *L'Être et l'Essence*, Paris, 1947, p. 7.

what is the case, to know reality as it is without deforming it, in a word, as Heidegger puts it, "to let beings be." It is abundantly clear that this is the meaning of the intention that man pursues from first to last throughout his cognitive life. He constantly strives to find a more adequate idea of the real. As the ancient philosophers put it, "truth is what is."

B. The Object of this Intention

The object (taking this term here in its very widest sense) at which the cognitive life is directed is *reality, whatever it is and as it is,* with all its aspects, possibilities and implications. The reality that I am and the reality that is other than myself; the manifold of beings in their particular properties, their individuality, together with what they all have in common; what makes things this and not that, as well as the bonds that bind them together in the unity of being; the inexhaustible series of the manifestations of a particular being, together with the principle that makes them follow one another in a definite series (what we call the "essence" of the thing); and finally what in fact is or has been, as well as the capacities that lie in things, particularly our own capacity for being together with its accompanying meaning and complex of values, all these are elements of reality. In short, what humanity is pursuing and trying to grasp more firmly through the glow of truth that underlies all its activities is what we have called above "the concrete in all its concreteness," "existence with its inseparable context," or again "the diversity of beings in being, and the being of beings."

Being and the "World". It is this that St. Thomas expresses by saying that the proper object of the understanding (taking understanding not so much as a distinct faculty but rather as the very end of the cognitive life, that which ultimately inspires it) is being itself. Being is for St. Thomas what the moderns call "the final enveloping factor," "the horizon of horizons"; it is the noematic correlate which defines the basic cognitive intention from the noematic point of view. It is, as Merleau-Ponty says, "the teleology of consciousness" looked at as an "operative intentionality."[31] One can, then, say that being plays the role in Thomist noetics which the "world" does in the phenomenology of Merleau-Ponty. The analogy is striking. For both of them the primary noematic factor in cognitive life is neither an idea, nor a fact, nor a sum of facts, nor a noumenal world hidden behind the facts, but our own existential

---

[31] *Phénoménologie*, p. 456.

"orbit." This existential context is a concrete whole which is prior to and interior to its parts, so that some speak of it as "a material *a priori*."

However, though the analogy is striking, there is an equally striking difference between the two views, one which is much more than a question of terminology. For by taking the "world" as the noematic correlate of our basic intentionality and then defining it as "the totality of perceivable things and the thing of all things,"[32] one is already perilously near to reducing the basic cognitive intention to one of its particular functions. Perception becomes the original modality of consciousness; reflection may easily be regarded as nothing more than a psychological turning back on perception, a perceiving of oneself perceiving. True, the world is said to be an enveloping factor. But it is no longer really the ultimate enveloping factor; it is no more than a part of it. For, besides the "world" in this sense, there are consciousnesses which are towards-the-world and which are only possible through their intrinsic reference to the world, just as the world itself is only possible as a world-for-man because it is bound up in its very being with the being of man.

Being as "the Cradle of All Meanings." We must, then, take *being*, rather than the world, as the common ground on which all particular meanings rest, as "the cradle of meanings." This is important, not only to preserve the originality and unity of cognitive life amid the diversity of its movements, but also to preserve the originality of the unity of being over and above its particular determinations. To say that being is the noematic correlate of the primitive intention that unifies and envelops the diversity of our cognitive activities, is to say that being cannot be grasped in its fullness by any one of these activities taken separately. Neither perceptual experience on its own, nor the abstract idea as such, nor reasoning divorced from experience, is sufficient for the task. Hence, being cannot be correctly described in terms borrowed from one particular type of cognitive activity. Being is neither a fact, nor an idea, nor a logical dialectic; it is beyond all that, not at all in the manner of a hidden world veiled by the world of facts, of ideas or of reasoning. We attain being through perceptual experience, with the help of abstract concepts, and by the mediation of reasoning. This doctrine enables us to safeguard the unity of cognitive life together with the diversity of the activities that go to make it up in their characteristic originality.

------

[32]"Le primat . . .," p. 124.

C. The Structure of Cognitive Life: Pre-Reflective Life and Reflection

Nobody denies that the cognitive life of man has a structure, that is to say, that it develops through a diversity of functions and activities. The problem is, however, to determine the role which each of these play in together constituting the unity of knowledge and making possible the unity of truth. The same danger arises here once again. To substitute for the basic cognitive intention one of its particular manifestations is to favor one at the expense of the others, taking from the others their originality by treating them as derivative. Empiricism consists in exalting perception at the expense of the idea, while intellectualism consists in affirming the primacy of the idea at the expense of perceptual experience. The true primacy belongs to the original cognitive intention which underlies and envelops both at once. Moreover, if perceptive or pre-reflective life and reflection are both grounded on the same primitive intention, it follows that neither exhausts this intention. Each refers to the other as its necessary complement in virtue of an intrinsic dialectic. Making *being* the noematic correlate of the primitive intention (in scholastic terms, the proper object of the intelligence) is the only means of escaping the choice between empiricism and intellectualism, while preserving the element of truth contained in each of them. This is what we must now attempt briefly to show.

Reflection. Reflection (as we shall understand it here) is a going back over the perceived datum with a view to understanding it more profoundly. Etymologically, to "comprehend" as Brunschvicg pointed out, means "to take simultaneously," to establish relationships, to bring back the diversity of data to the unity of an idea or a system or ideas.[33] Comprehension involves a twofold process of interiorization which tends to take away the twofold exteriority characteristic of contingent experience. In empirical experience facts are, as it were, *exterior to each other* and appear to us as *outside ourselves*.
In the understanding, on the other hand, they are grasped as somehow *interior* to each other, as demanding each other, as constituting a whole whose meaning lies in its being somehow prior to its parts. A triangle is understood to the extent that one sees the diversity of determinations that can be predicated of it. All these are contained together in the notion of "what the triangle is," namely a space enclosed between three intersecting straight lines. The reason for affirming these

---

[33]*La modalité du jugement,* p. 81, *seq.*

determinations is not because they impose themselves on me from without, but because I grasp them from the point of view of the enveloping
unity given in the idea of the triangle, an idea which arises in me due
to the fact I construct the triangle. In understanding, it is as if I went out
to meet things on the initiative of the mind. The idealists concluded
from this that the understanding which is involved in reflection is a
spontaneous creative factor constituting objects, a "form of interiority,"
whose norm is no longer reality. In understanding, the mind in a certain sense turns away from things in order to realize its own possibilities,
its own rational *a priori*, and to develop itself. Thanks to the effort of
understanding, consciousness understands itself, but this understanding
does not take a grip on reality. The real remains what is utterly "other
than consciousness"; it is impenetrable to the mind. Now this analysis
is simply incorrect.

What man seeks in reflection is not to discover the structure of the
understanding but rather to understand reality better. He wishes to
uncover the relationships that lie within it, the why and the wherefore
of the facts, the real unity which underlies and envelops its diversity.
In short, reflection is a reconquest of the concrete. Far from leading us
away from reality, it claims to carry on and strengthen our contact with
being, to reaffirm that closeness to things which perceptive life confers
on us. Thus reflection has a reference towards pre-reflective life, just as
pre-reflective life tends to lead towards reflection.

Pre-Reflective Life. Pre-reflective or perceptive life has itself a very
complicated structure, due to the fact that it makes me participate in
the primary cognitive intention in the manner of an embodied spirit,
that is, of a consciousness which is towards-the-world-through-a-struc-
tural-and-organized-body. My dealings with the world take place through
the medium of my different senses; in a general way, I reveal reality in
two series of experiential elements that are irreducible to one another.
Older philosophers spoke of internal and external experience. Now no
experience is either purely external or purely internal. Nevertheless, my
perceiving attention can direct itself either to the world of nature,
of which my body is a part, or to the living experience of my being as a
being-towards-the-world and of my body as belonging to me.

All this calls, of course, for numerous qualifications. Since perceptual
life is grounded on the primitive cognitive intention, each element of
perception carries me beyond itself and beyond the inexhaustible flood
of experiences that go to form pre-reflective life; each demands also
its necessary complement in reflection. The unity of the world as the
"horizon of horizons," or more precisely, the unity of being as "the

ultimate enveloping factor," is not the product of a summation; it comes from the fact that being is the noematic correlate of the primitive intention, and consequently the ultimate and enduring meaning of partial aspects and elements of experience. For this reason, the perceiver is aware that he does not exhaust reality in his perception. The perception itself invites him to examine it and its datum once again, not only to discover more detail in the datum and to see himself as a perceptive consciousness, but especially in order to look more deeply into the whole experience, and to understand reality better. This reflection takes place at different levels. We can direct it principally towards beings or groups of beings considered as beings of such and such a kind (physical nature, living things, human existence, the different spheres of culture), so as to throw light on their meaning and structure. But we can also look upon beings from the point of view of their "insertion" in being, and seek for the meaning of beings, the meaning of being-in-general, the ultimate essence of truth and value.

D. THE SUBJECT OF COGNITIVE LIFE

Immanence. Every epistemology implies a theory of the subject. The Thomist doctrine of the subject once again presents striking analogies with modern conceptions. For St. Thomas, as for modern writers, knowledge is a constituent element of subjectivity.[34] To know the object is for the subject a way of realizing itself, of developing itself as a subjectivity. Mediaeval philosophers expressed this by saying that it is an *immanent operation*. Not that they had an immanentist conception of consciousness. "An immanent operation is one that springs from the acting subject and remains within it as *something that perfects it*." Moreover, St. Thomas held, as do modern writers, that the intentional character of consciousness implies that human subjectivity awakens to itself only in revealing the object. It is revealed in revealing. "The sensible object in act is the sense faculty itself in act," and again, "the thing understood in act is the intellect itself in act." It follows that the

---

[34]The term "subject," as applied to man, is ambiguous. It has three basic meanings. First, it can mean the *suppositum*, that which is properly signified by the subject of a judgment. But the reality thus signified in the case where the subject is man, is usually a concrete individual, apprehended as part of the material world, and situated here and now in space-time with certain properties, like rationality and life, that mark him off from other beings. By "subject" one may also mean the subjectivity as it appears to itself in living experience. (Hence the modern definition of man as an "embodied self" rather than the "rational animal" of the Aristotelian tradition). Finally, it may mean the ultimate synthetic unity which makes me appear to myself and to others as an embodied spirit and as a body endowed with reason.

noesis and *noema* correspond to each other. In order, therefore, to determine the subject's manner of being, we must look to the kind of being involved in cognitive life and ultimately to the kind of being that belongs to the object known, not indeed as it exists in itself, but as it becomes through knowledge an object for us, contributing to awaken us to ourselves and render us actually subjects.

Intersubjectivity. Another striking resemblance lies in the fact that the subject is for both alike an individual subject, bound up with the body and open to being in the intersubjectivity. St. Thomas strongly opposed the view held by some of his contemporaries that the power which enables us to regard being as a whole, the agent intellect, is an impersonal separated one.[35] Since we attain the knowing subject only through the manifestations of cognitive life, it follows that once again we are faced with the same recurring danger. When one reduces the primitive cognitive intention to one of its manifestations, one fails to grasp the nature of the subject of the *Cogito*. For this reason, empiricism is not only a doctrine about truth and being, but also a theory of the subject. The subject is then merely the meeting place of a series of impersonal processes. Idealist intellectualism implies a characteristic conception of subjectivity. The subject of the *Cogito* becomes a universal thinker outside the world. The Kantian noetic, which is more a juxaposition than a synthesis of rationalism and idealism, leads to the theory of the double *Cogito*. As for existential phenomenology, we have shown above that although it is dominated by the idea of embodied being and although its phenomenological descriptions of the living experience of the body go far beyond everything that has been done up to the present, it still remains only a half way house in its ontology of the subject, for the good reason that it tends to identify philosophy, an integral knowledge of the whole reality, with phenomenology alone.

A Broader Concept of Existence. If it is true that our uncovering of reality as a whole is accomplished only through a multiplicity of activities, and particularly through two series of irreducible experiential elements, it must be admitted that the ultimate synthetic unity which is the source and ground of man's existence as an embodied subjectivity, can be thought neither in terms of physical objectivity nor in terms of descriptive psychology, whether it be phenomenological or immanentist. This ultimate unity, which is the ground of the diverse manifestations of our existence, belongs to the trans-phenomenal order. It can only be

---

[35]See, for example, *Summa Theol.*, I, q. 79, a. 4 and a. 5, ad 3.

thought by means of much wider concepts than those used by phenom-neology. Thus it would be necessary to use a concept of existence very much broader than Merleau-Ponty's. For him, "existence" means "the active relationship of the subject to the term within which it projects itself." [36] Now an idea of being that would be valid even for the "trans-phenomenal being of the phenomenon"[37] stands as the key to the thought of St. Thomas. By existence, says Gilson, St. Thomas understands:

> the existential act whence spring the fruitful operations thanks to which each subject progressively extends its conquest of nothingness, each according to its type of essence, with increasing liberty as one ascends the scale of beings.[38]

Substance. We also need a more comprehensive notion of the subject, one which will be valid for transphenomenal being. Once again, Thomism can provide this notion. It is the idea of substance. It is true that this idea has been so ill interpreted by Descartes and Kant that it is irksome to have to retain the same term. It necessarily makes us think of the "extended thing" and the "thinking thing" of the Cartesians, of the "*substantia* phenomenon" of Kant, or, worse still, of a world of lifeless noumena hidden behind phenomena. It is not necessary, however, to be an adept in the history of philosophy to know this never was St. Thomas' conception. In his view, substance is nothing other than the trans-phenomenal unity which is the ground of the series of manifestations of the existing thing. This unity is not stituated behind or underneath these manifestations, but saturates and envelops them, so that it is, as it were, "indicated" in them. For this reason, the notions of existence and substance are, in St. Thomas's eyes, inseparable. The proper act of substance is to *exist* (in the sense we have given this term), just as the proper characteristic of existence is to make an existing thing subsist in itself and manifest itself.

5. The Relevance of Thomism to Contemporary Thought

Having completed our analysis of cognitive life, we can now in-dicate those characteristic Thomist doctrines which seem to be most relevant to contemporary discussion.

---

[36] *Phénoménologie*, p. 203, n. 1.

[37] *L'Être et le Néant*, pp. 16 and 30. According to Sartre, this trans-phenomenal being is not to be found *behind* the phenomena; the phenomena point it out, so to speak, and require it. This is similar to Aquinas' view.

[38] *L'Être et l'Essence*, p. 309. Existence thus understood is what St. Thomas calls *esse*, that which is most intimate to things.

A. The "Natural light"

The *lumen naturale* for St. Thomas—and the same is true for contemporary writers—is not absolutely synonymous with what we have called above the primary indubitable factor (or the primordial significant datum) which is the perpetual foundation of our idea of truth. In tackling the problem of the *lumen naturale*, the source of understanding, we are on the plane of the analysis of human existence (*Dasein*), or, in other words, we are concerned with what older philosophers called the psychology of knowledge.

In every age, philosophers have made use of the idea of *light* to describe and explain the cognitive life of man. In this they are in accord with common usage, which puts as the end of all science and all reflection "seeing clearly" or "throwing light on the matter." But if it is true that "to know" is not synonymous with "to undergo," that truth is not the product of the physical influences of the world on me, and that all our cognitive activities proceed from an operative intentionality, it must be concluded that cognitive life is a sort of actualization of an openness towards being, which is part of what we have called our "nature." This openness towards being, this possibility of seeing clearly, of revealing ourselves to ourselves in uncovering reality, is not something we have invented, but a gift of nature that we have to exploit, to actualize in our dealings with the world.

This suggests the idea of a *lumen naturale*, a natural source of understanding. Empiricism alone takes no account of this useful analogy. In the context of rationalist intellectualism, the *lumen naturale* becomes either a world of innate ideas, or an ensemble of rational *a priori*, or the "*a priori* identity of the consciousness of self." St. Thomas has recourse to the idea of a *lumen naturale* (which he borrowed from Aristotle) precisely because he *denies* that we have innate ideas. Since the primitive cognitive intention, with that openness towards being which goes to define it, awakens to itself only in our living give and take with the world, its presence makes itself felt only in the gaining of knowledge. It is in uncovering the world that cognitive life and all it implies are revealed to us. Thus it is through completed knowledge, thanks to a process of analysis (which Aristotle called "abstraction"), that we come to speak of the operative intentionality that lies in us and the *lumen naturale* it involves. From this, as St. Thomas clearly saw, many important consequences follow.

B. The Transcendentals

In the first place, since there lies in us an operative intentionality that envelops and animates all our cognitive activity, it follows that the meaning of this intentionality saturates and underlies all particular meanings. We can discover it through a process of abstraction and grasp it, as it were, separately. This is just what we do when we formulate the general concepts we have called "transcendentals" or *prima intelligibilia*, namely being, unity, truth, goodness and the like. It is impossible for man not to possess some understanding of the meanings that terms like "being", "truth" and "value" designate, as well as of the noetic acts that correspond to them. Since these primary intelligible factors are ultimately due to the presence in us of the primitive cognitive intention, it follows that they are the expression on the level of explicit knowledge of the meaning of this intention. Knowledge of the primary intelligible factors is something which goes with being a man, and the active intellect is its source.

These *prima intelligibilia*, though naturally known, are not innate. If they were, they would be knowledge properly so called, "monads" of truth, as it were, independent and self-sufficient. We would be committed to a representationalist conception of knowledge. The proof that they are not innate is that we can express them only in abstract terms, that is, in terms whose meaning implies an intrinsic reference to the concrete as given in sensation.[39] There is a third point. From what we have just seen, it follows that the elucidation of the meaning of these primary intelligible factors can be undertaken seriously only in the context of an existential description of man as a being-towards-the-world, in the light of what we have called the "existential indubitable." To consider them in isolation is to run the risk of making them into vacuous statements, formal logical axioms; it is to miss the real meaning which makes them so basic to all thought. This meaning comes from their manifesting and expressing the intention which animates all our life of knowledge and makes us appear to ourselves as a self-with-others-in-the-world. Thus we rediscover what we said above on the originality of Thomism.

C. The Notion of "Being"

The originality of St. Thomas, we said, does not lie in his attachment to a small number of first principles taken in their widest possible meaning, but in a very special way of arriving at these principles and of interpreting their meaning. They are never taken in isolation; they can be understood only in the context of the primary significant datum.[40]

---

[39]E. Gilson, *Le Thomisme*, Paris, 1942, p. 298.
[40]See Section 1 of this chapter.

Take the concept of being, for instance. Being is truly "what comes first to the understanding," and the notion of being is the first of all concepts. "Being is what the intellect first conceives as best known; it is that in which all other conceptions are resolved."[41] It is not, as Jean Wahl would have it, a pseudo-idea; it would be, if taken in isolation, for then it is the emptiest of all notions, and nothing can be derived from it. To say that the concept of being is the most universal of all notions, applying to everything that is, so that there is nothing outside its reach, is a tautology devoid of intelligible content or illuminative power. This is not surprising, since, if it is looked at apart from concrete existential experience, the notion of being is separated from its meaning, from the intention that animates it. But when it is examined in the context of this experience, it reflects and expresses my existential openness. Indeed it alone can express this. For this reason, it is the intelligible *par excellence*. It is through the idea of being that we intersubjectively grasp the whole as anterior to its parts and yet penetrating them all. Now this is the very core of all understanding, since to comprehend is to take together, to grasp the parts from the point of view of the whole, attaining them in their concrete interconnection.

In grasping the whole through the idea of being, we affirm that the genuine whole, the really ultimate enveloping factor, is neither the world as opposed to consciousness, nor consciousness as outside the world, nor my individual consciousness as a grasp of the world, but *being as comprising an intersubjectivity of individual consciousnesses together open towards the world*. The whole is, therefore, no longer split in two, and the danger of the double *Cogito* is finally removed. The "for-itself" does not end up by absorbing the world (as in idealism), nor does the world absorb it (as in empiricism), but each retains its originality. The abyss that grew up between being and understanding has now been bridged. The Thomist holds not only that the form profoundly penetrates matter, but also that essence penetrates existence.

Essence. Essence, as we have seen, is what makes the appearances of an existent thing follow a definite pattern. It is, as Sartre puts it, "the meaning of the object, the source of the series of appearances that reveal the object,"[42] while existence is the ultimate existential act, that which makes beings to be and to manifest themselves.[43] It is characteristic of Thomist existentialism that it does not, strictly speaking, *separate* essence

---

[41]St. Thomas, *De veritate*, q. 1, a. 1.
[42]*L'Être et le Néant*, p. 15.
[43]See Gilson, *L'Être et l'Essence*, p. 325. "Every being exists thanks to the fecundation of an essence by an act of existing."

and existence, nor make existence a useless repetition of essence; it gives existence a genuine primacy as the "first intelligible."[44]

It thus leaves behind all forms of idealism of meaning. From this point of view, one can say that Thomism is characterized above all by its attention to the transcendental, *being*, in its primitive meaning. This meaning is basically a requirement of fidelity to the concrete in all its concreteness, in all the diversity it manifests and the unity that penetrates it.

It is interesting to note that the term "being," from the time of Descartes on, began to lose the comprehensiveness and suppleness it had for the medievals. The intellectualists equiparated it with "intelligible," or with the copula in judgments. They thus tended to oppose "being" to "reality" (or "existence"), to signify that which is capable of being perceived.[45] Brunschvicg gave "being" three different senses, first, the interiority of the predicate to the subject, second, real existence affirmed on the grounds of the "experiential shock," and finally, a sense compounded of these two. Merleau-Ponty chooses "to accept the usage which makes the term "being," designate existence as a thing, or predication."[46] To "being" he opposes "existence," therefore, since the latter designates the manner of being which is proper to man.

D. Non-Contradiction

It is this fidelity to the concrete which is the secret of the Thomist interpretation of the principle of non-contradiction, which St. Thomas calls "the strongest or most certain principle," the one that stands over all our reflective life and flows directly from our understanding of the meaning of the word "being." "Since this principle depends on our understanding of being . . . it is naturally first in the order of the second operation of the mind," (that is, of judgment).[47]

Considered in isolation from concrete human experience and from the primitive cognitive intention which animates us, the principle of non-contradiction becomes the supreme rule of formal logic, (in the form, "that-which-is cannot at the same time be affirmed and denied") but it now loses its illuminative power. To say that if Peter is seated, he cannot at the same time be standing, is a useless and practically meaningless tautology. This is not surprising, since formal logic abstracts from the existential sense of living thought. If the supreme principle is to recover its illuminative power, it must be put back into its existential

---

[44]See the excellent final section of Gilson: *L'Etre et l'Essence*, pp. 321, ff.
[45]See, for example, J. Lagneau, *Célèbres leçons*, pp. 249-50.
[46]*Phénoménologie*, p. 203, n. 1.
[47]*Comm. in Metaph. Arist.*, bk. 4, lect. 6.

context, and seen as reflecting and expressing the primitive cognitive intention and its noematic correlate. To say: "Peter is at this moment seated and hence it will always remain true that he was seated at this moment," is to declare that no one will ever be able to deny this state- ment. Every man who henceforth takes it on himself to elaborate a synthesis of the world will have to take account of this fact. Being as a whole must be such that there is room in it for this event.

What is commonly called the *principle of identity* is, in fact, in its application a first spontaneous explicitation of the primitive cognitive intention, an aiming at being-as-a-whole. In making this explicit- ation, I do not go beyond time, but rather bring about at the present moment a sort of synthesis of time, both mine and that of others. If the principle be taken in this sense, it comes close to being also a principle of sufficient reason. This latter is another way of expressing the fun- damental demand animating our approach to the world, which is to situate every piece of the pattern in its proper place, to understand the part in terms of the whole, in short, to be properly responsive to the real.

E. ETERNITY OF TRUTH

The so-called "eternity" of predicative truth is not the eternity of God, though it is more than the simple "non-temporality" of formal logic. In its existential context, it reflects my participation in being as an embodied self who pursues his vision of being through time and in intersubjectivity. Merleau-Ponty remarks that "the non-temporal is what is acquired, settled . . . . To say that an event takes place is to say that it will always be true that it has taken place."[48] He adds, however, that in making an affirmation, one is not satisfied simply to "fix" the past, giving it an inalienable position in the succession of time. For while I fix the past, I am also integrating it into my vision of the future and making a synthesis of time in being. The fact that I apprehend the world through its partial and necessarily one-sided aspects does not destroy the universality of truth for me. When I say, "this pencil is red," I convey not only that I see a certain kind of object as red, but also that whoever tries to work out the nature of the synthesis between the world and perception must take account of what I say and of other facts (e.g. a certain retinal structure) implied by what I say.

The predicative judgment is, therefore, not just a useless repetition of perception. It is even more than an expression of perceptive life in- tended to be communicated to others. The characteristic of judgment

---

[48] *Phénoménologie*, p. 450.

is to situate the perceived datum in being, against the horizon of horizons; in this sense, it constitutes the primordial type of understanding or (as St. Thomas would put it) of "reflection." Scholastic philosophers correctly took judgment to be the seat of truth,[49] seeing in it a "conception of the mind" or a "word," not an immutable completed representation, therefore, but an understood intention, a reality existing in the intentional order.[50] This recalls, once again, the difficult problem of the relation between predicative, objectivized thought with its conceptual and discursive character, and "open" thinking, or thought as an effort to unlock the secrets of the real. We have seen enough of this problem by now to know that it is in judgment alone that the primary cognitive intentionality expresses itself fully. Thus, reflection (of which judgment is the basic manifestation) is not simply a psychological turning back on perception. Speaking of a "primacy" of perception is, therefore, ambiguous. Reflection also has a certain "primacy," or originality; as we have seen, perception and reflection are two different dialectically linked manifestations of the primitive cognitive intention. Thus, if we must speak of "primacy," it is to this latter that we should attribute it.[51]

F. God and Historicity

It remains to say something of a problem that has cropped up frequently in these pages, namely, that of reconciling the affirmation of God with the historicity of man. In the light of what has just been said, the idea of God, involving an identity between being and thought, can no longer be called contradictory or vacuous. It would be so only if we began (as Brunschvicg and Sartre do) by splitting being in two and declaring that "the duality of being and thought is primitive and irreducible,"[52] "being" having been previously described as "impenetrable to the mind," as simply "the-other-than-consciousness." It is evident, of course, that a perfect coincidence of being and consciousness, of the in-itself and the for-itself, is not within the range of human possibilities. To say with Sartre that man's "passion" is to lose himself as man "so that God may come to life,"[53] is to make a claim which has meaning only in idealism, according to which the total reflection that is the object of philosophy is the awakening of the divine consciousness which

---

[49]St. Thomas, *Summa Theol.*, I, q. 16, a. 2.
[50]St. Thomas, *De potentia*, q. 9, a. 5.
[51]See especially J. Maréchal, *Le point de départ de la métaphysique*, vol. 5, Louvain, 1926, and A. Hayen, *L'intentionnel dans la philosophie de S. Thomas*, Paris 1942.
[52]*La modalité du jugement*, p. 98.
[53]*L'Être et le Néant*, p. 708.

slumbers within us. But, says Sartre, "we lose ourselves in vain. Man is a useless passion."[54] It would be more correct to say that such a "passion" does not exist. When St. Thomas tells us that there is within us a natural desire for God, he does not mean that we desire to become God. This would be to deny our characteristic autonomy, our *esse proprium*. But the existential openness which is characteristic of man can be satisfied fully only by the encounter with God. St. Thomas adds that we cannot bring about this encounter by our own powers, since God is beyond the range of human possibility. Encounter with God can only be the fruit of God's initiative, that is, in theological terms, of supernatural grace.

Our Autonomy Preserved. It has not been our intention here to write a treatise on metaphysics nor to formulate a proof for God's existence, nor to give a foundation for belief in God. What we have said is intended merely to reply to the belief, so widespread among our contemporaries, that the affirmation of God as the first truth and the ultimate foundation of truth cannot be reconciled with the historical and incomplete character of human knowledge.[55] This belief would be justified if the idealist interpretation of a being were the only true one. But it is without foundation if the affirmation of the existence of God is made in the context of a theory of knowledge such as we have just outlined. The affirmation of the Divine *Esse* does not cancel our *esse proprium*. We preserve our autonomy as creatures. The God of Thomist philosophy is a transcendent Creator who makes the world *exist*. As St. Thomas constantly repeats, to claim that God is the first source of being and truth in the ontological order (*quoad se*) does not mean that God is the proximate norm of partial and imperfect truths as far as we are concerned (*quoad nos*). If we believe that Einstein's physics is more adequate than that of Newton or that Thomism is nearer the truth than Fichte's idealism, it is not because we have compared our human thinking with God's knowledge of His Creation.

In chapter two, Merleau-Ponty was quoted as saying:

When it is not useless, the recourse to an absolute foundation destroys even that which it is supposed to support. If I believe that I can, on the basis of evidence, link up with the absolute principle of all thought and all evaluation . . . my judgments automatically take on a sacred character.[56]

The affirmation of God, as we have described it, in nowise implies that

---

[54]*Op. cit.*, p. 718.
[55]See the conclusion of Chapter 2.
[56]*Sens*, p. 190.

we can "link up" in this way with God, making Him an absolute norm for judgment. This would obviously be to destroy God's transcendence. It may be mentioned in passing, however, that some Thomists in speaking of St. Thomas' "Fourth Way," do in fact seem to fall into this trap. Their argument for God's existence runs somewhat as follows: it is impossible to speak of an imperfect, incomplete truth unless by making implicit reference to a perfect and infinite Truth, the norm of all partial truths. The implication is that our awareness of the imperfect character of our knowledge is gained by some sort of comparison of our knowledge with God's perfect knowledge!

The Foundation of Human Truth. Divine revelation aside, the foundation of human truth will always be *our* conception of the world, the experience of *our* existence as a participating existence. The standard of truth for us can only be fidelity to this foundation. It is characteristic of Cartesian and idealist intellectualism to neglect this vital distinction between the *prius quoad nos* and *prius quoad se*. For this reason, intellectualism, as a theory of truth, leads to idealism, that is to say, to the identification of being and phenomena, and hence to one form or other of metaphysical monism. But if the foundation and norm of truth for us (*quoad nos*) is not God but our own existence, with the existential orbit that is inseparable from it, it is clear that neither the affirmation of God nor later reflection on His mystery nor a special recourse to God will in any way change this *prius quoad nos* in its autonomy or in its historical character. Even if one takes account of supernatural revelation, the historical character of our existence is left intact since God's order of grace and faith does not compete with that of the man of science nor of the philosopher. The greatness of the supernatural lies in God's constituting Himself God-for-us, the ultimate meaning of our existence. In order to show this, it will be necessary to touch on problems which are not purely philosophical. This we shall do in the remaining chapter.

In conclusion, we believe that we have shown that modern philosophy would be making a mistake were it to ignore the philosophy of the Middle Ages, just as modern Thomism would be unfaithful to the spirit of St. Thomas if it thought that it could do without the contribution of modern thought. A Thomism shut in on itself can never be a living philosophy, capable of answering the needs of contemporary thought. The problem of the present value of Thomism is principally a practical one. It is in reactivating the past, in making it live, that we find the past taking on a real meaning for us. For a living and contemporary Thomism is not something existing once and for all, but something always to be achieved.

CHAPTER SIX

THE LIFE OF FAITH AND THE
FREEDOM OF INQUIRY

Up to the present we have been concerned mainly with doctrines, with theoretical interpretations of "existence" and of our link with the world. However, Christian faith is more than a doctrine, it is a way of life, an original way of exercising existence. The Faith confers on human life a Divine meaning, and it is incumbent on the Christian to take account of this meaning, realize it in his everyday life, whether personal, professional or social. The reality we call "the modern world" is more than a bundle of speculations about the world. It is a new way of experiencing existence, of emphasizing certain values and promoting them with greater intensity than in the past. This expression "modern world" immediately brings to mind another: "modern humanism." The question arises: can Christian faith, which is essentially bound up with the idea of revelation, be reconciled with the humanism of today, and in particular with the demand for *freedom of enquiry* that is characteristic of our time? There are many who maintain that this reconciliation is impossible. They freely concede that the wisdom of the Gospel has played a most important role in the growth of Western humanism, and that it can still bear much fruit for the good of humanity. But they hasten to add that Christianity, as a body of dogma and as a Church, has seen its day; it has no place in a world dominated by the sense of being-in-history and of the autonomy of the mind's quest for knowledge. This problem is one which concerns both theology and the philosophy of culture.

4. History of the Problem

The encounter between the Faith and humanism, or, if you will, between grace and nature, first became a problem for the conscience of Christendom during the second century of the Christian era. In Apostolic times, the message of the Gospel was the treasure hidden in a field about which Christ had said that whoever finds it hides it and then goes away and sells everything he has in order to buy the field.[1] This is just what the first Christians did. They formed small communities which they lived a life apart, on the edge of the established society.

---

[1]Matthew, XIII, 44.

But the day soon came when the coming of Christianity was recognized as one of the great events of history. Its adherents came from every stratum. Some, like St. Justin, coming from the pagan world, had lived in extremely cultivated circles. Christianity could not ignore this world of culture forever. As the number of the faithful who had previously received a philosophical education increased, people were forced to take into consideration "the wisdom of this world," that is to say, the philosophical currents of the moment. It became important to discover those elements of Hellenistic wisdom which were compatible with Christian belief, so that they could be utilized along the road leading to Christ. Thus, the age of the "apologists" began. Their principal preoccupation was to bring together Christian belief and all that was best in the philosophies of their day. It is important to note that this synthesis offered no very serious difficulties. It was a question of comparing two "wisdoms" by taking two conceptions of existence, one of which was considered to be the true one, and by evaluating the other against it.

A. Faith and Reason

In the Middle Ages, the problem becomes more complicated by reason of the fact that, over and above the opposition between sin and grace, which was uppermost in the thought of the Fathers, there occurs a further antinomy, that between the natural and the supernatural. The term "philosophy" has no longer quite the same associations as it had in the dialogues of St. Justin. For him, "philosophy" was practically synonymous with "wisdom"; it stood for a work of the Logos in us. For medieval man, philosophical truth becomes a work of natural reason, something distinct from the truth that comes down directly from heaven and is transmitted to us by faith. There is more than just the joy of a great discovery in the infatuation of the thirteenth century with the works of Aristotle. It is the first Christian realization of the autonomy of philosophical reason. There is no longer question of comparing two wisdoms; it is a matter of relating the wisdom that comes down from above with the philosophy which is the work of human reason. The problem of the proper relation between faith and reason now for the first time can be clearly posed.

Aristotle was the supreme representative of this natural reason. His authority was so unquestioned that certain commentators like Averroës spoke of a double standard of truth, while others supposed that conflict between faith and philosophy could not be avoided and that it was for the Faith to give the final decision in such cases. According to the latest historians, Siger of Brabant is to be ranked among these latter. He did not, strictly speaking, hold the theory of the "double truth." For him, there was only one definitive truth, the truth of Revelation. Philosophical truth could, however, sometimes be out of agreement with the Faith. To those who thought this opinion scandalous, Siger replied that "to philosophize is simply to find out what the philosophers, and above all Aristotle, have thought."[2] This may have been a useful way of getting out of the difficulties, but it did not solve the problem.

Against this over-simple opinion, St. Thomas formulated his celebrated declaration that faith and reason are necessarily compatible with each other. This doctrine evidently marked a decisive stage in the evolution of the problem. He affirms the consistency proper to natural reason. There is in us a *lumen naturale* which permits us to attain by our own powers, not all truth, but a certain number of assured and irrevocable truths. Among these truths, there are some that faith confirms and makes more precise, and others which faith presupposes; faith itself is an adherence to truths revealed directly by God. But, whatever their origin, these different truths cannot contradict one another; for, although there are many roads leading to truth, truth itself is essentially one. The ultimate basis of this unity is that all truth comes in the long run from God, either by direct supernatural revelation or by the mediation of creatures, which are the work of God and consequently manifest Him indirectly. The created order is a sort of natural revelation of God.

This doctrine became traditional in the Catholic Church and has remained so up to our own day. It has proved extremely fruitful. As we remarked in the preceding chapter, no philosopher has been so generous towards reason, while remaining as far as possible from rationalism, as St. Thomas. By retaining the unity of truth and reason in spite of the intervention of a supernatural revelation, he proclaimed that faith is a light for reason and that reason retains its functions even in the presence of faith. Faith itself calls on reason to justify belief and to carry forward its work of synthesis, taking account of every truth whatever its implication or origin. This doctrine makes theological reflection possible.

B. Faith and Empirical Science

Though St. Thomas' doctrine of faith and reason can be taken as definitely established, this does not mean that it constituted the last word on that subject. Rather was it a solution in principle, a governing

---

[2]E. Gilson, *La philosophie au moyen age*, Paris, 1947, p. 562. St. Thomas alluded to Siger's attitude in a sermon delivered before the University of Paris: "There are some who philosophize and maintain positions that are erroneous according to the Faith. When this is pointed out to them, they answer that this is what philosophy says but that they themselves do not affirm it—they are only repeating the words of the philosopher," Cited in *op. cit.*, p. 564.

rule in the work of synthesis; but it did not provide a methodology, a group of norms which would throw light on the difficulties that arise in practice. The Middle Ages could not give us a method of this sort simply because, in the absence of positive science, difficulties of *fact* were still practically non-existent. Natural reason was identified in practice with the philosophy of Plato and Aristotle. The task of making the necessary corrections in order to bring this philosophy into agreement with Revelation, though a challenging one, offered no more serious difficulties to St. Thomas than it did to St. Justin or to St. Augustine.

With the coming of modern science, however, the situation was transformed and the problem of the agreement of faith and reason entered into a new phase. The important thing about the trial of Galileo was not that he was condemned by the Holy Office, but that this condemnation was soon afterwards considered by theologians as unwarranted. For the first time in the history of Christianity, something that most people (wrongly) believed to be bound up with the Faith had to give way before natural reason.[3] Natural reason now held letters of credit of a very different kind from those issued on the authority of Aristotle. Empirical science had found its proper method.[4] The Galileo affair was

---

[3]Supporters of the view that the new ideas were incompatible with Revelation were to be found among Protestants and Catholics alike. In Germany, the Copernican system was opposed by Luther and Melanchthon; in Holland, it was condemned by the followers of Calvin as being "directly contrary to Divine Truth as revealed in Sacred Scripture." In Rome, the initial favor shown to Copernicus and, to a lesser extent, to Galileo, was succeeded by misunderstanding, distrust, and, finally, open hostility.

[4]The difference between old and new here was not so much one of *fact* (though there were, of course, the astronomical discoveries concerning the sunspots and the consequent doubt cast upon Aristotle's doctrine of the incorruptibility—and hence the eternity and circular motion—of the heavenly bodies) as of theory and interpretation. The issue was not nearly as clear-cut as it is often made to appear. On the one hand, theologians could—and did—stress the hypothetical character of the new physical theories which set them off so sharply from the largely analytic Aristotelian astronomy; they argued that hypothetical and "appearance-saving" constructs, while useful in science, could not be used as the basis of an inference to non-observed facts like the motion of the earth. Thus (it was reasoned) they ought to cede to Scriptural authority when questions like geocentrism arose on which (it was assumed) the Scripture could testify in a non-hypothetical way. This attitude was perfectly intelligible when it is remembered a) that the implications of the hypothetico-deductive method used in the new theories were quite unfamiliar and were not fully discussed until many centuries later; and b) that the astronomical theory involved *was*, in fact, at this stage still a purely descriptive one from which Galileo's inference about the motion of the earth could be made only with great logical difficulty. On the other hand, scientists could—and did—point out the dangers inherent in the literal interpretation of the Bible current during the Reformation and immediately post-Reformation period. This interpretation had not by any means the unanimous sanction of patristic tradition and it seemed to substitute Revelation for reason in what was evidently a task for man's God-given reason, namely, the rational understanding of Creation. Looking back on the controversy,

a victory for reason but it ultimately proved a great benefit to theology also.[5] Theologians were obliged to rethink their synthesis, and the Faith gained enormously in purity and grandeur. The question of whether the earth goes round the sun or the sun around the earth has no importance for the sanctification of the human race or for its eternal salvation. Pope Leo XIII later expressed the matter in these words:

> It was not the intention of the sacred writers, or more exactly, as St. Augustine reminds us, of the Holy Spirit speaking through their mouths, to teach men things that have no use for their salvation, that is to say, the internal constitution of the things we see around us.[6]

To make Revelation a rival of physics or of astronomy is not only to hamper the free expansion of the natural sciences, it is also to some extent a profanation of Revelation and its Divine Author. The storm over the Galileo affair eventually blew over, though rumbles are still occasionally heard. Towards the end of the nineteenth century, another apparent conflict arose when Darwin launched his theory of the evolution of species. After a period of often acrid debate, common sense eventually carried the day once more when men of science drew a distinction between evolution as a scientific theory and evolution as a philosophical thesis about the ultimate origin of things; theologians went back to St. Augustine and admitted that the Genesis narrative was scarcely meant by its author to be a scientific disquisition about the work of Creation.[6] The application of new historical and literary methods to the study of Sacred Scripture also gave rise to many extremely difficult problems; theologians have not yet quite succeeded in sorting out the relationships between Revelation and history. The scientific probity of Catholic exegetes and historians has counted for a great deal in this task, and once again theology, the science of what is revealed, has been profiting greatly from its contact with serious historical science, conscious both of the autonomy of its methods and of its limitations.[7]

---

it is clear that each side wished to maintain a wider competence for his science than it really possessed, and that each showed a more accurate appreciation of the limitations of the method of the other side than of the weakness in its own case. In bringing about the actual condemnation of Galileo, however, intrigue and passion played as least as great a part as logic did. See G. De Santillana's recent *The Crime of Galileo*, (Chicago, 1955) which gives a competent account of the complex issues involved.

[5]See E. L. Mascall, *Christian Theology and Natural Science*, London, 1956, Chapter one; G. Weigel, S. J., "American Catholic Intellectualism—a Theologian's Reflections," *Review of Politics*, vol. *19*, 1957, pp. 275-307.

[6]Encyclical, *Providentissimus Deus*, 1893.

[7]See E. Messenger, *Evolution and Theology*, London, 1931; P. Fothergill, *Historical Aspects of Organic Evolution*, London, 1952; C. Hauvet, *Beginnings: Genesis and Modern Science*, tr. by E. Emmans, Dubuque, 1955.

C. FAITH AND CIVILIZATION

But if the tension between empirical science and Faith seems less now than it has been in the recent past, the same cannot be said of the relations between Faith and civilization, understanding "civilization" in the sense of a search for values. It is frequently in the name of an historical humanism conscious of the necessity of constantly renewing the world of values that contemporary atheism launches its attack on Christianity and objects to its claim to be revealed and supernatural.[9] "Religion" said Marx, "is the opium of the people." "Christian morality"—for there is where the problem lies—"is mediocrity," said Nietzsche. His French disciple, Georges Bataille, elaborates on this theme: "This morality is not so much the answer to our burning desire for achievement as a barrier opposing such desires."[10] In Sartre's view, to affirm that God is the ultimate foundation of good is to believe in a world of values that are eternal and unchangeable, and to turn man into something fixed and determined; it is to suppress human liberty and make of man a sort of utensil, manufactured according to a special technique with a definite end in view.[11] In his eyes, the greatness of man lies in the fact that he freely creates himself and assumes the responsibility that this implies. "Life has no *a priori* meaning . . . it is for you to give it a meaning, and a value is nothing else than the meaning that you choose."[12] Let us recall once more the text of Merleau-Ponty we have already quoted so often: "The metaphysical and moral consciousness dies at the touch of the Absolute." In a word, the Christian is supposed to be a conservative and a reactionary by vocation. Christianity, which urges us to look for the things that are above us, and gives us a revealed and unchangeable morality, is supposed to make us less apt to face our tasks as men. Such is the reproach that modern unbelief makes against the Christian religion, and in particular against Catholic morality.

This objection is much more widespread than people think. It is to be encountered not only among those who openly attack the Faith, but also among those who are full of sympathy for Christianity, and even among a fairly large number of educated Christians. It is a plain fact that modern man is not impressed by a morality that is mainly negative, presented as a complicated code of prohibitions imposed from outside by an outside authority. He wants an "open" and creative

[8]See M. Cerfaux, "Révélation et Histoire," *Rev. Nouvelle*, 1951, pp. 582.
[9]See Chapter 2.
[10]*Sur Nietzsche*, Paris, 1945, p. 73.
[11]*L'existentialisme est un humanisme*, pp. 77 ff.
[12]*Ibid.*, p. 89.

morality, springing from the necessities of life itself and experienced not as a lessening or a denial of life, but as the affirmation of an existence going forward to master all the opportunities that lie before it. Many believe, though of course wrongly, that Christian morality, because of its revealed, dogmatic and immutable character, is a closed and negative one.[13] They conclude that Catholics are in a position of inferiority. They are supposed to be less free than others, poorly equipped to meet the problems of modern life, condemned to be always behind the times.

Thus we come back to the question posed at the beginning of our second chapter: "Is it true that belief in God and in an after-life stifles the sense of man and of history in us?" The moment has now come to look for a definite answer to this question. First, let us examine the two terms that we must bring face to face with each other: on the one hand, the life of Faith, and on the other, civilization as a search for values.

2. Supernatural and Faith

In approaching the problems of the supernatural, it is important to distinguish two things which almost coincide and cannot be understood without each other. These two things are the supernatural order or the mystery of Faith on the one hand, and the supernatural life of Faith on the other. The supernatural life is intelligible only in the context of the supernatural order, just as, at the level of natural existence, human life can be understood only in the context of an existential human order which encloses within it the individual person, allowing him to realize himself as an I-together-with-others-towards-the-world. It is impossible to define and describe the life of Faith, without making mention of the mystery.of Faith, which is the object of Faith, and in which we participate. The fundamental law of intentionality, according to which *noesis* and *noema* are correlative, is true of every domain of consciousness, even that of the life of Faith. If we neglect it, we are inevitably drawn into abstractions, and in the end we come to reduce the object of Faith to abstract truths. It is then easy to fall into the error of imagining that these abstractions are more significant than they really are, just because they are supposed to be revealed by God. They may be significant in the abstract. One may, if one wishes, dream of a world where God would come to teach us physics and economics. But would

---

[13]"The morality that (modern man) desires is a *living* morality, not just one deduced from absolute unchanging decrees. Because morality goes back to the very sources of life (rather than to dogmas), it responds to the needs of life: élan, growth, and so on." M. Lambilliotte, "Au delà des dogmatismes," *Synthèses*, no. 54, 1950, p. 264.

such a world still be a human world? It would, at least, no longer be *our* world, the world of concrete human existence, supernaturalized by Christ. It is partly because too little notice has been taken of this necessary correspondence between *noesis* and *noema* that men have so often confused the profane and the religious.

A. The Content of Faith (Noematic Aspect)

What then is the Christian Faith? What is its object? St. John has told us in unforgettable words, pregnant with meaning. "And we have come to know, and have believed, the love that God has in our behalf."[14] We Christians are distinguished from unbelievers by the fact that we have recognized the mystery of the God Who is Love, Who has shown Himself forth in His Son in the pouring forth of the Holy Ghost, and have placed our trust in Him. Christian faith is a well-grounded and trusting adherence to the mystery of God and His redemptive Love. The object of Christian faith is neither a thing, nor a group of things, nor a system of abstract truths and concepts, but *someone*, namely God Himself, with all that He is in Himself and all that He is and does for man. It is this adherence to God and to His redeeming intentions for man that we bear witness to in the Creed. The best way to know in whom and in what we believe and therefore to come to know the meaning of the Faith, is to consult the Creed.

God. According to this Creed, the mystery of Faith is first and foremost the mystery of God Himself and of His mercy for man: "I believe in God, the Father Almighty." God is Love, and the mystery of Love is shown forth entirely on His initiative. Hence the idea of *grace* or of gratuitous mercy: "In this is love, that God has first loved us."[15] Moreover God is also the ultimate term of this initiative. The purpose that God pursues through the saving Revelation of His mercy, is to bring us to the Divine Life and communicate to us His Glory, in short, to make Himself God-for-us-and-with-us, our last end, our highest value and our ultimate "possibility." Grace, St. Augustine tells us, makes us capable of being with God, *capaces Dei.* God's redemptive love moves in a circle. It comes from God and goes back towards Him in order that God may become "all in all." Thus God is mentioned at the beginning and at the end of the Creed: "I believe in God," "I believe in everlasting life"; and life everlasting is God.

---

[14] I John, IV, 16.
[15] I John, IV, 10.

The mystery of the love God comprises also the double mystery of the Word Incarnate and of the sending of the Holy Ghost. It is through the Word Incarnate and the gift of the sanctifying Spirit that God manifests Himself, communicates Himself to man and becomes Emmanuel, God with us, Our Savior and Sanctifier. The task of the Word in the order of Grace is to be the Word of God for us, the person who tells us of God and shows Him forth: "The only-begotten Son who is in the bosom of the Father, he has revealed Him."[16] The role of the Holy Spirit is to be the Spirit of God in us, making us able to love God and love our neighbor with the love of God. "The love of God has been poured out in our hearts by the Holy Spirit, whom we have received."[17]

The Church. The mystery of God also includes the Church and the Communion of Saints. The Church forms part of the mystery, and for that reason finds mention in the Creed as a mystery: "I believe in the Holy Catholic Church." The Church is not just the body of believers who have followed Christ's message down through history, in the way in which the Buddhists have followed the message of Buddha. It is also an institution founded by Christ on His Apostles. In the Church, the Risen Christ is still present: "I am with you all days until the consummation of the world."[18] Through the Church, the Holy Spirit carries on and brings to its fulfilment the work of Christ. For this reason, the Church is called the Bride of the Word, the faithful Spouse, bound to the Word by the bond of charity. It is God's dwelling place among men, the sacred place where men may meet their God. The Church can be compared to a sacrament or sign of the Real Presence of God in the midst of His people. In it we find pardon for our sins and the life of grace which is to bind us to God for all eternity. Our adherence to God in faith, through Christ, and under the inspiration of the Holy Ghost, welds us into a new and supernatural society, embracing not only believers on earth but also those who have died in the Lord and share His glory: "I believe in the Communion of Saints." The bond of charity that united them here below to God and to all the children of God is not dissolved by death. Established finally in the love of God, the saints continue to carry on the work of salvation, interceding for us with God.

The Blessed Virgin. It is in the context of the mystery of the Communion of Saints that the belief of the Catholic Church in the mystery of the

---

[16]John, I, 18.
[17]*Romans*, V, 5.
[18]Matthew, xxviii, 20.

Blessed Virgin Mary is to be understood. She is the first among the Saints, the Queen of Heaven. Even in the natural order, maternity cannot be taken as a mere biological event. It must be interpreted as playing a unique part in the human existential order from which it takes its meaning. This is even more true of maternity in the context of the mystery of the Incarnation and of the supernatural existential order that springs from it. Having been chosen by God as Mother of the Word Incarnate, Mary was placed in a unique position of nearness to God, united to God the Father, to Christ and to the Holy Spirit, by ties that belong to the order of love. These give her a place apart in the economy of salvation. This unique nearness of the Blessed Virgin to God in the Divine plan for the sanctification of mankind could not have stopped short at her death. Hence Catholic Faith believes that at this very moment Mary is together with God and with us, and that she shares in a special way in the glory of the Risen Christ and in the royal power that He possesses in its fullness for the sanctification of His Church and the salvation of the world.

If this be the sense and the content of the mystery to which we adhere by faith, then it is at once a mystery of *revelation*, of *redemption*, and of *sanctification*. This redeeming revelation is doubly Divine, because it both comes from God and has God for its object. It is the mystery of God-revealing-himself. It is essentially religious. A worldly revelation that would make of God the rival of the scientist is sheer nonsense.

This mystery of God's mercy transcends time and yet embraces time within it. The order of grace is, in its deepest essence, an invisible reality that lies outside history. But it also has an historical and visible aspect; for the mercy of God for mankind shows itself and realizes itself through a series of visible historical events that stretches from the creation of the world to the definitive setting up of the kingdom of God by the return of the Savior in His glory. At the centre of this sacred history lies the coming of Christ, and at the climax of the life of Christ stand the Cross and the Resurrection. All these events fulfil a twofold function in the economy of redemption: they reveal God, showing forth His redemptive will, and they bring God into contact with us by helping to carry out His plan of salvation and by setting up a permanent supernatural order.

Lastly, the fact that this supernatural economy is ultimately the work of God and of His gratuitous mercy does not mean that there is no place in it for man's cooperation. Man's participation in the salvation of the world takes on a very special form which in no way infringes on the sovereignty of God and the gratuitous character of salvation. This cooperation consists in our adhering to God and to His saving will, in manifesting our docility towards the Wisdom of the Word and the action of the Holy Spirit. Everywhere God holds first place. Hence the concepts of "predilection" (or predestination), of "mediation," of "ministry," that crop up everywhere that man is called to collaborate with God in the work of salvation. It is this adherence to God and to His Incarnate Word, Jesus Christ Our Savior, that we here call "faith." The term "faith" expresses the noetic act the *noema* of which we have been describing.

B. The Life of Faith (Noetic Aspect)

By baptism and by faith, we come into this existential supernatural order of which we have spoken. We are born again to a new life and called to participate in ever-increasing measure in the mystery of the life of God and of His redemptive love. This supernatural growth is in its turn the fruit of faith, that is to say, of an increasingly complete adherence to God and to His saving will. For this reason, the life of the faith is a "theological" life, a personal communing with God-in-person through the Word and the Holy Spirit. But this "personal structure" of the act of faith, far from shutting us up in ourselves, opens us up towards God and His saving will, which is at all times and in all its aspects a universal will. Even though the faith affects man in the depths of his personal being, it finds its fullest flowering only in *intersubjectivity*, in community.

Faith is a supernatural gift; it brings us into an existential order that is supernatural through and through, namely the order of the saving charity of God, which we call the order of grace. An adherence to God and to His Word is possible only if God makes us interiorly capable of it. The Word of God is efficacious; when God speaks to us, He at the same time creates in us the power of understanding Him; in this sense, too, faith is a supernatural grace. This gratuitous and supernatural character of faith does not mean that it does not demand of us an adherence that is both personal and free. The life of faith is like a dialogue with God in which God is the first and last to put the questions, and for this reason, faith is a call to prayer and finds its fulfilment only in prayer. This freedom which is bound up with faith, is, like all human freedom, connected with a definite situation, and consequently is a call to make ourselves free. The fact that most Christians are baptized without their knowledge and have received a Christian education almost in spite of themselves, is no reason to question the free character of faith. It is the same with faith as with all our judgments of value. Every value-judgment is a call to make ourselves freely receptive to the value, to accept it in our everyday existence and to promote it for ourselves and for others.

Because it is a theological life, faith develops an attitude of confidence and fidelity. This is the sense of the phrase, "believe in," in the statement, "I believe in God." To "believe in" someone is to have confidence in him, to entrust oneself to him, to place oneself at his disposal. By faith, we adhere to God and to His love for man. For this reason, faith is in practice inseparable from charity, a charity which in one undivided impulse goes out both to God and to our neighbor.

But faith is also a *light*, and includes within it a knowing. It is true, of course, that the mystery of God cannot be grasped in clear and distinct ideas nor fully conceptualized. We cannot comprehend God, as St. Thomas reminds us. Revelation, in giving to us a God who comes close to us, still does not destroy the Divine transcendence, but rather accentuates it further. God remains the completely-Other, the supremely ineffable One, and adherence to God by faith consists above all in accepting the truth that God's ways are not our ways. Yet it is also true that the idea of revelation would crumble and the preaching of God's message would be unthinkable, if there did not correspond to it *some* knowledge that can be expressed in concepts and judgments. This brings us to the problem of the expression of the mystery of faith, or in other words, of dogma.

C. The Notion of Dogma

What is dogma? The word has two meanings which must be distinguished with care. In everyday (as in philosophical) usage, it signifies an opinion or affirmation that is unjustifiable or at least unjustified. Its psychological counterpart (in phenomenological language, its noetic counterpart) is dogmatism. As Gabriel Marcel rightly said: "Dogmatism is more an attitude of mind than a doctrine. There is even a critical dogmatism, a dogmatic way of excluding dogmatism."[19] Unbelievers are usually acquainted only with this first usage of the term. Thus, in a famous speech made before the French Chamber of Deputies, Jean Jaures proclaimed:

> What must be preserved above all, what constitutes the inestimable conquest achieved by man through so much prejudice, suffering and strife, is this idea that there is no sacred truth, that is to say, no truth which men are forbidden to investigate fully. The greatest thing in the world is freedom of the mind. No interior or exterior compulsion, no dogma, must limit the unceasing search of the human race.[20]

---

[19]*Journal métaphysique*, p. 315.
[20]Speech delivered on the 11th Feb., 1895. Quoted in V. Hommoy, *Humanisme et livres de choix*, p. 369.

If it were necessary to identify the idea of dogma with that of prejudice, and the idea of sacred truth with that of a taboo out of bounds for human investigation, Jaures would be right. Since those identifications are incorrect as they stand, he is somewhat confused.

In its religious and theological meaning, the word "dogma" stands for the religious mystery that is the object of faith, or more precisely the *knowledge* that we have of this mystery thanks to revelation, as well as the *propositions* in which this knowledge is expressed. The noetic counterpart of dogma is not dogmatism, but faith. As we already remarked, faith is not a blind adherence, and in no way excludes further reflection on the object of faith. On the contrary, it demands such reflection. Moreover, as St. Thomas remarks, the dogmatic proposition that is used to express the mystery of the faith is not the object in which faith terminates. Faith is an adherence to God Himself and to the Wisdom of the Word *through* the dogmatic proposition. "The act of the believer does not terminate with the proposition, but with the thing."[21] Thus, if we are to believe in God, we must first have a true idea of God. But faith does not stop short at this idea. Through the idea, faith reaches out to God in person. Similarly, faith in Christ as the Word Incarnate and as the Savior of the World is not possible without real knowledge concerning the mystery of existence and life that Jesus of Nazareth carried within him. It is just this knowledge that is contained in the dogmatic proposition which expresses our belief in Christ. The same is true of all the other mysteries of Christianity.

To say that faith reaches out to God Himself and to the work of His redemptive love through the dogmatic proposition, is to proclaim once more the intentional character of the attitude of believing. Faith verifies what we might call the "second law of intentionality" (the first being that of the correspondence between *noesis* and *noema*). According to Husserl, the peculiar character of the intentional consciousness is to transcend itself while remaining immanent, to terminate at the object "in person" through a "matter," that is to say, through a "content of consciousness" which is immanent, and represents the object (for example, sensible impressions, concepts, judgments). It is the same with faith. Dogmatic formulae do not constitute its final object, but the intention of faith in some way animates these formulae. Through them the soul throws itself open to God Himself.

What is true of all cognitive "matter," of every predicative statement, is true also of faith. Within our predicative knowledge of the mysteries of faith, we must make a distinction between two components. On the

---

[21]*Summa Theol.*, II, IIae, q. 1, a. 2, ad 2.

one hand, there is an essential and stable nucleus without which the religious mystery would not be properly viewed nor correctly expressed. Without an authentic idea of creation, for example, faith in God is impossible. On the other hand, there is our human way of holding these mysteries in view, which will always include a mass of inessential representative and affective elements, and which may vary according to the culture of individual believers. Understood in its essential kernel of meaning, the idea that a child or a primitive convert has of God is fundamentally the same as that possessed by an adult or a theologian. In either case, it is truly an idea of the same God, the God of Jesus Christ. But it is nonetheless clear that secondary elements, either of the representative or the affective order, are different in the different cases. If the child thinks of God as having a beard, or the Negro represents the glory of God through the image of the majesty of a Negro king, this does not affect the essence of their faith nor the essential meaning of the proposition in which they express their belief in God. In the Semitic lands where the narrative of Genesis took shape, the beginning of the world would naturally be represented in accordance with the current cosmogony. But this in no way precludes this narrative's also giving a genuine idea of creation and an authentic belief in a Creator.[22] It is the task of the theologian to purify our knowledge of religious mysteries by distinguishing the essentials from what is accidental.

After this discussion of faith from both the noetic and the noematic points of view, let us pass on to the other side of our problem, civilization as a search for values.

3. The Sense and Structure of Civilization

It is a great merit of the existential philosophies to have brought out the point that man "humanizes" himself only in "humanizing " the universe and cultivates himself only in creating around him a world of civilization and of culture, and that, in consequence, it is characteristic of man to ask questions and to go on searching unceasingly.

This, then, is the paradoxical situation of man as an embodied being. On the one hand, he appears to himself as being haunted by an inexhaustible desire for liberty and liberation. He tends continually towards a more complete realization of all his possibilities, and he experiences this realization as the suppression of the state of servitude in which he is held by the material world. Primitive man is more the slave of matter

---

[22]See the Encyclical *Divino Afflante Spiritu*, (1943): "Holy Scripture teaches us the things of God, using the ordinary speech of men."

than its master. On the other hand, this liberation can only be accomplished with the aid of matter. Matter represents for man both an obstacle and a support, a prison that holds him captive as well as an instrument that enables him to set himself free. Even his most immaterial activities, his most "interior" actions, cannot be exercised without the aid of matter. There is no science without language, no moral virtue without moral behavior exteriorized in concrete actions. The recognition of man by man remains an impotent sentiment unless it is expressed in an economic, social and political order worthy of man. In a word, if we are to liberate ourselves, we must associate the world with our liberation. In scientific investigations for instance, we put questions to the world in order to uncover the structures and the possibilities that lie hidden in it. By means of technology and artistic creation, we transform it into a dwelling worthy of man. The purpose of economic, social, and political life is to improve relations among men and to create the conditions that are most favorable to the exercise of freedom.

A. OBJECTIVE AND SUBJECTIVE CULTURE

Objective Culture. The ideas of civilization and culture brings us into the territory of what Hegel called the "world of the objectivized spirit." The "objective" spirit is, however, inseparable from the "subjective" spirit, that is to say, from the life of the spirit insofar as it is constitutive of subjectivity. The words "civilization" and "culture" (here taken as synonyms) in common usage sometimes designate the culture of the subject, the flowering of his different faculties (in this sense, we speak of physical or intellectual culture, or a cultivated sense of the beautiful), and sometimes objective culture, that is to say, the ensemble of objective creations which make of brute nature a world of civilization (technology, works of art, spoken and written language, legislation, social institutions, etc.).

Subjective culture is, in reality, inseparable from objective culture, just as thought as an activity is inseparable from an objective body of thought. The relationship that holds between them is not one of mere juxtaposition, but a dialectical relationship in virtue of which each refers to the other and influences it. It is analogous with a dialogue. In order to liberate himself, man transforms the universe into a world of culture, while this world in its turn shapes man and impels him to free himself further, along different lines perhaps. Objective culture does not, of course, entail subjective culture by an impersonal causal necessity. Museums do not create a sense of beauty, nor do even the best treatises of philosophy automatically engender philosophers. The same is true in social and political life. "*Quid leges sine moribus?*" No regime will ever succeed in stamping egoism out of men's hearts. If the recognition of man by man presupposes a more humane economic order, it also demands a more conscious charity between men. Wherever man realizes himself as a being-in-the-world, liberty must take the first initiative.

Three Conditions. For this reason—and this is important for what follows—any genuine emancipation of mankind calls for the simultaneous fulfilment of three conditions. The progress of positive science and industrial technique constitutes, of course, the basic condition, but it is, of itself, not enough. Over and above this, there must be a more genuine recognition of man by man. By this we understand a greater respect for other people, a growing spirit of justice and brotherhood, expressing itself in institutions more worthy of man. Without this respect for the human person, no matter who he may be, or, in Christian terms, without an attitude towards our neighbor that makes us love him for himself, the domination of matter by science and technique can easily become an instrument for the subjection of man to man. Modern dictatorship is simply science and technology turning against man and his freedom.

There is also a third condition, namely, the proper education of man. The purpose of education is to free, expand, and harmoniously develop, all the possibilities that lie in man, and especially what is best and highest in him, his openness to the highest and most universal values. Without this education, man could still remain the slave of his passions, his instincts, his comforts. It is useless to raise the wages of the worker if he is not educated to make good use of them. Because man, by essence a "worker-being," only perfects himself in perfecting the universe, he is also an historical being, a facet which is amply illustrated by the history of civilization. As Merleau-Ponty says, "it is on work that history rests." Work is not "the mere producing of wealth, but, in a more general way, the activity by which man projects around him a human environment and goes beyond the natural data of his life."[23]

The Direction of Civilization. The history of civilization does not, of course, progress with the rigidity of a dialectical play of concepts giving rise to one another. But neither is it a tumult of events without order or succession, without lines or vectors. Hence the problem of the meaning of history. It is certainly true that the road followed by history is not a single uncomplicated highway. The immense variety of individuals and

---

[23]*Sens*, p. 215.

peoples, the multiplicity of values of which man is capable, go to make up a history of infinite complexity. There is not one civilization but many civilizations, each one with its own history. The same civilization advances in one sense and decays in another when one particular value is emphasized and another neglected. But in spite of all this, we can speak of the history of "the" world. This history is not just the sum of the histories of individuals and peoples.

Thanks to a better understanding of the laws of nature and to continuing advances in industrial technique, the world is being more and more unified. The horizon of man is progressively being widened; relations between men take on a more and more international character. The geographical and cultural barriers that separated peoples in the past are gradually being eliminated. The under-privileged peoples of the earth are beginning to receive the genuine advantages of modern civilization in a way that would have seemed impossible only a short time ago. The idea of a more authentic recognition of man by man, thanks to a more equitable distribution of the goods of the earth and a more genuine participation of all peoples in the world order, comes daily closer to realization. For all these reasons, one can say that the recent history of human civilization shows a definite overall meaning and direction.

Christian and Marxist Concept of History. There is a tendency at the moment to exaggerate the opposition between the Christian conception of history and that of the Marxist. The Marxist conception of history concerns phenomenal existence only. At this level, it is difficult to speak of a Christian conception of things. There is no specifically Christian view of the evolution of physics, medicine, economics or of political regimes. For the Christian, there is, however, as we have seen, a sacred, as well as a secular history. It is true that the former in a sense includes secular history within it. As Danielou remarks, "secular history is taken up into sacred history."[24] But this is no sufficient reason for holding that "the history of the world, in the true sense of the word, is essentially sacred history,"[25] or that "it is Christianity which makes history genuine."[26] This is playing on the word "history," and talking as if secular history was somehow not genuine history; the term "history" has, in fact, different meanings and belongs in the first place to the secular order.

---

[24]"Histoire marxiste et histoire sacramentaire," *Dieu Vivant*, no. *13*, 1949, p. 110.
[25]*Ibid.*, p. 101.
[26]*Loc. cit.*

B. Different Domains of Value

In order to throw light on the problem of this chapter, namely, the encounter between Christianity and civilization, it is above all necessary to note that human civilization has a structure, which we may describe as a "hierarchy of value-domains". Human existence, considered as an openness to values, holds within it self a great number of possibilities, and these give rise to an order of domains of values. It is beyond the scope of this essay to develop a philosophy of value, but a few central ideas will be presented.[27]

a) Biological Values. The first task that every civilization pursues is to make the world more habitable, to adapt it to the biological needs of man. Hence a first cultural domain, that of *values connected with life itself* and the goods necessary for life, such as a dwelling place, clothing, hygiene, comfort, etc. It is clear that the different techniques evolved by "the fabricating reason" play a fundamental role in the elaboration of these vital values.

b) Cultural Values. After these come what, for want of a better word, we may call *particular spiritual values* or *cultural values*, in the narrow sense that this word has in common use. Among these must be classed the "pure" sciences, different kinds of art, and, to some extent and in some respects, those economic and social institutions whose end it is to better human relationships and bring about the reign of order and peace in society.[28] This second cultural domain is not directly concerned with the biological life of man. In this sense, it is less utilitarian than the preceding one. But it is also distinct from the realm of moral values, because it comprises only those values which concern *particular* manifestations of spiritual existence, whereas moral judgment refers to the value of the person *as a whole*. Science, for example, does not refer to man as a whole; it is normally a good for him but may, at times, be turned against him.

c) Moral Values. It is not easy to define precisely what, from the phenomenological point of view, is the original character of moral conduct. One can, however, in a general way say that our conduct

---

[27]For what follows, consult the excellent study by A. Wylleman, "L'élaboration des valeurs morales," *Rev. Philos. Louvain*, *48*, 1950, pp. 239-46.

[28]A society which is peaceful and orderly constitutes in itself a value for man as a form of well-being. Looked at from another point of view, however, it is also an instrument in the service of biological, moral, and cultural values.

will be good or bad from a moral point of view according to the extent to which it has the character of being *a concrete and effective recognition of the dignity of the human person,*[29] or, if you will, of the value of the person as a whole. Man is called a "person" because he appears to himself as something for-itself, that is to say, as an end in itself existing for its own good. He is a kind of "embodied liberty." ("Liberty" here does not simply mean "free-will"). There is an eternal truth, then, in the Kantian affirmation of the primacy of the human person. For Kant, this affirmation is the supreme axiom of all ethics: "Act in such a way that you treat mankind, both in your own person and in the person of others, as an end and never as a means."

This concrete and effective recognition of the value of the person as someone with an inalienable dignity, as an end in himself, further implies the recognition and active support of a certain number of values which so concern the human person that their development is inseparable from that of the person. These values are, in a way, constitutive of personality. It is because man can appreciate, experience, and pursue, these values that he appears to himself as man, that is to say, as a being that rises above animal life and experiences his existence as constitutive of a "for-itself," an "I." Hence, to maintain and develop the sense of these values is to maintain and develop respect for the human person, while to neglect them tends to stifle the sense of humanity in the world. Thus, the attention given to these values is generally and spontaneously considered as the index of the moral worth of a civilization.

Respect for Life and Death. Among them, respect for life and death comes first, as a matter of course. Because man is a person, he experiences his life as his own, and the questions, "what is my life worth in the long run? what must I make of my life?" spontaneously suggest themselves to him. These are questions which an animal cannot ask, because it lacks the sense of existence as something that belongs to itself as a synthetic overall unity, constituting an "I." The animal lives in the sensory experience of the present moment. It is incapable of considering its existence as a whole, and asking itself what is the sense of this whole. This is why death has no *meaning* for the animal, while for man it automatically takes on a sense, indeed a sense which comes near to the sense of the Sacred. "Before the anguished prospect of death I feel myself face to face with my own responsibility. I suddenly realize that, in the long run, it is not worldly events, my successes or my failures, that will decide the sense of my life, but rather what I myself have done or will do

---

[29]See Wylleman, *loc. cit.*, p. 241.

with it. In the face of death, I am, as it were, alone with myself, and in this solitude I perceive myself as a whole."[30]

Hence the importance of the respect given to life and to death for any humanism that has a genuine care for the human person. This point is so elementary that it may seem unnecessary to insist on it. But the respect for life and the sense of death can easily atrophy. The unmentionable atrocities, the slaughter, the mass suicides we witnessed in the last war may doubtless appear as a normal result of the state of war. But they indicated an ebbing away of the very sense of life and of the most elementary respect for the human person.

Love of Truth. A second value that is inseparable from respect for the human person is the love of *truth*, of which sincerity is a particular form. If man raises himself above the animal level it is, among other reasons, because he is capable of distinguishing truth from falsehood, knowledge from ignorance, and personal reflective judgment from what Heidegger aptly called "the daily chatter of men," the opinions of the anonymous "they." For this reason, truth and sincerity spontaneously appear to him as surrounded with the aura of the sacred. Our nature is outraged at the knowledge that the truth is being violated or is condemned to hide itself under a bushel. An attack on truth is felt to be a crime against the dignity of the human person itself. There is much that is pertinent in the words of Jaures quoted some pages back, but once again the thing is in a way so evident that nobody would openly deny it. The sense of the truth is everywhere taken as a fundamental element of morality. In the modern world, nevertheless, respect for the truth is threatened from all sides. The demagoguery that surrounds us is the triumph of untruthfulness, calumny and deceit. The demagogue and the dictator are close to each other, and always appear in history as allies. The best way of subjecting the masses to slavery is to hypnotize them.

Love. A third moral value is *love*, in the sense that the medieval philosophers gave to this word. In this sense, love is that attitude of a man towards other men which makes him treat them as persons, as other "I's," as ends in themselves. Thus, genuine love is disinterested, unconditional and faithful.[31] It takes on many forms and many different names. Whether we call it friendship, conjugal fidelity, the solicitude of parents for their children, charity, its essence is in every case the same:

---

[30]See Chapter 3, Section 3 C.
[31]This is the *amor benevolentiae* of the medievals: the wishing of the good of the other for the sake of the other.

it goes out to the person as such, for himself. Our civilization has shown itself dangerously indifferent to this value too. Such sacred things as the family, conjugal fidelity, chastity, have been so ridiculed (in literature and the cinema, for instance) that the sense of love has almost disappeared. This sense is at the very core of the human personality. It is a refusal to treat the other person as the instrument of selfish pleasure, as a thing one discards when one has no further use for it. As Marcel has so well argued, fidelity and love are inseparable sentiments. A civilization which shows itself incapable of keeping these alive in the hearts of men is a humanism in decadence.

Liberty. A respect for *liberty* issues from the proper recognition of the human person, for man is essentially free. But the understanding of true freedom and of genuine liberation is a fragile thing; once again, the modern world often gives the impression of no longer caring about the meanings of words when it speaks of liberty and emancipation. Liberty is identified with arbitrary caprice and emancipation with licence. True liberty, the liberty that truly sets man free by freeing what is best in him, does not consist in doing whatever one wishes, or in following one's passions blindly, or in ridding oneself of all the cares and responsibilities that genuine existence brings in its train. To act freely is to act in the full knowledge of what one is doing and why one is doing it. It is to give a sense to one's life, and to accept this sense personally. Our acts acquire a meaning from the fact that they embody values and thus contribute to the acceptance of certain values in the world. Freedom and value are paired together, and true freedom, far from being opposed to the idea of duty, finds in it its highest expression.

Society. The constitution of an *authentically* human *society*, one really worthy of man, is also indispensable to the development of human personality. Man is a social being, not only because he is biologically connected with the whole of mankind by ties of flesh and blood, but also because he is spiritual. His openness to the highest values directs him towards other people and demands of him that he live in society. The highest values are also most universal ones, because by their very essence they go beyond the individual. Value, as Le Senne remarks, is contagious; it impels one to communicate it to others. The scientist who keeps his science to himself has no love for science and sins against the truth. The artist who cultivates his art only for egotistical ends is ignorant of true aesthetic joy.

Good, according to the medievals, must diffuse itself. Because man is naturally open to universal values, he is made for living with other people in society. If society is to be worthy of man and bring about a genuine recognition of man by man, it must reflect in its institutions and legislation a care for the human person and respect for all those values which are necessary for the development of the person. No society can, then, be authentically human unless it has a moral basis, unless it rests on "truth, justice and love."[32]

This brief description of morality, which we have called the third domain of value, has no pretensions to completeness. The important thing to remember is that the domain of morality is distinguished from the preceding ones by the fact that it directly concerns the recognition of the dignity of the human person. The human person is a unique value, having no measure in common with particular values, whether of the biological or even of the cultural order. The domain of moral values must also be distinguished from the religious one. This latter we shall treat as a fourth domain for convenience' sake, even though in a sense it lies outside the world of civilization, since it brings us to the Transcendent.

d) Religious Values. It is somewhat difficult to draw clear boundaries between the religious and the moral because of the influence that religious conceptions exercisie over moral life. It would be wrong, however, to confuse the two domains and to believe that moral sense depends on an explicit belief in God. There are sincere unbelievers of striking moral uprightness who are animated by a burning love for mankind. Nor should this surprise anyone. The idea of duty, the feeling of the dignity of the human person, the sense of the values that go to make up personality, all these are bound up with the experience of my existence in its totality, of myself as an "I." These sentiments are thus, in a way, innate in us. Though many people take them as direct indications of God and a starting point for a proof of His existence, they ought not be confused with the explicit affirmation of the existence of God, or with belief in Him. It is one thing to be able to show that God is ultimately the foundation of the moral order and that the idea of duty lacks consistency without this foundation, but quite another to have a living experience of duty and of the dignity of the human person.

The characteristic of religion is that it seeks for communion with the Absolute, the ultimate and transcendent principle of everything there is. Religion, says Le Senne, is

---

[32]Pope Pius XII, *Address on the occasion of the sixtieth anniversary of the Encyclical, Rerum novarum.*

the activity which leads us to seek in the depths of the soul an increasing participation in the fundamental energy of things and to ask of love that it makes us one with the inner generosity of the Spirit. In a word, we ask to be made creative by remaking and developing unceasingly our union with the original dynamic force that lies in all things.[33]

This definition is verified in a unique way in the Christian religion, since Christian faith leads us to participate in the very love of God, affirmed as the transcendent and immanent principle of all created things. The life of grace, as we have already said, is the work of the Spirit of God in us. It makes us able to love God with the very love of God, and obliges us to love our neighbor in God.

Because of this, religion makes us leave behind the world of civilization. This world is entirely due to our existence as beings-to-the-world, to the necessity that lies on us "of getting beyond the natural data of our life" and projecting around us "an environment that is human."[34] Not that religion, too, cannot be expressed in exterior actions and works (books, monuments, works of art). Far from being something imposed from outside on our being-towards-the-world, it makes us communicate with "the dynamic force that lies in all things," and gives to our existence its final meaning, the answer to the question: "what is life worth, in the long run?" It is natural, then, that religion should also express itself as a set of moral values.

From all this it follows that religion will automatically be reflected in civilization, even though it transcends it. It may, therefore, be said to constitute a domain of cultural values (in the broad sense) enveloping all the others. If taken in its deepest essence and according to its proper character, however, it rises above civilization; its purpose is not to make the world closer and more friendly to us, but to bring us nearer to God and make us a familiar of Him Who is above this world. It is here that the basic distinction between the secular and the religious, which is so important for our subject, finds its origin. This distinction is not simply a matter of words, it is a necessary consequence of the fact that human existence is dominated by two fundamental intentions which orient it in divergent directions. On the one hand, there is existence as being-to-the-world, and on the other this this same existence as openness towards the Transcendent, as being-for-God. It is another of the merits of phenomenology that it has shown that to these divergent intentions there necessarily correspond two different worlds of meaning and of value.

---

[33]*Introduction à la philosophie*, p. 347.
[34]Merleau-Ponty, *Sens*, pp. 215 f.

C. Relations Between Domains of Value

Before bringing this analysis of the idea of civilization to a close, a word must be said about the relationships that hold between the different domains of meaning and value that we have just described. These relationships are by no means simple. In the first place, each of these domains has a certain autonomy with respect to the others. It possesses its own life and develops according to its own rhythm. It is a fundamental characteristic of value that it has a consistency of its own and a certain "absoluteness." Every value is a good in itself. If it can later be utilized as a means to an end, it is only because it has in the first instance this value in itself. This autonomous character entails that the different value-domains should, to some extent, at least, develop independently of each other. One may be an excellent doctor and yet have no taste in artistic matters. One scientist may be a believer, another an agnostic. But this has nothing to do with the value of their science. There are civilizations where technology is still in its infancy, but where the moral and artistic sense is extremely refined. The opposite is also true.

Although the different domains of value are autonomous, still they are not to be taken as so many worlds placed side by side and shut off from one another. The autonomy of values does not mean that human existence in its receptivity to values reduces to a group of value-judgments or experiences of value without order or bond between them. What holds good of truth, holds also of value; the many activities of the "appetitive" life constitute an organic unity, and show forth in their diversity the unity of man as something existing for-himself. These values both reveal this unity and contribute to its development. Thus, the activities by which man pursues values and realizes himself with the aid of the world, manifest a certain interdependence with regard to one another and lean on one another in their development. Even though art differs essentially from technology, a considerable knowledge of technique is still indispensable to it; better technique can give birth to new kinds of artistic creations. Morality does not depend on the progress of science and industry, but science and industrial technique can and must be of service to morality. Thus, a more authentic recognition of man by man, thanks to greater justice and wider brotherhood among men and nations, presupposes a flourishing economy, and consequently a greatly developed technology.

This mutual interdependence of the different domains of culture is infinitely complex. Since these domains have a certain measure of autonomy, this interdependence must appear as a reciprocal relation. Any given value can at one and the same time be an obstacle and an instrument in respect of another value. Although technical progress can be pressed into the service of morality and religion, it can also adversely affect the expansion of moral and religious life. Poverty has always been considered to be the source of many vices, but too much comfort, and a life made too easy by the progress of mechanization, give rise to laziness and run the risk of dulling the most specifically human faculties. Though technique is indispensable to the work of art, the artist may easily become the slave of his technique. Books are necessary to the life of philosophy, but we all know that the present plethora of publications runs the risk of stifling personal reflection and leading to the death of philosophy. These remarks should be kept in mind when studying the encounter between belief and civilization.

4. The Encounter Between Faith and Civilization

Let us return now to the central question. Is it true that Christianity, at least as a dogmatic system and an organized Church, has had its day and that there is no longer a place for it in a world dominated by a sense of being-in-history and by autonomous searching for truth? The Christian Faith, by proposing to us an unchangeable revealed moral doctrine, is supposed to make us less able to face the world as men. Is it true that belief in a supernatural revelation lessens in us the sense of man and of history? This question is important, not only because it is still the source of interminable misunderstandings between believers and unbelievers, but also because an answer to it is for the Christian a positive task whose significance he cannot safely deny. If Christian faith is a light for man, and gives to human life its deepest and ultimate meaning, then Christianity has an earthly vocation. A Christianity divorced from the realities of this world is untrue to itself. The more Christians withdraw themselves from the world, the more easily the world becomes an obstacle for the Church. "The greatest fault of Christians in the 20th Century," as Cardinal Suhard once remarked, "would be to leave the world to shape itself and bring itself to unity without them."[35]

A. Difficulties to be Overcome

But if the giving of concrete shape to Christian faith in the world of today is an important task, it is also a most difficult and delicate one.

---

[35]*Essor ou déclin de l'Eglise,* p. 53.

We are no longer in the Middle Ages, and any attempt to go back to them would be simply foolish. Medieval Christendom was constituted by a sociological coordination of religious and civil power that is no longer possible today.[36]

> Until the Renaissance, the intellectual history of Europe (and the same might be said for its social and political history) is only a chapter in the history of the Church. There is so little lay thought that even those who fight against the Church are dominated by it, and think only of transforming it.[37]

The modern world, on the contrary, is a lay world, a world where the layman has become conscious of himself and of the autonomy of his own domain, a world that is organized "under the banner of duality."[38] It is very difficult to achieve a synthesis of the religious and the secular nowadays that would not be just a juxtaposition or, worse still, a confusion of the two domains. To live with our eyes fixed on heaven and to maintain alive in ourselves the sense of the terrestrial and the historical is by no means an easy thing to do. There is a way of having recourse to Revelation which constitutes a profanation of it, because it confuses sacred with secular knowledge and seems to make God a rival of the man of science. There is even a way of abandoning ourselves to God that would make of faith a shameful alibi invoked in order to avoid the trial involved in building a better world in which the mass of mankind could be free. The confusion of the secular with the religious and still more the abuse of the religious in the defense of secular interests are, of all the temptations that threaten Christian life, the most dangerous. Hence the great scandal of that social conservatism so often condemned by the Church, which, as every one knows, does great harm to the spread of the Faith.

Compatibility of Faith and Free Inquiry. To the question "is faith compatible with the free search of the mind?" it is not sufficient to answer: "It must be, because all truth and value come from God in the long run." It is obvious that in the ontological order God is the ultimate foundation of truth and value. However, we are not perfectly united with God, and our knowledge of the ontological order is limited. The problem that the modern world puts to us is above all a practical one which *we* must solve. The problem is to bring about a synthesis of truth and harmony of value in ourselves and in our world.

---

[36]See J. Vialatoux and A. Latreille, "Christianisme et laïcité," *Esprit*, no. 160, 1949, p. 522.
[37]H. Pirenne, *Histoire de l'Europe*, Brussels, 1935, p. 393.
[38]G. Thils, *Mission du clergé*, Paris, 1942, p. 15.

The problem of the reconciliation of faith and free inquiry is not unlike that of reconciling science and philosophy. In order to show that philosophy and empirical science do not conflict, it is not enough to say that scientific knowledge and philosophical truth are ultimately rooted in the unity of divine truth. The content of both must be examined, the type of rationality that belongs to each must be determined, and it must be shown that both represent manifestations of óne and the same *Cogito*, for they are nothing other than possible directions of the original cognitive intention that animates the *Cogito*. The same holds for the problem of the encounter between faith and free enquiry, between the religious and the secular. It is above all necessary to keep the content of the two terms clearly in mind. The synthesis of Christian belief and civilization can result only from an unflagging fidelity to the basic sense of things. Faith has nothing to fear from science or philosophy or the march of civilization, as long as the latter respect their own boundaries; conversely, neither science nor philosophy nor civilization has anything to fear from faith, when it is exercized in all authenticity and purity. As Mounier once wrote, "to break through the wall of misunderstanding which surrounds . . . the Christian message, it is not necessary to invent some new magic, but simply to rediscover Christianity, to give back to the Word its naked power."[39] The synthesis of faith and civilization requires a constant return to the principles and wellsprings of both. This is what remains to be shown, on the basis of the analysis already given.

We have seen that the distinction between the secular and the religious, as well as the possibility of their union, is part and parcel of the very structure of human existence. This fundamental distinction, is a consequence of the fact that man exists as an embodied spirit called to realize himself in the world, without being, for all that, limited to this world alone. Man perfects himself only in perfecting the universe, in projecting around him a human environment, a world of culture. Nevertheless, man is not purely and simply a being-towards-the-world. The world of culture does not exhaust all the possibilities contained in his existential openness. Human existence also has a religious dimension, a possibility of opening itself to the Transcendent. There is, as St. Thomas said, a desire for God in the depths of human nature. This expectation of God is just what grace and faith come to fulfil, but a way that surpasses all expectations. From all this, two pertinent conclusions may be drawn about the encounter of faith and secular culture.

---

[39]"L'agonie du christianisme,' *Esprit*, no. *122*, 1946, p. 724.

B. TRANSCENDENCE OF FAITH

Revelation is Essentially Religious. The religious dimension of our existence is not, properly speaking, a prolongation of its secular dimension. Because we exist as embodied beings, we must, in order to liberate ourselves, enlist on our side the secular world in which we live and make it closer and more friendly to us. But God is not part of this world nor is He the sum of the things that go to make it up. God is the Transcendent, that which is beyond and other than the world. The fact of a supernatural order into which we enter through faith does not take away from this transcendence. Christian belief insists on the transcendence of God, and yet dwells also upon His gratuitous mercy in constituting Himself God-for-us, our last end, and the ultimate meaning of our existence. The order of faith is the order of God revealing Himself, manifesting Himself, and communicating Himself to sinful humanity through the Word Incarnate and the pouring out of the Holy Spirit.

Thus, the Christian revelation is essentially religious. It comes from God and has God for its object. The Christian mystery to which we adhere by faith is a *religious* mystery, the mystery of God Himself and of His mercy for men. Of course, this mystery embraces man also within it, and supernatural revelation brings us light on man. But it concerns man primarily in his relations with God, in the meaning his life has before God. What Pope Leo XIII said about the Bible holds for the whole sweep of Christian Revelation. "It was not the intention of the sacred writers . . . to teach men things that are of no use for their salvation, such as the internal constitution of visible things."[40] Similarly, Pope Pius XII wrote that "Sacred Scripture teaches us the things of God, using the ordinary speech of men."[41]

Religion is not a Substitute for Civilization. Now, as we have shown, the purpose of empirical science and of secular culture as such is not to

---

[40]Encyclical, *Providentissimus Deus.*

[41]Encyclical, *Divino Afflante Spiritu.* To say that Scripture teaches us the things of God while using the ordinary speech of man does not imply that one can "restrict inspiration to certain parts of Sacred Scripture to the exclusion of others (Encyclicals *Providentissimus Deus* and *Divino Afflante Spiritu*). This would reduce Scripture to a set of isolated propositions; it would then no longer have the unity of meaning requisite to make it a significant whole. There are difficult problems involved here which belong to the domain of exegesis and semantics. To throw light on them would call for a profound study of the structure of what we call the "meaning" of a sentence and of a book, and, in a more general way, of the structure of speech as a manifestation and an instrument of the intentional life. The semantical problems of theology have been exercising many members of the language analysis group in England of late. See, for instance, B. Mitchell (ed.), *Faith and Logic*, London, 1957; S. Toulmin, R. Hepburn, A. MacIntyre, *Metaphysical Beliefs*, London, 1957.

direct us towards God and bring us into communion with Him, but *to make us at home in the world and bring this world closer to us.* For this reason, the progress of science and civilization can neither satisfy nor suppress the need for religion, and conversely there is no danger that religious faith, lived in all its purity, will disturb the work of mankind in search of cultural values. It was Comte's illusion that science would one day make religion superfluous, just as it was Marx' to think that a communist organization of society could of itself bring about the disappearance of the need for religion. The religious dimension of our existence is not an epiphenomenon or a sublimation of the secular, but springs from another intention, another source, and has a life all its own.

Grace and Nature. The theological axiom, "grace does not destroy nature but perfects it," must be properly understood if it is not to give rise to confusion. It does not mean that in the domain of things secular the Christian has an especially privileged position, or that the unbeliever can be but a second-rate physicist, doctor, economist. The term "nature" is ambiguous, inasmuch as human nature, being open to values, has many different possibilities and capacities. As such, Christian faith is meant neither to throw light on nor to perfect the secular life of the Christian. It makes him able to commune with God and confers on Him the love of God and of His neighbor. By this very fact, as we shall see in a moment, it heals, purifies, and elevates his moral life. It is through Christian morality that Christianity has had an influence on the secular history of the world. This is, of course, not meant to imply that outside of Christianity there can be no morality, but rather that Christian belief, by introducing an extremely elevated conception of the human person, gave rise to a morality which could not but influence the history of the world in the direction of a spiritual and personal ideal.

C. IMMANENCE OF FAITH

From Faith to Morality. This distinction between the religious and the secular does not imply that there are two totally separate existences, parallel to each other or superposed one on the other. In the order of grace, God constituted Himself God-for-us, our last end, our supreme value, the ultimate meaning of our life. Faith is neither theoretical nor abstract; it is an existential and concrete reply to the supreme question, the question of the *ultimate meaning of existence*, the sense of existence *as a whole* as it affects the "I," the person. For this reason, the life of Faith, by the very fact of its making us receptive to the Transcendent, affects our self in its profoundest level of existence, in that region, at once central and enveloping, once described as "the center of the soul where God has His dwelling." It follows that the life of Faith gathers together within it all the elements of secular and historical existence. It gathers them up, giving them a new sense, a new dimension, without weakening either their specific content or their proper historical structure. This synthesis of Faith and the secular within concrete human existence comes about through Christian morality. The life of Faith is, we have said, a communion with God which terminates in God directly. It cannot but give rise to a morality. In theological terms, the theological virtues of faith, hope and charity necessarily blossom forth into moral virtues supernaturalized by grace.

Morality of Love. For the Christian, the coming to be of a human subject in the world is not, as it is for the atheist existentialist, an "absolute" or an "ontological" event which is inexplicable and unjustifiable.[42] In the Christian context, human existence is justified at its deepest levels. It has a primary and undeniable meaning, one which comes not from ourselves but from God, namely, that *God loves us*. The task of the Christian is to accept this ultimate meaning of his life freely, to realize it in his daily conduct, and to promote it for himself and for others. Faith is a personal adherence to God and to His love for man. Christian belief, if it is to be a genuine and lived belief, must, then, give rise to Christian morals. Since he has become the child of God, the Christian ought to live as a child of God, honoring God's intentions for mankind, loving God above all things and his neighbor for the love of God, in imitation of God, without respect of persons. "Your Father in Heaven . . . makes the sun rise on the good and evil and rains on the just and unjust . . . You are to be perfect as your Heavenly Father is perfect."[43] Christianity is not just a message of supernatural salvation; it is also a morality. This morality is a morality of love, in the highest sense of the word.

Morality of the Person. Being a morality of love, Christianity is a morality of the *person*, centered around a most elevated conception of man. In the context of the Gospel message, the dignity of the human person takes on a splendor without precedent in the history of civilization. To the Christian, man's greatness derives from the fact that God loves him and that his life has, therefore, a meaning before God. Far from les-

---

[42]J. P. Sartre, *L Être et le Néant*, p. 121.
[43]Matthew, V, 45, 48.

sening the original and unique character of the human person, Christian belief gives man his highest perfection, since it calls him to a personal and indefectible communion with a personal and eternal God. It is in this that the superiority of Christianity over the atheist ideologies lies. These ideologies, no matter what their proponents may say, represent a real danger for humanism. For if God does not exist, if man is not made for God, what finally is to become of man? He is just a part of the universe like any other, an ephemeral moment in the evolution of the cosmos, a handful of electrons scattered finally by death. If this once be granted, thinking of the living man as a mere collection of electrons, as a thing among things, becomes fatally easy. This needs not necessarily follow, of course, and many have too high a feeling for human dignity to take the step. "If God does not exist, everything is permitted," wrote Dostoievsky. It is only too true, as Cardinal Saliège remarked, that "materialistic doctrines develop the sense of force and violence in man . . ., unbelief ends up by making him a savage."[44]

D. From Love to Morality

Dynamic Morality. Christian morality is, of course, a revealed morality, having its roots in Christian dogma. But it would be a poor interpretation of Christian revelation and Christian dogma that would permit one to conclude that Christian morality is "closed," static, opposed to progress. The term "dogma," as we have seen, is not synonymous with "dogmatism." It ultimately signifies the mystery of the love of God for man. Modern man "feels the necessity of and has a longing for a morality of life," wrote Lambilliotte in the passage already quoted. Christian morality is above all a morality of life, because its foundation is the communion of man with God which grace and faith provide, and also because it is basically a morality of love. "Thou shall love they neighbor as thyself." Is there any ethical principle more dynamic or more creative than love? Christian morality is no mere negative morality, made up of prohibitions. Is there anything less negative than love? The Christian view of justice, for example, cannot be reduced to the simple command, "Thou shall not steal." It also implies the obligation to keep on improving the attitude towards ownership, to review it as the occasion demands, and to adapt it to the evolution of economic and cultural life. Christian morality, properly understood, is no code of fixed rules which can be applied from the outside, like the yardstick of the physicist or the geometer. It is made up of an ordered ensemble of

---

[44]*Menus propos*, vol. 4, pp. 26-7.

value-judgments, centered around the recognition of the inviolable dignity of the human person. Like a concrete and effective value-judgment, the moral life of the Christian is powered by a dynamic attitude of mind, a group of virtues which inspire him to action and give rise to concrete forms of conduct appropriate to his situation here and now in the world. Being a morality of virtues, the Christian ethic, more than any other, is essentially inventive, creative, and dependent on free choice.[45]

Its Central Principle. This moral choice is not an empty nor an arbitrary one; it is virtuous, that is to say, it is animated and directed by what scholastics called the "virtues." There is, at the origin of Christian moral choice, a stable and unchanging vision. This is the constant and effective recognition of the great dignity of every human person, taken not only as an end in himself existing for himself, but also as a child of God, loved by God and called to possess Him. Christianity demands of Christians that this effective recognition, this constant and active preoccupation with the person and with everything that is necessary for his development, be the very breath of their life, the unwavering inspiration of all their actions, the rule of their conduct everywhere and all times. This is where the great principles of Christian morality expressed in the Ten Commandments derive their universal and immutable character. It is preposterous to claim that the presence in Christian morality of universal and eternal principles automatically makes it "lazy" and "closed," with no place for inventiveness and choice. The universal principles of morality are only the expression, on the level of objective thought, of the universality, constancy and intransigence of Christian love. This love is the central normative principle of Christian life, its fundamental command, its initial, constant and final direction; in a word, love gives Christian living *its sense*. Nor is this sense, properly speaking, something that the Christian invents for himself, since it comes directly from God and from God's intentions for man. The task of the Christian is to discover this sense and then to accept it freely, to embody it in his concrete conduct, to promote it everywhere and at all times, in order to further the reign of charity in the world as far as in him lies.

In order to show the superiority of existentialist morality (a "morality of choice and invention") over Christian morality (like all others than his own, a "closed morality"), Sartre, in a very famous passage, tells the story of one of his pupils who sought him out during the war to

---

[45]A. Wylleman, *loc. cit.*

ask his advice.[46] "This young man," he writes, "had the choice before him at that time between setting off for England to enrol in the free French Forces . . . or remaining with his mother to help her live." "I had only one reply to make," Sartre tells us, "you are free, make your choice, invent your solution. No general moral principle can point out for you what is to be done," It is hardly necessary to point out that this is a highly untypical example of moral choice, one where both courses are in themselves good, though indirectly involving undesired evil side-effects. Far from lending credence to Sartre's general theory of moral choice, it proves absolutely nothing; it is, in fact, simply throwing dust in the reader's eyes. A Catholic moralist would, indeed, have given a similar reply. "To set out for England," he would have said, "is a good and virtuous act, just as to remain with your mother and help her gain a living is also good and virtuous. It is up to you to make your choice, bearing the full responsibility for your actions and knowing what you are doing and why you are doing it." "*Ama, et fac quod vis*—only love, and then do what you will," said St. Augustine.

Sartre conveniently forgets to add that there was a third possibility for the young man, namely to go over to the enemy, betray his country and denounce his fellows, in order to have the money to lead an easy and self-centered life. The Catholic moralist would have said—and probably Sartre would not disagree with him—that this third possibility was unlawful and evil. The choice which shows forth moral judgment is not arbitrary, then, but receives its direction and foundation from values. Among these values, there is one above all which we in no way invent, namely the inalienable dignity of the person, the ultimate meaning of human existence as a person, as a whole. It represents on the level of practical life the first indubitable, the primordial significant datum, the origin of all particular meanings.

Christian Humanism. It is through the fidelity of Christians to the moral teaching of Christ that Christianity is called on to enter into the secular history of the world; it is this, too, which makes Christianity an historical factor of immense significance for humanism in every age. Christendom, as a living community of believers, is not merely an instrument in the hidden hand of God working for the salvation of the world. It is also a humanism, an original, intensely spiritual and personalist way, not only of conceiving human existence, but of accepting it, exercising it, and promoting it for oneself and others. A young and vigorous Christianity exercises a spiritual force of incalculable impor-

[46]*L'existentialisme est un humanisme*, pp. 39-47.

tance, capable of influencing and directing the march of history in a sense that is highly humanist and personalist. It is hardly necessary to insist that the world of today is crying out for a force of just this kind. Dominated as it is by technology and called to realize the immense task of emancipating the masses, it needs more than ever the "extension of soul" of which Bergson spoke in *Les deux Sources*.[47] Christianity could supply this extension to the world of today. But this presupposes that the Christian must not make of his faith in the hereafter an alibi to dispense him from working here below to build a better world, one more worthy of man. It also supposes that the Christian is not going to take his baptism and his knowledge of the catechism as a diploma that frees him from the task of seeking for truth in community with others.

We now have our answer to the question raised above: Is it true that belief in God kills the sense of man and of history? Is it true that the metaphysical and moral consciousness dies at the touch of the Absolute? The answer is: in principle, certainly not; in practice, it all depends on ourselves. If our recourse to the Absolute is genuine, if our faith is truly a life in God, a loving openness towards God and, through God, towards man, Christianity cannot fail to express itself in a true and healthy humanism. Not that Christianity is first and foremost a humanism, but it is a humanism none the less.

5. Conclusion: the Need for Dialogue

Now that the time has come to terminate this long dialogue with contemporary thought, we cannot escape the impression that we have only sketched an introduction to the dialogue proper. Many of the problems raised in the course of these pages have been touched on very lightly. Moreover, we have confined ourselves to the domain of philosophy, whereas, if it were to be complete, a comparison between Christian belief and contemporary European thought would have to be extended to domains such as moral teaching, social thought, the philosophy of religion, and even theology.

A. The Duty of the Christian

Among the conclusions that emerge from our study, there is one on which we should like to lay particular insistence, namely, the usefulness of dialogue. In his encyclical *Humani generis*, Pope Pius XII reminds Catholic philosophers and theologians that they have no right to ignore

---

[47]*Les deux sources de la morale et de la religion*, Paris, 1932, p. 335.

or neglect contemporary doctrines. Indeed, he adds that "they have the obligation to possess a profound knowledge of them." He goes on to give some of the grounds for this obligation. For those who wish to see, these are simply different ways of proclaiming the necessity for dialogue.

External Ground of this Duty. In the first place, the Pope tells us, one can only cure the sick properly if one knows them properly. Christians are not the only ones to aver that the modern world is sick; they are, however, convinced that the trouble is more deep-seated than most people think. They believe that, if modern society is sick, it is above all because man is sick, because the respect for the human person has diminished, and ultimately because the sense of God and of His love has dimmed. The Gospel of Christ is not simply a message of supernatural salvation; being before all else the Gospel of love, it can also become an historical force in the spiritual and moral order capable of restoring health to the earthly life of man, of bringing justice and charity more to the fore in the relations between men, thus encouraging the growth of a more humane social order, and, in a general way, of endowing human civilization with an extremely elevated conception of the person.

But whatever the dimensions and causes of the sickness from which our world is suffering, one thing is certain; the task of every man here on earth, and of the Christian in particular, is to fight against evil in all its forms, to heal sicknesses of body as well as of soul, to see a "neighbor" in everyone who suffers and to hasten to soothe his wounds. To cure sickness, however, we must first understand it. We must find out the nature of the sickness and get to know its causes; we must recognize, too, healthy forces which are still present, without whose cooperation even the best remedies may remain ineffective. If it is to be fruitful, then, the Christian apostolate must exert a constant and sincere effort to understand better the world of today. Although it must denounce the failings and errors of our time, it must also recognize its points of greatness, its merits, its insights, or else it may easily lose its grip upon it. This is all the more important when it is remembered that Christianity is not simply one truth among others or one value added to others, but a synthesis of truths and values from the point of view of the ultimate truth and the ultimate sense of things. Because of this, a Christianity which proved incapable of effecting the synthesis between faith and those partial truths and genuine values that it encounters in the world, would be doomed to failure right from the beginning. This, in turn, underlines the importance of a philosophy (and, *a fortiori*, of a theology) that is living and contemporary, one which takes account of the aspirations of the modern world and speaks its language.

Internal Ground of this Duty. The theological synthesis brought about by the dialogue between faith and the modern world is important, not only for the Christian apostolate among unbelievers but also for the expansion and progress of faith within the Church. The Pope stresses the fact that "even in false doctrines there may lie hidden an element of truth," one which it would be wrong for the Christian to neglect or not to know. In the eyes of the Christian, any truth, however small it may be, no matter what its object or its origin, is something precious. It characteristic of the Christian approach to believe in the unity of truth and of reason. But if the truth is one, and if this unity is not the unity of a collection, it follows that all truths should throw light on one another. It is true, of course, that the aim of Revelation is to make us receptive of the Transcendent and to uncover for us the mystery of God and of His Redemptive love; it is, therefore, not an extension of the positive sciences and of profane cultural values in any sense. But it would be wrong to conclude from this that the Christian mystery constitutes a universe of its own, completely isolated from the secular world. The mystery of the Faith envelops man and mankind, since it implies a plan of redemption for each man in particular and for mankind in general. Hence the immense importance for theology, not only of a deeper understanding of the Bible and the Fathers, but also of a better knowledge of man, his nature and his structure, his historical and prehistoric past, his possibilities and aspirations, his psychic life and the biological substructure of his psyche.

Truths which at first sight seem foreign to the faith can, at a given moment, become highly relevant to the development of theology. Pope Leo XIII, speaking of ecclesiastical history, once said: "The historian of the Church will be in a better position to bring out its Divine origin if he has been honest in discussing the trials that the faults of its children, and even on occasion of its ministers, have made it undergo,"[48] The same can be said of the history of the Jewish people in Old Testament times. Or take archaeology. By revealing to us a human world whose dimensions keep expanding beyond our wildest imagining, it cannot fail to stimulate the reflection of the theologian and thus will, in the long run, lead to a more magnificent and more exact picture of the merciful love of God for sinful humanity. The same is true of modern psychology. By uncovering the mysterious bonds that link the conscious life of man with the life of instinct, it raises difficult problems, it is true, for the philosopher and the theologian. But this must ultimately throw

---

[48]Letter to the clergy of France, 8th September, 1889. (*Acta Leonis XIII*, vol. 7, p. 295.

fresh light on the central doctrines of grace, freedom and sin. Because truth is one, theology is bound to be respectful of and anxious for the progress of human knowledge, welcoming all the acquired truths that it meets along its way, fully prepared to separate what is valuable in them from what is not.

B. THE ROLE OF ERROR

Even error has a part to play in the discovery of truth, as we all know. It is only through much painful groping in the dark that human knowledge advances. As Pope Leo XIII said, "we must leave men of science the time to think and to make mistakes."[49] Error is much more of a stimulus to reflection than ignorance is! "False doctrines provoke the mind to a closer scrutiny of accepted philosophical and theological truths."[50] It is, of course, very difficult to define the precise role of error and untruth in the discovery of the truth.[51] One thing seems certain, however. It is not error as such which brings about the advance of knowledge, but its link with the truth it hides and yet somehow indicates. It is something like the way in which the negative of a snapshot gives an idea of what the positive is like. This link between error and truth can take on many forms. The most important is what Jaspers has called "the inversion of the truth." It often happens that a truth, which is at first glimpsed with great perspicacity, is inverted so as to become an error because, by reason of its apparent importance, it comes to eclipse all other truth and becomes a sort of dictator. Error in philosophy often comes about in this way as we have seen. A partial truth is made central and enveloping; what is really only an aspect of being takes on the guise of a first principle. Yet there *is* a partial truth in it to begin with. This explains why philosophical systems which have long ago been by-passed retain their interest for us. Examples that come to mind are the Platonist realism of ideas, the rationalist intellectualism of Descartes and Spinoza, and the Kantian critique.

These are all reasons why the Christian who has a care for his faith should never break off the dialogue with his contemporaries. These reasons, already cogent for the Christians of St. Justin's age, are more than ever relevant today.

---

[49]Quoted by Bishop Keppler, *Vraie et fausse réforme*, tr. by C. Bègue, Fribourg, 1903, p. 31.

[50]Encyclical *Humani generis*, Part II.

[51]We must be particularly grateful to some of our contemporaries (Jaspers and Heidegger, for instance) who have discussed this point more methodically than was ever done before.

C. Dialogue with a Modern

One of the general characteristics of our age is the unification of our planet it has brought about. Modern techniques have shortened cultural and geographical distances. The daily encounter between the most diverse opinions and convictions, between workers and thinkers from every land, is one of the marks of our civilization. This makes a great difference to the situation of modern man as compared with that of his ancestors. Living in a closed and homogeneous society, the Christian of the Middle Ages had practically no contact with unbelief. The modern world, on the contrary, even more than the world of St. Paul, is "open to every wind of doctrine."[52]

Bacause the man of today receives less support from his environment, he has a more lively consciousness ot the complexity of the truth and the difficulty of disputed problems than his predecessors had. To someone who has never left his own environment, everything is apt to appear simple and obvious. His conscious life, religious and otherwise, is dominated by the idea that everything is "quite natural." In the Middle Ages, Christian belief was considered the most natural thing in the world, and one needed to be very original indeed and to have quite a revolutionary temperament not to accept it as everybody else did. But the anguished experience of disagreement about the great problems of existence is an integral part of man's daily situation nowadays. For this reason, he has become more demanding where religion is concerned. If he does not understand the meaning or the importance of a religious belief or practice, he will tend to disregard it. The twentieth century believer who sees that he has to profess his faith in a world where unbelief appears to advance daily, wants to know what he believes and why he believes it. Likewise the modern unbeliever will respect a religious belief only when it is consciously and willingly accepted and faithfully lived up to. It would seem, then, that one of the most characteristic traits of the modern mind is its insistent demand for sincerity and loyalty towards oneself and others. As Congar remarks in his great book *Vraie et fausse réforme dans l'Eglise*, there is in the heart of modern man a "desire for true gestures," a desire for words and attitudes which get out of the rut of anonymous custom and faithfully and spontaneously express what a man thinks and believes deep down in himself. Certainly this "desire for true gestures which really correspond to what they claim to signify . . . has always been demanded by the Christian character, but

---

[52]*Ephesians*, IV, 14.

it is now called for just as insistently by the modern ideal of sincerity."[53]

The intellectual who is a Christian, particularly if he be a philosopher or theologian, has the obligation of trying to meet this demand for sincerity and of manifesting the living testimony of a faith whose implications are fully accepted and which is, therefore, open to all the problems of our time. This faith will, of course, involve a sincere adherence to religious dogma, but it must also know how to avoid all appearance of dogmatism. It is evident that, to accomplish this mission, the intellectual must live in continual contact with the world. He will have to be "present everywhere in regions of intellectual conflict"; he must get used to "looking at the problems of men and nature in the new dimensions in which they henceforth pose themselves."[54] If he is not capable of seeing the unbeliever's point of view and of taking seriously the difficulties that the unbeliever feels bound to raise against the Faith, he will do immense harm to the Christian cause; for he will give the impression that Christian belief is a dogmatic attitude which cannot be reconciled with the respect for the complexity of problems and the desire for absolute sincerity which are the mark of the modern mind. It is vitally important that Christians should pursue their dialogue with modern thought in sincerity and fidelity. It is mainly by the conflict of ideas that human thought passes from the stage of pre-reflective, anonymous and dogmatic contentedness, to the reflective, personal and free awareness which alone can show forth the truth in all its persuasive power.

---

[53]Paris, 1950, p. 50.
[54]Pope Pius XII, *Message to the Pax Romana Congress*, 1950.

SUBJECT INDEX

Absolute, the, and historicity, 39 ff., 163 f.; and naturalism and intellectualism, 48 f.; in Spinoza, 117. See also *God.*

Abstraction, and the Absolute, 49; and incomplete knowledge, 53; and rationalism, 85; and the concrete, 46; Thomistic doctrine of, 142 f. See also *Reification.*

Act, notion of, 49.

Action, notion of, 101 f.

Affectivity, and knowledge, 74 f. See also *"Befindlichkeit"*

Analogy, in most philosophies, 138.

Analysis, limits of, 98 f.

Anguish, importance of, 90 f.

Antepredicative, notion of, 30; and truth, 51. See also *Prereflexive, Consciousness.*

Apologetics, and conversion, 75.

A priori experience, 27.

Aseity, and monist intellectualism, 17.

Atheism, practical, 73. See also *Existentialism.*

Autonomy, inadequacy of, 93 f.; and God, 63 f.

Becoming, concept of, 42.

"Befindlichkeit", notion of, 90 ff.

Being, and metaphysics, 27; and truth, 50; in Marcel, 63, 93 f.; and the concrete, 87, and analysis, 98 f.; and the trans-phenomenal, 112 f.; idealist conception of, 117; and consciousness, 117 f.; contingency of, 125; unity of, 138, 147; and knowledge, 150 f.; primary datum, 158 f. See also *Primary intelligibles, Esse.*

Being-to-the-world, characteristic of human existence, 15; nature of, 29, 59 f.; modern consciousness of, 37; and history, 39.

Buddhism, 173.

Causality, impersonal, and responsibility, 15; and the supernatural, 15; and presence, 30; validity of, 114 f.; vagueness of, 157 f.

Certitude, limits of 53; and faith, 95. See also *Evidence, Truth.*

Christendom, medieval, 190.

Christianity, and historicity, 39 ff.; and free inquiry, 165 ff.; and humanism, 197 f. See also *Faith, God.*

Church, the, nature of, 173.

Civilization, as a work of man, 38; as a search for values, 170 ff.; conditions of, 180; Christian and Marxist conceptions of, 184 ff. See also *Culture.*

Cogito, notion of, 34; ontological status of, 59; Merleau-Ponty on, 61; nature of 122 ff.

Comprehension, notion of, 54 f.; 152 f. See also *Understanding.*

Concept, abuse of, 80 f.; excessive mistrust of, 103 ff.

Concrete, two meanings of, 86 f.

Consciousness, antepredicative, nature of, 30; and rationalism, 82 f.; impersonal, 123 See also *Prereflexive, Consciousness, intentional.*

Consciousness, intentional, not primarily knowing, but being with, 19, 28; and noesis-noema, 31; and evidence, 52; ontological status of, 59 f.; 113 f., 116 f.; and reflection, 122 ff.; in Thomism, 148. See also *Intentionality, Intention, Knowledge.*

Consciousness, predicative, nature of, 30.

Consent, necessity of, in coming to God, 92 f.; and universality of knowledge, 99; to being, 118.

Critical Foundation, notion of, 98 f.

Culture, objective and subjective, 179 ff. See also *Civilization.*

"Dasein", nature of, 14, 29 ff., 50.

Datum, See *Primitive Fact.*

Death, meaning of, 183 f.

Despair, sense of, 91.

Determinism, and naturalism, 48. See also *Evolution.*

Dialectic, existential, 27; and presence, 30; and history, 39; in Hegel and Hamelin, 137.

Dialogue, necessity of, 5, 198 f.; and presence, 30; and intersubjectivity, 46 f.

Dogma, notion of, 176 f.; and dogmatism, 202 f. See also *Faith.*

Duration, Bergsonian idea of, 43, 137.

AUTHOR INDEX

IMPRIMATUR

Lovanii, die 8 Martii, 1958

H. van Waeyenbergh

ep. gilben., rector universitatis.